INDIAN PHILOSOPHY AND TEXT SCIENCE

INDIAN PHILOSOPHY AND TEXT SCIENCE

Edited by

TOSHIHIRO WADA

MOTILAL BANARSIDASS PUBLISHERS
PRIVATE LIMITED • DELHI

First Edition: Delhi, **2010**

ISBN: 978-81-208-3405-7

MOTILAL BANARSIDASS
41 U.A. Bungalow Road, Jawahar Nagar, Delhi 110 007
8 Mahalaxmi Chamber, 22 Bhulabhai Desai Road, Mumbai 400 026
203 Royapettah High Road, Mylapore, Chennai 600 004
236, 9th Main III Block, Jayanagar, Bangalore 560 011
Sanas Plaza, 1302 Baji Rao Road, Pune 411 002
8 Camac Street, Kolkata 700 017
Ashok Rajpath, Patna 800 004
Chowk, Varanasi 221 001

Printed in India

By Jainendra Prakash Jain at Shri Jainendra Press,
A-45 Naraina, Phase-I, New Delhi 110 028
and Published by Narendra Prakash Jain for
Motilal Banarsidass Publishers Private Limited,
Bungalow Road, Delhi 110 007

PREFACE

In 2002 the Graduate School of Letters, Nagoya University, received a five-year national grant to establish an international center of excellence (COE) in the humanities. This grant enabled us to conduct the 21st Century COE Program, entitled 'Integrated Text Science' and headed by Professor Shoichi Sato. As part of this project we held eight international conferences, one of which was devoted to research on the texts of classical India. This conference was held under the title of "Conflict between Tradition and Creativity in Indian Philosophy: Text and Context" in December 2005. Its proceedings was published by the Graduate School of Letters, Nagoya University in 2006, containing five papers.

The present book includes these papers, of which three have been revised. Fortunately four additional scholars have contributed to this book. Accordingly, this book has got a new look, and, we hope, will attract more readers.

I am grateful to the Graduate School of Letters for permission to reproduce the five papers mentioned above, with or without revision. I would also like to thank Arm Corporation, Nagoya, for preparing the fine camera-ready sheet of this book.

T. Wada
July 2008

NOTES ON CONTRIBUTORS

JOHANNES BRONKHORST (Ph.D., D.Litt.)
Professor, Faculté des Lettres, Université de Lausanne
Specialty: Indian Philosophy (Sanskrit traditional grammar, realism, Vedānta, Mīmāṃsā, Sāṃkhya, Yoga, Buddhism, Jainism, and materialism)
Publication: *Tradition and Argument in Classical Indian Linguistics* (1986); *The Two Traditions of Meditation in Ancient India* (1993); *Why is there philosophy in India?* (1998); *Langage et Réalité* (1999); *Greater Magadha* (2007).

SHOUN HINO (Ph.D.)
Professor, Department of Liberal Arts, Gifu Pharmaceutical University
Specialty: Vedānta philosophy, Hindu religion, and Shin-Buddhism
Publication: Advaita Tradition Series 12 vols. (coauthored, 1982–2005); *Three Mountains and Seven Rivers* (co-ed., 2004); "Soteriology of Shin Buddhism" (2006)

KATSUNORI HIRANO (Ph.D.)
Global COE Assistant Professor, Graduate School of Letters, Nagoya University
Specialty: Indian realism (Nyāya and Vaiśeṣika) and text science
Publication: "The Definition of Universal in Vaiśeṣika Philosophy" (2002); "On the System of the Commentary Texts in Indian Philosophy" (2003); "Some Aspects of the Differential Cognition in the *Vyomavatī*" (2006); "The Configuration of Texts: A Way for Interpretation of the Text" (2008).

PARIMAL G. PATIL (Ph.D.)
John L. Loeb Associate Professor of the Humanities, Committee on The Study of Religion and Department of Sanskrit and Indian Studies,

Harvard University
Specialty: Intellectual History and Philosophy of Religion in Southern Asia, Buddhist Epistemology, and Sanskrit Intellectual Practices
Publication: "On What Is It That Buddhists Think about?" (2003); "Traditionalism and Innovation: Philosophy, Exegesis, and Intellectual History in Jnānaśrīmitra's Apohaprakaraṇa" (2006); "Dharmkīrti's White-lie: Jnānaśrīmitra on the Intellectual History of Buddhism in India" (2007); "History, Philosophy, and Philosophical Study of Sanskrit Texts" (forthcoming).

SHIGERU SAITO (Ph.D.)
Visiting Lecturer, Nagoya University
Specialty: Indian Buddhism
Publication: "Synonyms of Ātman in Early Abhidharma Buddhism" (2006); "The Oral Tradition of Commentary in Pāli Buddhism: Pārāpariya and Pārāsariya" (2006); "On the Establishment of the Thirty-seven Dharmas Leading to Enlightenment" (2007).

MASAHIRO SHIMODA (D.Litt.)
Professor, Graduate School of Humanities and Sociology, University of Tokyo
Specialty: Indian Buddhism
Publication: *A Japanese Translation of the Tibetan Translation of the Mahā-parinirvāṇa-sūtra* (1993); *A Dictionary of Mahāyāna Sūtras* (co-ed., 1997); *A Study of the Mahā-parinirvāṇa-sūtra* (1997); *Basic Literature in Religious Studies*, (co-ed., 2007).

TAKANORI SUZUKI (Ph.D.)
Visiting Lecturer, Graduate School of Letters, Nagoya University
Specialty: Indian realism (Nyāya and Vaiśeṣika)
Publication: "Udayana's Theory of Inference in His *Kiraṇāvalī*" (2002); "The Theory of Inference in the *Vaiśeṣikasūtra*: Interpreted in Candrānanda's Vṛtti and the Upaskāra" (2006); "Uddyotakara and Vācaspati: Development of the Theory of Inference in the Nyāya School" (2006).

TOSHIYA UNEBE (Ph.D.)
Associate Professor, Graduate School of Letters, Nagoya University
Specialty: Indian philosophy of language and Buddhism, Thai Buddhist

manuscriptology

Publication: "The 'Grammarians' Objection' Presented in Sthiramati's *Trimsikābhāṣya* and Bhartṛhari's Argument on the Secondary Application of Words" (2004); "Inference Based on *Vyapadeśa*: Bhartrhari's Remark and Related Discussions in Nyāya and Buddhist Treatises" (2006); "Three Stories from the Thai Recension of the *Paññāsa-jātaka*" (2007).

TOSHIHIRO WADA (Ph.D., D. Litt.)

Professor, Graduate School of Letters, Nagoya University

Specialty: Indian logic, philosophy of language, and realism (Nyāya and Vaiśeṣika)

Publication: *Invariable Concomitance in Navya-Nyāya* (1990); *Three Mountains and Seven Rivers* (co-ed., 2004); *The Analytical Method of Navya-Nyāya* (2007).

CONTENTS

INTRODUCTION

Toshihiro WADA

The present book aims at clarifying various aspects of Indian philosophy by applying concepts used in text science towards their analysis. Text science attempts to establish universal rules which apply to all forms of human expression. If we regard all human expression, 'including behavior', as communication, it contains a meaning-system whether it has the form of language or not. Human expression may be classified as language, figure, body action, and so forth; we consider all these forms of expression to be *texts*, for which there must apply universal rules. The aim of text science is to explain how these rules function throughout various types of *texts* and thus provide a better understanding of human behavior.

It may be sometimes difficult to differentiate text science from communication theory. As long as spoken or written language is being dealt with, they do not essentially differ. Text science, however, deals with certain issues which communication theory does not, such as the relationship between the meaning of a *text* and its context or cultural background, the genesis of *texts* or *text* groups, the relationship among the different versions (*texts*) of a text written by one and the same author, the relationship between the successive commentaries (*texts*) of one *text*, and so forth. Since *text* stands for anything meaningful, as mentioned above, text science can delve into meaning-systems underlying even art, such as pictures and sculpture, and human behavior, such as rituals.

One of the most important concepts text science makes use of is that of context, which functions as the factor determining the meaning of a *text*. All the contributors to this book have made particular use of this concept in their analysis. 'Context' indicates not only the linguistic structure surrounding a particular expression, but also the non-linguistic structure surrounding it, such as the speaker, the hearer, the social or cultural circumstances, etc., of that expression. Moreover, the term 'context' can be used to mean other *text(s)* independent of but relating to the text in question or intellectual framework which impels one to interpret each text as forming the whole. It is in the second or third sense that all the contributors will use this term in the following chapters.

Context will lead us to a new understanding of, for instance, a written *text*. When we encounter a *text* contradicting a general tradition or presupposition in India, we attempt to take a specific tradition, some fact, or wider presupposition as the context and thus are able to solve this contradiction by viewing the *text* from the viewpoint of this context. If this context allows us to understand other *texts* more coherently, it is a useful method of interpreting all those *texts*. Here the direction of analysis is from context to text. It is also possible to move from text to context. We can arrive at a new context from *texts*, such as commentaries, which context cannot be discovered through reading only one of those *texts*. Such a context will certainly help us coherently interpret other *texts* related to the *texts*. The concept of context and these two directions of analysis may not be necessarily new tools to scholars of Indian studies, who often adopt this method unconsciously. However, we aim to use this method consciously here. It is an underlying principle of this book that in order to understand *texts*, written in Sanskrit or other languages, we need to turn our attention towards factors outside of them, such as information provided by other areas of study, which factors we call context.

To classify the nine papers contributed to this book, it might have been better to take the text-context viewpoint. However, this way of classification is not so familiar to scholars of Indian studies. Moreover, since text science deals with non-language meaning-systems as well as language meaning-systems, this classification would have only limited use here. It is also a fact that it is more difficult to present theories on non-language meaning-systems than on language meaning-systems, and much more difficult to connect both types of systems. As the papers in this book do not deal directly with non-language meaning systems, it is not necessary to enter into a comparison of language and non-language meaning systems here, though such a topic deserves much future work by researchers.

In this book we have adopted the orthodox classification, i.e., Buddhism or non-Buddhism, and the schools of Indian philosophy. Nine papers have been organized into four parts: (I) General, (II) Buddhism, (III) Vedānta, Mīmāṃsā and Vyākaraṇa, and (IV) Nyāya and Vaiśeṣika. Below I have provided brief summaries of the nine chapters.

Chapter 1: "The Context of Indian Philosophy" by Johannes Bronkhorst vestigates the importance of co:ntext in interpreting philosophical texts of assical India. In one case he has attempted to explain the reason for the iticism by Bhaṭṭoji Dīkṣita (ca. 1600) of his teacher by taking notice of the ligious affiliations of both; In another case Bronkhorst has shown how the :bate between Kumārila (ca. 7th century), a Mīmāṃsaka, and the Buddhists ıncerning the existence of universals reflected their social background; umārila being a Brahmin would quite naturally believe in universals like 3rahmin-ness', which would distinguish him fundamentally from other ıman beings. In general, Bronkhorst has revealed the importance of public :bates as the context of philosophical texts or systems, and has claimed at the difference between the philosophical systems of the Sarvāstivāda ıd the Theravāda schools resulted from the fact that the former system :veloped from a context in which debate played an important role, and at the latter developed from a context in which debate did not. Finally, ronkhorst objects to the practice of trying to understand Indian philosophy / merely looking at questions and issues it has in common with modern /estern philosophy; instead Indian philosophy has to be understood within s own historical context.

Chapter 2: "Some Reflections on the History of Buddhist Canons ı Ancient India" by Masahiro Shimoda attempts to interpret Buddhist :ripture, in particular the teachings associated with Śākyamuni Buddha's :rfect awakening and the issues concerning it, as texts which can be ıfluenced by their context. Shimoda has started with the episode of "the ɔd Brahmā's entreaty of the Buddha to his discourse", which raises vo significant issues: (1) words cannot adequately convey the truth : experience of the Buddha, and (2) no truth would come to the world ithout the the utterance of words by the Buddha. Words are the medium ɔr conveying Buddha's experience, and they exist in particular forms in articular historical contexts. Shimoda has shown how the context of the uddha's teaching changed over the first two to five hundred years after is enlightenment: the Buddha's words first heard directly and individually ıerished by his disciples became public in Buddhist communities after is death. At first transmitted orally they later were consigned to writing ıd became scriptures. Shimoda recommends a rethinking of the history of uddhism from the viewpoint of text-context instead of reconstructing a istory by dealing with scriptures merely as documents.

Chapter 3: "The Gandhāran Disturbance in the Late 4th Century CE as a *'ontext*" by Shigeru Saito has as its field of inquiry Gandhāran Buddhism.

Saito has constructed a context using the travelogue entitled *Gao seng fa xion zhuan* (高僧法顯傳) by the Chinese pilgrim Faxian, who visited north India in the early 5th century. In 402 CE Faxian visited the Gandhāran region. The number of temples and monks he notes in Puruṣapura, the capital, is much less than what he reports in other places, which, according to Saito, indicates the decline of Gandhāran Buddhism. Saito argues that this decline was caused by the Gandhāran Disturbance which occurred between Sapur II's expedition to the east and Kidāra's unification, i.e., between ca. 350 and ca. 410 CE. This context can explain why the Buddhist scholars Asaṅga and Vasubandhu moved from their home in Puruṣapura to the east during this period, which facts are referred to in the *Da tang xi yu ji* (大唐西域記); this context also explains why nine priests left Ji bin (罽賓) and went to China to translate texts into Chinese, as referred to in the *Gao seng zhuan* (高僧傳).

Chapter 4: "Consuming Scripture: Philosophical Hermeneutics in Classical India" by Parimal G. Patil investigates how Kumārila assigns significance to Vedic texts. Patil has addressed three questions: (1) What counts as scripture? (2) Wherein lies its authority? (3) What can be said about philosophical theology on the basis of scripture, and how can this be justified through exegesis, and other commentarial and 'quasi-commentarial' practices? He claims that these questions form an 'intellectual context' in which all scriptual statements should be properly understood, and that to properly interpret a scriptural statement is to make good use of it. Patil calls this model of hermeneutics 'principled consumerism'. He emphasizes that Kumārila's intellectual context will help us understand the creativity and innovation of Hindu theology.

Chapter 5: "The Beginnings of *Bhakti*'s Influence on Advaita Doctrine: The Teachings of Madhusūdana Sarasvatī" by Shoun Hino clarifies how Madhusūdana, who was active in the 16th century, introduced *bhakti* into the tradition of the Advaita Vedānta school. In this school *bhakti* is not an essential means of obtaining liberation, but he synthesized it into the Advaitic way to liberation. Some factor, in other words, context, impelled him to do this, and it is his faith in Kṛṣṇa from a younger age. From the viewpoint of this context Hino has indicated two important points: (1) Madhusūdana maintained the importance of *bhakti* as a driving force for progressing through the stages of liberation, and (2) he held the already established idea that *nididhyāsana* is, in the end, to be equated with *bhakti*. This chapter shows that even the Advaita Vedānta school, whose founder, Śaṅkara, gave only minor importance to *bhakti*, could not survive without incorporating *bhakti* into its teachings.

Chapter 6: "Bhartṛhari on Text and Context" by Toshiya Unebe examines the relationship between the understanding of the meaning of a sentence (*text*) and its context in Bhartṛhari's *Vākyapadīya*. Unebe has shown that in understanding the meaning of a sentence, Bhartṛhari takes into consideration the situation, or circumstances (*prakaraṇa*), in which the sentence is uttered. This situation corresponds to our concept of context. Unebe further examines the argument between the Grammarians and the Mīmāṃsakas on whether one should deal with a passage containing many verbs as a single integral sentence (*ekavākya*) or separate sentences. This argument presents what literal context is, according to both schools. Bhartṛhari's view is ultimately related to the concept of *pratibhā*, a flash of understanding. Understanding of a text (whether a word or a sentence) is neither that of the meaning of all the linguistic elements which constitute it, nor that of the meaning of the other texts surrounding it, but an instantaneous and intuitive cognition encompassing the entire *context* including literal context.

Chapter 7: "New light on the Commentary Texts of Ancient India: A Genesis of the Inherence Chapter in the Commentaries on the *Padārtha-dharma-saṃgraha*" by Katsunori Hirano explores the system through which the commentaries convey information and advances a new theory to explain their genesis in ancient India. Hirano has taken up the commentaries on the *Padārtha-dharma-saṃgraha* of Praśastapāda (ca. 550–600). They are generated via combination with already known information; that is, the 'texture' of quotation of the commentaries is composed of information drawn from preceding texts. Introducing the quotation theory, Hirano has focused attention on the way in which information is quoted or drawn from the preceding commentary texts, such as the *Vyomavatī* of Vyomaśiva (ca. 900–960), the *Nyāyakandalī* of Śrīdhara (ca. 950–1000), and the *Kiraṇāvalī* of Udayana (ca. 1050–1100), implicitly and explicitly. In addition, a social context, as the necessary conditions for the genesis of the commentary texts, has been offered.

Chapter 8: "Text, Context, and Author's Intention: Two Frames of Reference in the Vaiśeṣika school" by Takanori Suzuki attempts to explain the different conceptions of *śabdapramāṇa* (language as a valid means of obtaining true cognition) in the Vaiśeṣika tradition. Suzuki claims that those conceptions are rooted in two major currents in the tradition, which Suzuki calls 'context'. He has dealt with the commentaries on the *Padārtha-dharma-saṃgraha*, i.e., the *Vyomavatī*, the *Nyāyakandalī*, and the *Kiraṇāvalī*, as in chapter 7. The first two commentaries (*texts*) regard *śabdapramāṇa* as one variety of inference as does the *Padārtha-dharma-saṃgraha*, while the third one regards it as a means independent of inference as the Nyāya school does. Thus, Suzuki has constructed the context which gives birth to the different conceptions in one tradition, and has laid a foundation for future research on such a context.

Chapter 9: "The Genesis of Sanskrit Texts and Their Context in Navya-nyāya: From Gaṅgeśa's *Tattvacintāmaṇi* to Its Commentaries" by Toshihiro Wada, based on the quotation theory like chapter 7, deals with the way in which commentaries are composed and what context impels them to arise in their extant forms. The present chapter takes up the Vyāptipañcaka Section of the *Tattvacintāmaṇi* and two commentaries thereon: the *Tattvacintāmaṇi-sārāvalī* of Vāsudeva (second half of the 15th century) and the *Tattvacintāmaṇi-prakāśa* of Rucidatta (first half of the 16th century). This chapter too supports the conclusions of chapter 7.

* I would like to thank Dr. Charles Pain for correcting my Englsih.

I
GENERAL

CHAPTER 1

THE CONTEXT OF INDIAN PHILOSOPHY

Johannes BRONKHORST

I.

Indian philosophy has a long and rich history. Numerous texts have survived, and we know that many others have been lost. Many thinkers were involved in writing these texts, and many more studied them. The contents of these texts have been researched, and are still researched, by modern scholars in many countries. These studies inform us what Indian philosophy was about. We learn from them that there were many different schools of philosophy, and also thinkers who did not belong to any one school in particular, who rather elaborated ideas of their own. By and large these thinkers, and their ideas, were associated with the main religions of South Asia. Brahmanical thinkers produced philosophies that are brahmanical, Jainas produced Jaina philosophies, and Buddhists produced Buddhist philosophies. This distinction into some major groups is only approximate, for the different philosophies influenced each other. We know that the Jainas were deeply interested in the philosophical developments that took place around them. The Buddhist and brahmanical thinkers, too, followed closely what others had to say. They informed themselves about the ideas of others, and frequently borrowed some of these, often without explicitly saying so. The shared concerns of all these philosophers—whether brahmanical, Buddhist, or Jaina—is also attested by the fact that they had a number of problems and concerns in common. They may have provided different answers to shared problems, but the fact that their problems were sometimes the same shows that these different philosophers were not isolated from each other.

Who were these philosophers, and why did they compose their sometimes difficult treatises? Asking this question means showing an interest in the context of the different Indian philosophies. We can, of course, ignore this question and concentrate exclusively on the *contents*, rather than on the *contexts*, of India's philosophical texts. Much can be learned from analyzing their contents, even about the relationships between the different schools. The texts themselves often criticize alternative positions, and argue against them. Modern scholars can analyze these arguments, and evaluate them. This is what modern scholars often do, and rightly so. In one sense, this is all the modern scholar who is interested in philosophy has to do. The philosophical arguments are all there in the text, they are part of the *contents*, and not of the *context*. And yet, other issues may be at stake, issues that do not, or only superficially or indirectly, find expression in the texts themselves. In some cases a discussion about a highly technical point of philosophy may cover a difference of opinion of a much more banal kind.

In order to illustrate this observation, I will first briefly mention a relatively recent Sanskrit author who was both a philosopher and a grammarian.[1] I take this example because here, exceptionally, we have a fair amount of contextual information. The name of this scholar was Bhaṭṭoji, or Bhaṭṭoji Dīkṣita, and he lived around the year 1600 CE in Benares. Bhaṭṭoji has remained famous until today as a result of a number of technical grammatical treatises which he composed. The most well-known of these is the *Siddhānta Kaumudī*, a text which is still used in India to teach Sanskrit grammar to students. Another text composed by Bhaṭṭoji is a long and extremely learned commentary on his own *Siddhānta Kaumudī* (called *Prauḍha Manoramā*). Whereas the *Siddhānta Kaumudī* was written for students, this commentary is meant for specialists. One has to be quite advanced in traditional Sanskrit grammar in order to understand it, and one might be inclined to think that this learned text is very far removed from the every day life of its author. A closer study reveals that this is not the case.

Bhaṭṭoji's commentary, in its learned discussions, frequently compares different points of view, different interpretations of the ancient grammar of Pāṇini. Bhaṭṭoji discusses these interpretations, discards some of them, and accepts others. Rarely does he specify who held the interpretations he discards, with the result that the text makes the impression of being an even-handed discussion of ideas, without entering into personal matters.

Bhaṭṭoji's contemporaries knew better. Those among them who were themselves learned grammarians, knew that many of the views discarded in this commentary, were the views of Bhaṭṭoji's teacher, i.e., the scholar from

1. For details, see Bronkhorst [2005a].

whom Bhaṭṭoji had learned grammar to begin with. And criticizing one's teacher, in the milieu to which Bhaṭṭoji belonged, was an extremely serious matter. Instead of showing respect to his teacher, Bhaṭṭoji was here doing the opposite. Bhaṭṭoji did not use inappropriate words, certainly. He did not even admit that he was criticizing his teacher, and modern scholars might not have noticed it. But the descendants and other pupils of his teacher needed no time to find out what was happening, and they reacted. They wrote grammatical treatises which tried to destroy all the points of view which Bhaṭṭoji had presented as his own. Once again, the style of these treatises is very learned and highly technical. There are only some odd remarks, usually at the beginning or end of these treatises, which reveal that their authors held a personal grudge against Bhaṭṭoji, that they could not forgive him for having behaved in an inappropriate manner toward their teacher.

But why did Bhaṭṭoji behave in this inappropriate manner? The situation is not completely clear, but it seems likely that there were reasons for this which our texts do not even hint at. One explanation that has been suggested is the fact that Bhaṭṭoji and his teacher had different religious affiliations. Both were, of course, Brahmins, and both were Vedāntins. But whereas Bhaṭṭoji was an Advaita Vedāntin, his teacher was a follower of the school of Vedānta created by Madhva some centuries earlier. We know about these religious affiliations from other sources. The grammatical treatises of Bhaṭṭoji, his teacher, and all the others who became involved in this long drawn-out debate, do not mention this issue. It is only our knowledge of the context which allows us to guess what was going on below the surface of polished and erudite discussions of details of Sanskrit grammar.

I have taken the example of Bhaṭṭoji because, being a relatively recent author, we can find out things about him and his personal life. His own works, but also those of his teacher, and those of some of his critics, have been preserved, and with them various introductory verses and final colophons that throw light upon the situation. Besides this, there are other sources of information that have survived, and which allow us to piece together a coherent picture of what happened. We know a lot about Bhaṭṭoji and his family: we know the name of his father and of various other members of his family; we also know the names of some of his pupils and the pupils of his pupils. We are similarly informed about his teacher and the children and pupils of his teacher. And we have works composed by many of these people, and other information about their lives. In some cases we know who financially supported these scholars.

About earlier philosophers in India we do not have such detailed information. Great and important thinkers of classical India, among them the Buddhist Nāgārjuna and the Vedāntin Śaṅkara, remain completely unknown to us, except through their own works. We are not sure when exactly Nāgārjuna and Śaṅkara lived, or where they wrote the works that made them famous. We do not know the names of their fathers and of their pupils. We do not know for sure at what age they died, and whether their lives had been peaceful or otherwise. We are ignorant as to who supported them, and what encouragement they received from their surroundings. And what I have just said about Nāgārjuna and Śaṅkara—perhaps the two most famous philosophers of classical India—is equally true for practically all other Indian philosophers of that period. Sometimes there are legends, but these legends are often late and unreliable, or mere inventions. All this makes it extremely difficult to situate the philosophers of classical India in their respective contexts. The temptation to abandon hope and to concentrate exclusively on the contents of the surviving texts is therefore great.

However, I am of the opinion that this would be a mistake. We need all the contextual information we can get about our philosophers, for sometimes this is the only way to understand what underlies their philosophical thinking. Sometimes, as in the case of the grammarian Bhaṭṭoji, the deeper motivation may be philosophically insignificant, such as a family feud or a difference in sectarian affiliation. In other cases the deeper motivation is of great philosophical interest. As an example I will briefly present a case to which attention was drawn a few years ago by a Swiss scholar, Vincent Eltschinger. He discusses it in his book *«Caste» et philosophie bouddhique* ("Caste" and buddhist philosophy) that came out in 2000.

Buddhist and brahmanical philosophers of the first millennium CE were engaged in a long and technical debate about the existence of universals. At first sight this is a purely philosophical question, with parallels in the history of European philosophy. The question, as it presents itself in India, can be explained with the help of a simple example. We know that the nouns of our language can be used to designate a large number of objects. The word "cow", for example, can be used not just for one cow, but for all the cows that exist in the present, in the past, and in the future. The same can be said about practically all other nouns, such as "house" or "car". If we stick to the example "cow", we may wonder whether all these cows—past, present, and future—have something in common that justifies this common denomination. Is there such a thing as "cow-ness", a universal that is different from each single cow but that is yet connected with each of them? The same about houses: is there a universal "house-ness" that justifies the application of the word "house" to so many different objects? Brahmanical philosophers had a tendency to accept that such universals exist; Buddhist thinkers denied their existence.

This purely philosophical debate took a special turn in the seventh century with Kumārila Bhaṭṭa, a brahmanical thinker, and Dharmakīrti, a Buddhist. Kumārila applied his belief in the existence of universals to the classes, or "castes", of society. Being a Brahmin, he claimed that all Brahmins share a universal "Brahmin-ness", which distinguishes them fundamentally from all other human beings, just as the universal "cow-ness" separates all cows from other animals, such as horses. Dharmakīrti and his followers did not accept this line of reasoning. They did not think that Brahmins were essentially different from other human beings.

Here, then, we see how a purely philosophical debate took on a social dimension, dictated by the fundamental interests of the philosophers involved. In studying these debates it is imperative to know the different social backgrounds to which thinkers like Kumārila and Dharmakīrti belonged, the former being an orthodox Brahmin, convinced of the intrinsic superiority of the Brahmins, the latter a Buddhist, and as such sceptical with regard to all such claims. This opposition between Brahmins and Buddhists was not created by Kumārila and Dharmakīrti, to be sure. The opposition had been there right from the beginning. A number of *Sūtra*s in the ancient Buddhist canon depict discussions between the Buddha and one or more Brahmins, in which the claim to superior status of the Brahmins is rejected, or even made fun of. With Kumārila and Dharmakīrti this opposition took on a distinctly philosophical dimension, it became part of the philosophical debate of that time. The historian of philosophy will need to be able to place this debate in its historical situation, he will need to be aware of the context in order to fully understand the contents.

II.

A completely different example of a philosophical development which was, perhaps, closely related to a social phenomenon is constituted by a concept which came to play a role in buddhist thought, viz., that of the teaching-body (*dharmakāya*) of the Buddha.[2] We know that worshipping the bodily

2. For details, see Bronkhorst [2005b].

remains of the Buddha was an important aspect of the religion of Buddhist laymen and monastics alike. These bodily remains were often preserved in *stūpa*s. However, the Buddhist preoccupation with dead bodies was highly impure in the eyes of their brahmanical neighbours. Their sensitivity to the impurity of death and all that is associated with it did influence the Indian Buddhists, too, as may be illustrated by the fact that they tended to turn their attention from the bodily relics to the *stūpa*s, their containers, which became objects of worship in their own right. It is also striking that bodily remains of the Buddha tended to be accessible, to at least some degree, in regions which Buddhism did not share with Brahmanism—China, Tibet, Ceylon, but also northwestern India—, but hardly ever in regions where Brahmanism was important. It is perhaps in these regions that Buddhist thinkers developed the idea that the real body of the Buddha was not his physical body, but rather his teaching (*dharma*). There are, as a matter of fact, canonical statements to that effect. It was but a small step from here to postulating an entity called *dharmakāya*, teaching-body, and to maintain that that is the body of the Buddha that should be worshipped. The *dharmakāya* did indeed undergo a long and interesting development in buddhist thought, and came to be identified, in various texts, with different important concept, among them *dharmadhātu* and *tathāgatagarbha*; most importantly, many Buddhists came to look upon the *dharmakāya* as the absolute.[3] This long development, if the hypothetical reconstruction of the historical background of the *dharmakāya* here presented is correct, began, and finds its original explanation, in the Buddhist reaction to brahmanical social pressure.

III.

These last two examples show that knowledge of the social context of Indian philosophy sometimes helps the modern researcher to understand certain details of the positions taken by its practitioners. However, we also need knowledge of the social context to understand that there was such a thing as Indian philosophy at all. In a way this is self-evident. If one wishes to understand why there is philosophy in the modern world, it is important to know that there are institutions, such as universities, which provide modern philosophers with the support they require, such as jobs, teaching opportunities, funds for publications, etc. Without such support, modern

3. For a more detailed presentation, see Bronkhorst [2000: 163 ff.].

philosophy would have a hard time to survive. The situation in classical and medieval India was not different in this respect. These philosophers, too, had material and intellectual needs. They, too, needed an income, or at least shelter and regular meals; they needed access to libraries, manuscript libraries in their case; they needed to be able to pass on their knowledge, first of all to students, we may assume, but also to a network of other philosophers who read their works, etc. The Indian philosophical texts that have come down to us say very little about these earthly and banal realities, yet it is undeniable that, if the circumstances had not been right, many authors might not have been able to write their texts, or, even after writing them, these texts would not have been read and preserved.

All this amounts to saying that the very fact that there is such a thing as Indian philosophy cannot be separated from the circumstances that made this possible. It seems *a priori* likely that there might not have been philosophy in South Asia if there had not been people who had the leisure to create and continue it. But the existence of such a group of people, in and by itself, might not yet have guaranteed the presence of a philosophical tradition. To some extent these people had this leisure, they were given this leisure, because other members of society thought that the study of philosophical issues was particularly important and represented a fundamental value of society as a whole. This we know is true. Most schools of Indian philosophy agreed that philosophy is necessary for those who wish to attain liberation from the cycle of rebirth which they all believed in; and liberation from rebirth is the highest aim there is.

So far so good. The elements considered so far do not, however, explain why Indian philosophy took the forms it actually took. They would explain the existence of wisdom teachings, perhaps in different varieties for different currents of thought. They do not explain why classical Indian philosophers went out of their way to argue for their positions, sometimes going to the extent of criticizing the positions of other thinkers, they do not explain why these philosophers developed logical rules and rules of debate, why they presented their views in the form of ever more coherent wholes, why they created systems of thought rather than mere collections of wise statements. Why did they do all this? Why did they not leave each other alone, concentrating each on his own method to attain liberation? Liberation, in most religious currents of India, is a highly personal attainment, quite independent of social considerations; why then should the way leading to it pass through philosophical debates whose aim is to convince, or refute others? Obviously the Indian philosophers did all they could to convince each other, to show that the other thinkers, if they really thought things out clearly, should change their opinions and convert to their own points of view.

At first sight one might think that Indian philosophers were concerned with convincing each other because this was part of their missionary intention. We know that Buddhism made a conscious effort to convert people, and that it was extraordinarily successful in this. Jainism, too, we can be sure, made efforts to convince people of the value and importance of their path to liberation. In spite of this, I think that the urge to convert provides at best a very small part of the answer to our question. Buddhism and Jainism did not, or not primarily, carry out their missionary activity by means of philosophical debate, but by preaching their respective doctrines. And Brahmanism, as is well known, was not interested in missionary activity in the ordinary sense at all: no one could become a Brahmin who was not already a Brahmin; agreement or disagreement on complex philosophical issues could not change that.

The correct explanation of the elements of Indian philosophy just mentioned, as I see it, is different. These elements are in an important sense the result of a social custom. They are the consequence of a feature of the social context, that has accompanied Indian philosophy for most of its history. This feature, this social custom, is the existence of public debates between philosophers of different persuasions.

The history of Indian philosophy is full of references to debates that presumably had taken place between prominent representatives of different schools of thought. Many of these accounts may be legendary, or fully imaginary; others may be less than reliable because coloured in favour of one of the parties involved. It would yet be extremely interesting if someone were one day to make the effort of collecting all those accounts, whether from brahmanical, buddhist, or Jaina sources, whether reliable or not. Such an overview might even include the *paṇḍitapariṣad*s, the "assemblies of wise men", that are still sometimes held in India, and that are occasionally organized at international Śanskrit conferences. These *paṇḍitapariṣad*s are, to be sure, no more than fossilized survivals. But living debates, with sometimes serious consequences for the participants, accompanied Indian philosophy for most of its history. We know, for example, that the brother of Bhaṭṭoji, the philosopher and grammarian whom we referred to above, won a debate at the court of a South Indian king called Veṅkaṭappa. Given that this debate took place at the court of a king, we must conclude that this king allowed, or even encouraged, this debate to take place.

King Veṅkaṭappa was not exceptional in organizing, or allowing, such debates at his court. As a matter of fact, he continued a very long tradition in doing so. It is this social custom—it is really a social custom—which, I believe, made Indian philosophy what it is. Participants in such debates could win much, they could also loose all they had. Participating in such debates was not, therefore, a matter of mere amusement. It was through such debates that philosophers of different orientations combated each other, and tried to obtain a maximum of advantages for themselves and for the groups they represented. But since the stakes were so high, every potential participant had to prepare himself as well as he could. He had to be able to present his views, or those of his school, in such a way that an outside judge, sometimes the king himself, would be convinced by them. In practice this meant various things. First of all, mere wisdom teachings would not impress anybody. Teachings had to constitute coherent wholes, free from inner contradictions and loose ends. Second, the debater should, to the extent possible, know the ideas of his opponent, including whatever weaknesses it might contain. It would of course be very impressive to be able to show, during a public debate, that the opponent held incoherent or even nonsensical views.

As I said above, debates are not a recent phenomenon in Indian philosophy. For the middle of the first millennium CE—the classical period of Indian philosophy, we have a number of reports from foreign visitors. We will look at two of them in some detail. The first of these two derives from the Chinese Buddhist pilgrim Xuanzang (or Hsüan-chuang); since he is called Genjō in Japanese, I will use that name in what follows. Genjō has left us a detailed account of his visit to India in the first half of the seventh century of the Common Era. In this account he regularly mentions debates between representatives of different schools of thought. The debates he refers to normally took place in the presence of a king, and tended to end in victory for one of the two parties, and defeat for the other. According to the biography of Genjō composed by his pupil Huili, Genjō himself volunteered to participate in a debate on one occasion. The event is described as follows:[4]

> At that time a heretic of the Lokāyatika school came to seek a debate and wrote his argument in fourteen points, which he hung on the door of the monastery, while he announced, 'If anybody is able to refute any one point of my argument, I shall cut off my head to apologize!'

4. Li [1995: 132 f. (modified); translates pp. 245a–c].

> After the passage of several days, nobody came out to accept the challenge. The Master [=Genjō] then asked his personal servant to take down the poster, destroy it, and trample the broken pieces under his feet. Being greatly enraged, the Brahmin asked, 'Who are you?' The servant said in reply, 'I am a servant of the Mahāyāna-deva.' The Brahmin, who had already heard of the fame of the Master, was ashamed of himself and did not say anything more. The Master sent for him and brought him to the presence of the Venerable Śīlabhadra [Genjō's teacher at Nālandā Monastery], with various virtuous monks as witnesses, to start a debate with him about the principles of his school and the theories founded by other heretical sects as well.

The debate as recorded in Huili's account is somewhat one-sided, presumably because the Brahmin opponent is too shy to speak in the presence of Genjō. Genjō first demonstrates his knowledge of a number of brahmanical ascetic and philosophical schools, and then refutes one of them, supposedly the one to which his opponent belongs, in detail.[5] At the end of this the text sums up the result:

> In this manner the argument was carried on with repeated refutations; and the Brahmin remained silent and said nothing. Then he rose to his feet and said with apology, 'I am defeated, and I am ready to keep my word.' The Master said, 'We Buddhists do not take any man's life. I now make you my slave, and you should work according to my orders.' The Brahmin was glad to obey the Master's orders with reverence, and was brought to his living quarters. All those who heard about this event praised it with delight.

It is unlikely that this passage accurately presents what happened. It is hard to believe that a Brahmin who was seeking a debate would accept total defeat without as much as uttering a word. But nor would we expect historical accuracy in a document that primarily sings the glory of Master Genjō. It will be interesting to see what kind of arguments supposedly led to his victory in debate.

The text does not offer much in terms of arguments, with one notable exception. The Master is recorded to have dealt with the Sāṃkhya system of thought in a rather more detailed manner. First he presents an outline of

5. Surprisingly, Genjō refutes the Sāṃkhya school of thought, even though his opponent is a Lokāyatika. On this question, see my forthcoming article "Pañcaśikha and Lokāyata".

the system, which agrees with what we know about it. After this exposition he draws attention to what he considers its lack of coherence. It is not likely that a real Sāṃkhya would have felt defeated by the reflections brought to bear on their system by the Chinese pilgrim. It is yet interesting to see that Genjō is here depicted as presenting what is an accurate description of the main features of the Sāṃkhya philosophy, and that, having presented this outline, he tries to show its inner incoherence. The fundamental assumptions of this philosophy do not, according to the position attributed to Genjō, justify the functions it ascribes to the various entities it postulates.

Accounts like this are extremely interesting, and give us a glimpse, if ever so faint, of situations India's philosophers may have been familiar with. In the present context it is noteworthy to see what could be at stake in such debates. Genjō's unfortunate opponent was lucky to get away with his life, and be merely reduced to the state of being Genjō's slave. We do not know to what extent we are here confronted with an exaggeration on the part of Genjō's biographer, but we will see that death as a result of a lost debate is a recurring theme. But even without death or loss of individual liberty, there can be no doubt that debaters could lose their reputation once and for all, and with it whatever privileges were reserved for their group or community. Winning a debate could be very advantageous. Elsewhere Genjō reports that Śīlabhadra, the same Master also mentioned in the preceding passage, had once defeated a Brahmin in a debate, after which he had received from the local king the revenues of a certain city.[6]

Let us now turn to the second example, situated a few centuries before the time of Genjō. It depicts a debate between a Buddhist and a Sāṃkhya in which, this time, the latter is victorious. The story is found in Paramārtha's *The Life of Vasubandhu*. The main character is the Sāṃkhya teacher Vindhyavāsa, who modified the Sāṃkhya doctrine and came to think that the doctrine set forth by him was the greatest, and that nothing could be superior to it. However, Buddhism was flourishing in the world at that time. Vindhyavāsa therefore resolved to refute it. The text continues:[7]

> Accordingly he went to the country of Ayodhyā and beat the drum of dispute with his head and said:
> (The translator of this passage explains in a note that, according to a commentator, 'it was customary for a king in India to keep a drum

6. Watters [1904–05/1973: II: 109–110].
7. Takakusu [1904: 283 f.]. Cp. the discussion in Larson & Bhattacharya [1987: 131 f.].

at the Royal Gate. When a man wants to appeal to the Court or to challenge a dispute, he has to beat it.')

'I will dispute (with any Buddhist Śramaṇa). If I am defeated my opponent shall cut my head off; but if, on the contrary, he is beaten, he shall give me his head.' The King, Vikramāditya..., being informed of the matter summoned the heretic and asked him about it, whereupon the latter answered: 'Thou art, O King, the Lord of the Land, in whose mind there should be no partial love to either Śramaṇas or Brahmins. If there be any doctrines prevailing (in thy country) thou shouldst put them to the test (and see whether) they are right or wrong. Now I intend (to dispute) with a disciple of Śākya-muni [=the Buddha] to determine which party is the winner or the loser. Each should vow to stake his own head.' The King thereupon gave him permission and despatched men to ask all the Buddhist teachers of the country in the following words: 'Is there anyone who is able to oppose this heretic? Whosoever thinks himself competent should dispute with him.'

At that time the great Teachers of the Law, Manoratha, Vasubandhu, and others were all absent travelling in other countries. ...

There was at home only Buddhamitra the teacher of Vasubandhu. ... This Teacher of the Law was formerly very learned, but he was now advanced in years and therefore weak in mind and feeble in his speech. He said: 'Now the great champions of the Law are all abroad. The heretic is strong and obstinate and must not be let alone any longer. I will now see to it myself.' He informed the King, who appointed a day on which he summoned a great assembly to the hall of discussion, where the heretic and the Buddhist teacher were to meet and dispute.

The heretic said: 'Will you first set forth your opinion? Or will you refute the opinion first set forth by me?' The priest replied: 'I am like a great ocean which swallows up all that comes. You are like a lump of earth which will be submerged if it comes to the ocean. You may do as you like.' His opponent said: 'Then you had better set forth your own opinion (first). I will refute it.'

The Buddhist teacher, thereupon, set forth his doctrine of impermanence and said: 'All composite things are in process of destruction every moment, why? because they disappear in the end.' He further supported this by various arguments. The heretic opponent could repeat all these arguments of the Buddhist priest after once hearing them and began to criticise them one by one by processes of reasoning. On being requested to commit to memory and repeat these refutations the priest

> failed to do so. He could not even re-construct his own arguments, though requested to do so.
>
> Thus the Buddhist priest was completely defeated. The heretic said: 'You are a Brahmin by caste and I also am a Brahmin. We are not allowed to kill. I will beat you on the back instead, in order to show that I am the victor.' He did so. The king gave him three lacs of gold as a prize. On receiving the gold he distributed it among the people at large and returned to the Vindhya mountain where he entered a rocky cave.

The story has a happy ending after all, for Vasubandhu, after his return, composed a work criticising the Sāṃkhya doctrine in such a competent manner that the heretics had nothing left for them to fall back upon. In this way, without meeting Vindhyavāsa, Vasubandhu took full vengeance on him and wiped off the disgrace put upon his teacher.

IV.

These examples show that loosing a debate could have serious consequences, and winning one could have serious advantages. It is not surprising that debating manuals were produced, some of which have survived. Public debates had to be won, and all possible means were used in order to attain that goal. This included trickery, but also straightforward, and soundly based, criticism of each other's positions. It is this aspect of the debate tradition which has no doubt exerted a lasting influence. Criticism directed at others and criticism received from others had the unavoidable effect that all participants in these debates straightened out their own positions. Incoherent or inconsistent views might not survive scrutiny, not by an opponent in debate, but neither by the thinker who did not wish to be exposed by those who disagreed with him.

It is in this way that a social custom—viz., organizing public debates, preferably at the court of a king or local ruler—was responsible for one of the most striking features of Indian philosophy: the search for coherent systems of thought. Interestingly, we know much more about the effect of this social custom than about the social custom itself. Our sources inform us in great detail about the systems of thought that were elaborated, and only occasionally about the debates that took place. The connection between these two seems to me yet close enough to allow us to draw conclusions with regard to periods from which we have very little information about the social context. I suggest that, wherever Indian philosophy gave rise to coherent systems of thought, we can conclude from this that a debate tradition made this possible, or even necessary. Note at this point that not all of Indian thought is coherent and systematic. Most of the religious literature of India contains ideas which are not put into the straightjacket of a system of thought. Examples are the early *Upaniṣad*s, the philosophical portions of the *Mahābhārata*, and much else. Systematic thought in India dwindles in comparison with the quantity of non-systematized thought. Yet it is systematic thought that interests us at present, because it reveals something about the social context in which it could arise and flourish.

If, with this in mind, we look at the earliest manifestations of systematic thought in India, our attention is inevitably drawn to the scholastic development which Buddhism underwent during the last centuries preceding the Common Era. Buddhist scholasticism of that period, called *abhidharma*, has mainly survived in two bodies of texts, belonging to two schools of Buddhism. One of the two, belonging to the Theravāda school of Buddhism, shows an ongoing refinement, but little or no attempt to develop a coherent system of thought. The other school, Sarvāstivāda, is altogether different. Several texts of its canonical "Basket of scholasticism" (*abhidharma-piṭaka*) show that serious attempts at systematization were made in this school. Since the innovations concerned were made on the basis of traditional material, the result is often quite complex, and this is not the place to deal with them in full detail.[8] Only some striking features must here be mentioned. The Sarvāstivāda conception of the world is essentially atomistic. The macroscopic, and therefore composite, objects which we are acquainted with from everyday experience do not really exist. What really exist are the ultimate constituents, called *dharma*s. A particularly important composite object is the human person which, too, does not really exist. The atomistic understanding of the world also finds expression in the belief in momentariness: nothing exists for more than a single moment.[9] Various questions linked to this atomistic vision of the world are raised and often answered by introducing an appropriate *dharma*. The question, for example, how different bundles of *dharma*s stick together so as to form different persons (remember that persons do strictly speaking not exist), is answered with the introduction of a *dharma* called *prāpti* 'possession'.

8. For a slightly more detailed, but still incomplete presentation, see Bronkhorst [2000: 76–127].

9. Momentariness is not explicitly mentioned in early Sarvāstivāda Abhidharma texts, but can quite safely be attributed to their authors; see Bronkhorst [1995].

Other difficulties were connected with the belief that mental events occur only one at a time in one person. This leads to difficulties in the case where someone observes, say, his own desire. This activity involves two mental events, the observation and the desire, which cannot simultaneously exist. When the observation is present, the observed desire must of necessity be non-present. Observation of a desire is therefore only possible if a non-present object (the desire) exists. The Sarvāstivādins concluded from this that past and future exist. This particular view, incidentally, is responsible for their name, Sarvāstivāda, the "position (*vāda*) according to which everything (*sarva*) exists (*asti*)". Sarvāstivāda, as will be clear from this very brief presentation, made a major effort to rationalise its teachings, Theravāda did not. Sarvāstivāda played a major role in the tradition of debate that came to involve all schools of philosophy, whether Buddhist, Brahmanical, or Jaina; it seems even likely that the Sarvāstivādins were the first to adhere to this tradition of debate in India. Theravāda played no such role, and indeed left India before this tradition of debate had attained a prominent position.

What can we conclude from these attempts at systematization carried out, apparently for the first time, by the Sarvāstivādins of northwestern India? I am tempted to conclude that the same social context which made systematization possible and necessary in later times, existed already in the last centuries BCE in northwestern India, perhaps for the first time. The Buddhists of that time and region clearly felt the need to present their more sophisticated views in such a manner that outsiders would not easily find systematic weaknesses in them. Just like their later colleagues, they had to defend their positions, quite possibly during public debates.

This conclusion raises a number of questions. Who were the rulers in northwestern India who might organize debates at their courts or elsewhere? With whom might the Buddhists of northwestern India have been asked to debate? Who were their opponents? Don't forget that we have no evidence of the existence of systematic brahmanical thought during this early period. What is more, there are good reasons to think that there were few, if any, Brahmins in the regions inhabited by the Buddhists of northwestern India—primarily Gandhāra, perhaps also Bactria. These regions were ruled, for at least some of the time that concerns us, by Greeks. We know that Hellenistic kings in general cultivated the presence of philosophers at their courts, and encouraged debates between them. Is it possible that the social context which was to accompany Indian philosophy practically throughout its long history, the debates that made the formulation of critical and systematic philosophy a necessity, is it possible that all this began at the Greek courts of northwestern India? I think there is much that pleads in favour of this possibility.[10] We know that a number of Greeks from that area were interested in Buddhism, even converted to that religion. The text called "The questions of king Milinda" shows that, in the imagination of at least some later Buddhists, the Greeks and their kings, most notably Menander, had participated in discussions with Buddhists. It is also known that, even after the Greeks had lost power in northwestern India, their influence took centuries before ebbing away completely.

V.

At this point you may raise the following objection. You will admit that a certain knowledge of the context is required to understand at least certain issues dealt with in Indian philosophy. You are even willing to grant that context has to be considered in order to understand that there is such a thing as Indian philosophy at all. However, you will say, what we need to know about this context is relatively little. Two of the cases we have discussed show this. Yes, to understand some aspects of Indian philosophy we need to know that many Indian philosophers were Brahmins, people who claimed a privileged status in society, while others, most notably the Buddhists, did not accept that claim. And yes, you will continue, to understand the inner dynamic of Indian philosophy one must know that public debates were a recurring phenomenon throughout its long history. However, you will insist, both these contextual features are as old as Indian philosophy; they have accompanied it from beginning to end. Even after the disappearance of Buddhism from the Indian philosophical scene, debates continued, as we saw in the case of Bhaṭṭoji. In other words, you will conclude, only contextual features that have not changed in any essential manner need to be known to understand Indian philosophy. Other contextual features, features that changed over the period of two thousand years or more since the beginning of systematic philosophy in India, such other features are of little importance for the study and understanding of this tradition.

This objection is not justified in my opinion. It is true that two of the four examples so far discussed concerned contextual features of great temporal endurance. Both the brahmanical claim of social superiority and the tradition of public debate had a long life, as long as Indian philosophy itself. Yet it

10. Cf. Bronkhorst [1999].

would be a mistake to look upon these two features as constants, as some unchangeable and permanent background to the development of Indian philosophy. They were not, as a matter of fact. Some schools of thought developed in environments where there were neither tradition of debate, nor sophisticated opponents ready to criticize their thought in detail. There is also reason to think that the tradition of debate was not always equally strong. I will briefly discuss one example for each of these two cases.

I have already briefly mentioned the Theravāda school of Buddhism, contemporaneous with the Sarvāstivāda school which we studied in some detail. Both these schools developed and preserved an important body of scholastic literature, called *Abhidharma*. The Sarvāstivāda school, as we saw, remodelled their *Abhidharma* into a coherent system of thought. The Theravādins did no such thing. This can be seen by considering one of their texts, which is one of the earliest surviving texts in India dedicated to criticising the positions of others. It is called *Kathāvatthu* "Text dealing with disputes", and was composed, according to tradition, 218 years after the death of the Buddha.[11] It criticises in its oldest portions a position which we know was held by the Sarvāstivādins, mentioned earlier. An analysis of the criticism presented in the *Kathāvatthu* shows that its author had not understood, and had perhaps no knowledge whatsoever of, the arguments used by the Sarvāstivādins to justify their position. The Sarvāstivādins held that past and future exist, and their argumentation, as we have seen, was built on their fundamental belief that no two mental events can simultaneously occur in one person. The author of the *Kathāvatthu* presents instead an argument that is totally nonsensical.[12] The *Kathāvatthu*, then, is a text which criticises the positions of others without being properly informed about them (at least in this case). No need to say that its uninformed criticism carried little weight. The Sarvāstivādins did not, and did not need to, change their views as a result of the criticism expressed in this Theravāda text. What is more, the Theravādins felt no need to tighten up their own views and develop them into a coherent whole. The question is why? The answer I propose is that the *Kathāvatthu* was written in a part of India where public debate had not yet forced its author or authors to introduce coherence in their own thought, and had not yet urged them to inform themselves with regard to the details of the opinions they disagreed with. The authors of the *Kathāvatthu* were under no pressure to do all this,

11. Hinüber [1996: 70 f.].
12. Bronkhorst [1993].

and the result of this is visible in their text.

Regarding the tradition of debate, our information about it is only lacunary, and I have already given expression to the desirability of further research in this domain. It seems yet clear that this social institution was during some periods more active, more alive, than during others. In order to illustrate this, I return once again to the philosopher and grammarian Bhaṭṭoji Dīkṣita, discussed at the beginning of this paper. I have told you already that this thinker lived in Benares, around the year 1600 CE. Bhaṭṭoji and his nephew Kauṇḍa Bhaṭṭa are known for the new development in the so-called "philosophy of grammar" which they initiated. In this philosophy they made use of a new technical terminology that had been created some centuries earlier by thinkers of the Navya-Nyāya, i.e., "New Logic", school of thought. Bhaṭṭoji and Kauṇḍa Bhaṭṭa introduced this terminology into grammatical thought, from where another school of thought, that of Vedic Hermeneutics (Mīmāṃsā), appears to have borrowed it to use it for its own purposes.

The question that presents itself here is the following. Why did it take several centuries before the new technical terminology was taken over by grammarians and Vedic Hermeneuts? And why was it then taken over by both grammarians and Vedic Hermeneuts, almost simultaneously, in the city of Benares? The new terminology was apparently used for several centuries inside one school, with hardly anyone bothering to take notice (even though Prof. Wada informs me that certain Vedāntins may have started using it somewhat earlier than the grammarians and Vedic Hermeneuts). How can this be explained? The answer, as I see it, lies in the fact that Benares around the year 1600 CE was a centre where debate between representatives of different schools of thought had been revived, for reasons which are too complex to analyse here at present. For some centuries before this time, philosophical schools existed and even flourished in a certain sense. However, they remained largely isolated from each other. A new centre and a new political and social situation were required to oblige these philosophers again to take serious notice of what happened in other schools of thought.

VI.

I think I have said enough about the changeability of the context in which Indian philosophy began and developed. To conclude, I would like to very briefly touch upon an aspect of Indian philosophy which is claimed to be central to it. I had occasion to point out that most schools of Indian philosophy agree that philosophy is necessary to attain liberation from the cycle of rebirth. How practical was this claim? How serious were Indian philosophers about reaching this aim during this life? Was this claim mere lip-service to a high ideal, without practical consequences, or did Indian thinkers combine the study of philosophy with other activities they believed were necessary to reach the highest goal?

It is not possible to answer these questions in general terms that are valid for all Indian philosophers. The seriousness with which thinkers dedicated themselves to the attainment of liberation may have differed from one school to the next, from one person to the other. In many cases it is extremely difficult, or even impossible, to find information that may allow us to answer these questions. It is for this reason all the more interesting to refer to some recent studies that throw light on the practical commitment to liberation among Buddhist monks of northwestern India during the first centuries of the Common Era. I am referring to the studies of Gregory Schopen, more specifically to those that have recently been brought out in a collection called *Buddhist Monks and Business Matters* (2004). Many of these studies are based, at least in part, on a detailed analysis of portions of the large collection of monastic rules known by the name Mūlasarvāstivāda Vinaya, which appears to date from that period. It is not possible to do full justice to Schopen's volume here. All I can do is quote a short passage which contains a clear statement about the issue that interests us:[13]

> Forty years ago André Bareau said not just about [the Mūlasarvāstivāda Vinaya] but about all Buddhist monastic Codes: "It is true that the Vinayapiṭakas ... do not breathe a word about the numerous spiritual practices, meditations, contemplations, etc., which constituted the very essence of the Buddhist 'religion'." And although this is something of an exaggeration, still it should have given pause for thought. Our Code, for example, does refer to ascetic, meditating monks, but when it does so in any detail, such monks almost always appear as the butt of jokes, objects of ridicule, and—not uncommonly—sexual deviants. They are presented as irresponsible and of the type that give the order a bad name. There are texts in our Code where, for example, ascetic, cemetery monks manage only to terrify children; where ascetic monks who wear robes made from cemetery cloth are not even allowed into the monastery, let alone allowed to sit on a mat that belongs to

13. Schopen [2004: 26].

> the Community; tales whose only point seems to be to indicate that meditation makes you stupid; texts about monks who meditate in the forest and cannot control their male member and so end up smashing it between two rocks, whereupon the Buddha tells them, while they are howling in pain, that they, unfortunately, have smashed the wrong thing—they should have smashed desire; and a tale about another monk who meditated in the forest and, to avoid being seduced by a goddess, had to tie his legs shut. The goddess being put off by this then flung him through the air, and he landed—still legs tied—on top of the king, who was sleeping on the roof of his palace. The king, of course, was not amused and made it known to the Buddha that it would not do to have his monks being flung around the countryside in the middle of the night. The Buddha then actually made a rule forbidding monks to meditate in the forest! Texts and tales of this sort are numerous in our Code.

Remember that these remarks are made about the Mūlasarvāstivāda Vinaya, an expression which Schopen translates either "the Original Vinaya of the Sarvāstivādins" or "the Vinaya of the Original Sarvāstivādins" (p. 25). Either way a link with the Sarvāstivādins is implied by its very title. The Sarvāstivādins, you may recall, were among the first systematic philosophers of India. Schopen's observations suggest that these philosophers, who in theory subscribed to the connection between philosophy and liberation, were in practice united in a monastic corporation which had no place whatsoever for monks who wished to meditate.

This is not the occasion to elaborate the implications of these observations. It is however clear that here we may be confronted with a situation in which the context and the contents of the philosophical writings concerned do not easily fit together. The question does require further reflection, but it does seem allowable to conclude that these Buddhists from the first centuries CE only paid lip-service to the ideals which were supposed to be the justification of their philosophical efforts.

VII.

Indian philosophy is not a collection of timeless truths. Like everything else, its doctrines were produced in certain times and in certain places—in other words, within a context. Extracting Indian philosophy from of the context in which it was created is doing it an injustice. Worse still, it may deprive us of possibilities of understanding which only an awareness of context can provide. Why did Indian philosophers accept these ideas rather than others? Why did they defend them the way they did? What was philosophy good for in their eyes? These and many other questions can only be answered by situating the texts and their authors in their own environments, by finding out what was important for them, which were the problems they had to deal with, etc. Any other way of trying to understand Indian philosophy, for example by merely looking at questions and issues that it has in common with modern western philosophy, is fundamentally mistaken, and may give rise to major misunderstandings. Context, seen in this way, is not an extra, an indulgence for those who are interested in it. Trying to understand Indian philosophy in its own historical context is obligatory, the only way one may hope to arrive at an optimal understanding.

References

Bronkhorst, Johannes

1993 "Kathāvatthu and Vijñānakāya", *Premier Colloque Étienne Lamotte* (Bruxelles et Liège 24–27 septembre 1989), Université Catholique de Louvain: Institut Orientaliste Louvain-la-Neuve, pp. 57–61.

1995 Review of Rospatt [1995], *Asiatische Studien / Études Asiatiques* 49(2): 513–519.

1999 *Why is there Philosophy in India?* Amsterdam: Royal Netherlands Academy of Arts and Sciences.

2000 "Die buddhistische Lehre" in *Der Buddhismus* I: *Der indische Buddhismus und seine Verzweigungen*, Die Religionen der Menschheit, vol. 24,1, Stuttgart: W. Kohlhammer, pp. 23–212.

2005a "Bhaṭṭoji Dīkṣita on sphoṭa", *Journal of Indian Philosophy* 33(1): 3–41.

2005b "Les reliques dans les religions de l'Inde" in Lars Göhler (ed.), *Indische Kultur im Kontext. Rituale, Texte und Ideen aus Indien und der Welt. Festschrift für Klaus Mylius*, Beiträge zur Indologie 40, Wiesbaden: Harrassowitz, pp. 49–85.

Eltschinger, Vincent

2000 *«Caste» et philosophie bouddhique: Continuité de quelques arguments bouddhiques contre le traitement réaliste des dénominations socials*, Wiener Studien zur Tibetologie und Buddhismuskunde 47, Wien: Arbeitskreis für Tibetische und Buddhistische Studien Universität Wien.

von Hinüber, Oskar
1996 *A Handbook of Pāli Literature*, Indian Philology and South Asian Studies 2, Berlin / New York: Walter de Gruyter.

Larson, Gerald James, & Ram Shankar Bhattacharya
1987 (eds.) *Sāṃkhya: A dualist tradition in Indian philosophy*, Encyclopedia of Indian Philosophies, vol. IV, Delhi: Motilal Banarsidass.

Li, Rongxi
1995 (tr.) *A Biography of the Tripiṭaka Master of the Great Ci'en Monastery of the Great Tang Dynasty*, translated from the Chinese of Śramaṇa Huili en Shi Yancong (Taishō, vol. 50, No. 2053), BDK English Tripiṭaka 77, Berkeley, California: Numata Center for Buddhist Translation and Research.

von Rospatt, Alexander
1995 *The Buddhist Doctrine of Momentariness: A survey of the origins and early phase of this doctrine up to Vasubandhu*, Alt- und Neu-Indische Studien 47, Stuttgart: Franz Steiner.

Schopen, Gregory
2004 *Buddhist Monks and Business Matters: Still more papers on monastic Buddhism in India*, Honolulu: University of Hawaii Press.

Takakusu, Junjiro
1904 "The Life of Vasu-bandhu, by Paramārtha (A.D. 499–569)", *T'oung Pao*, Série II, vol. V, pp. 269–296, 620.

Watters, Thomas
1973 (1904–05) *On Yuan Chwang's Travels in India. (A.D. 629–645)*, Delhi: Munshiram Manoharlal, Reprint.

II
BUDDHISM

CHAPTER 2

SOME REFLECTIONS ON THE HISTORY OF BUDDHIST CANONS IN ANCIENT INDIA

Masahiro SHIMODA

1. Between Religion and Scripture

"Founded religions" such as Christianity, Islam and Buddhism have ideas, concepts, and thoughts expressed by words embedded in books that are specially designated as *sacred scripture*. Once accustomed to this characteristic, people tend to take these sacred writings to be the origin of these religions. When we pay attention to how things are temporally ordered, we will find it obvious that some of the constructs of a religion were first expressed orally, and then, at some later point in time, were compiled in the form of written scriptures, and not the other way around. Despite this self-evident phenomenon, people seem to inherit canonical scriptures not only as writings to read and understand, but as objects of worship. These scriptures, immersed in this secondary characteristic irrelevant to the primary aim of writing, end up in being enshrined in the recesses of altars.

Once a religion entrusts a major part of its existence to written materials, the religion starts to regard the image emerging from the writings as the eternal figure of the religion. The religion and the scripture at this stage are inseparably related as though they were mirrors reflecting each other's contents. Even in the midst of historical changes, the religion repeatedly returns to the self-image preserved in the writing and continues to attach to it. Tensions and conflicts arising in the encounter between changing realities and fixed canonical scriptures can be eased by interpretation. As a result, an impression comes to be shared among people that the canonical scriptures are protected from the effects of temporality.

To locate in a proper context a religious scripture provided with the aforementioned characteristics is not a simple task. A scripture that is a product of a past goes beyond the past in terms that it, when read, affects the present of the reader of the text. Canonical texts in this respect show "a past to affect the present," not of an inert past that ceased to effect on the present. This, then, leads us to call into question the generally accepted attitude of reading a *sūtra* in Indian Buddhism by reconstructing its historical context. This way of reading that confines the *sūtras* in the already closed historical past, fairly common among modern academic societies, though, needs reconsideration. Attention should be paid to another way of reading that takes a note of a dialogue to be invoked between the past of the text and the present of the reader.

In this regard, the distinction between "the documentary aspect" and "the work-like aspect" that is proposed by Dominick LaCapra comes to our attention.[1] When a reader deals with a text as a "document" comprised of historical sources, LaCapra argues, he or she recreates the historical context of the text one-sidedly, and, at this time, it is only the text that is subject to change. On the other hand, when one reads a text as a "work," a dialogue arises between the reader in the present and the work from the past, and, on this occasion, not only the text but also the reader will go through changes as he or she reads along with the text.[2] The more a text from the past deserves to be qualified as a classic, the more likely is it that the text has the power to resist a conventional understanding by drawing a reader into serious emotional or intellectual conflict to change the reader's world-view as well as his or her own self-image.

The work-like aspect of a text seems effective in considering the formation process of Buddhist scriptures in ancient India; *sūtras* have functioned in the world of Buddhism more as "works" than as "documents," for it is dialogues being continuously conducted between the compilers and the readers of the texts that developed and modified the *sūtras* in the process of transmission. To properly understand a *sūtra* endowed with these characteristics inherited in a history, a process by which a text has been transformed through a continuous dialogue is of primary significance.

---

1. LaCapra [1983].
2. It should be noted that LaCapra's definition of the relation between "work" and "text" is not commensurate with the now widely accepted analysis provided by Roland Barthes in his influential essays, "From Work to Text," and "Death of the Author." In these essays, "work" specifically implies a one-to-one relation between author and his creation, and "text" implies (among other things) the inability to pinpoint a single individual as the creator of the textual object—which itself lacks a clear border from "other texts." See Barthes [1977].

2. Truth, Person, and History in Buddhist Texts

"In the beginning, was *not* the Word." Unlike the above-mentioned relationship between a religion and its canonical scriptures commonly confirmed in the other founded religions, we should start to investigate with this rather strange statement, as far as the Buddhist canons are concerned. Contrary to our expectation that Buddhism began with the Buddha's first discourse, a number of life-stories of the Buddha agree on the point that the Buddha, having reached the supreme awakening, showed a strong hesitation to deliver his teaching through the medium of the word.

These legends describe with one accord that the Buddha blessed with the pleasure of the supreme awakening in the midst of deep meditation came across an idea that the *Dharma* he had finally reached was too profound for people to understand. Overwhelmed by this notion, fearful of the possibility of failure in his effort to teach, the Buddha decided to retreat into his experience of meditation, keeping silent in an individually-enjoyed state of meditative bliss. Seeing this, Brahmā, the supreme god in the ancient Indian religious world, appeared in front of the Buddha, pleading with him three times to deliver his teaching, by pointing out that no truth would ever be revealed if the Buddha did not speak. This entreaty by Brahmā to open up the discourse eventually woke the Buddha up to reality, encouraged him to turn a merciful eye to those in struggle around him, and, at last, succeeded in persuading him into making a firm declaration of a resolution to preach for the miserable beings.[3]

The distrust by the Buddha of the efficacy of words is understandable.

---

3. Regarding this topic, see Shimoda [2001] [2004b]. As I mentioned in these papers, this tale may sound rather odd to modern-day Buddhists, who are accustomed to seeing the Buddha as savior. Previous studies generally gave to the story such a conventional interpretation as they aimed at ensuring Buddhism authenticity in the Indian religious world by making the supreme god pay homage to the Buddha. This interpretation, not being entirely wrong in explaining the secondary effects brought about by the event, is far from satisfactory when we take into account the following two points. First, the advantage of enhancing the relative position of Buddhism to Brahmanism is utterly outweighed by the disadvantage of degrading the Buddha's image as savior. This is the most crucial scene in which the truth, once discovered by the Buddha, is about to be transmitted to and shared among the people suffering in pain and misery. The Buddha's attitude in wishing to retreat into an inner life of personal contentment, instead of showing compassion for the poor, would irretrievably damage his image as savior. Second, this story, in view of its syntactical structure, apparently operates not so much to enhance the Buddha's image over that of the god Brahmā as to emphasize the Buddha's hesitation to speak on the Dharma. For the materials of this story, see: Sakamoto (Goto) [1992].

Words have been maintained and transmitted as social property in a society, and they are valid insofar as the members in the society share common experience by using those words. We may ask, at this point, a simple question of whether a word can convey a definite meaning to others who do not have the same experience. If the Buddha was conscious that no one had reached the same state of mind that he had, he may well have felt disinclined to communicate to the people of the rank and file in the society by using words. Once consigned to words, one's experience, however profound it may be, would be imprinted on the surface of the meaning of the word that has been commonly shared in the society, and would be understood as nothing other than a tiny, daily event.

The tension between the word and experience is so important a subject that it appears repeatedly in Buddhist literature in different guises through the ages.[4] Nevertheless, the Buddha's firm resolution to give the first discourse, trusting the efficacy of the word as a means of conveying experience, opened up a path for the next generation. The effort to formulate experience into language, at first, makes the speaker recognize in a clearly articulated form an experience he or she have had in a more or less amorphous state, and then, with that effect, induce the hearer into the similar, or perhaps the same experience. Even though the word by nature is not the truth, it works as an effective means to clarify one's own experience, and lures others into a similar structure of experience.

This attitude of Buddhism toward the word and experience represented by the Buddha at his first sermon is in stark contrast with that of the monotheistic religions that operate from the premise of the sentence "in the beginning, was the Word," and that cannot go without the presence of prophets who are "entrusted with the word of God."[5] In Buddhism, by contrast, the word itself is not the truth, and the truth lies in what the word conveys and realizes. A true word leads one to the truth, and when one reaches the truth through the word, one can abandon the word in the same way as one abandons a raft after he or she managed to cross a river.[6] We

4. For this topic, see Shimoda [1996]. This paper is based on previous several studies on this theme such as: Edgerton [1929]; Poussin [1936/7]; Eliade [1958]; Schmithausen [1981]; Vetter [1988].
5. Although "the Word" here is, not to mention, an English equivalent of "logos" in Latin, and does not precisely correspond to "words" in the daily use of the term, this interpretation, in terms that "logos" means something that has essential connection to verbal development, might well be acceptable.
6. MN i 134.30–135.26.

find in this attitude no sign of the consecration of the word.

The episode of "the god Brahmā's entreaty of the Buddha to his discourse" raises another significant issue of how the word is evaluated in Buddhism in relation to the Buddha as engaged in history. Buddhism, with the historical figure Śākyamuni Buddha as its founder, needs the word of the Buddha for the truth to appear on the earth. This may be rephrased in a general formula as follows: "the truth of Buddhism is manifested in specific words at specific historical occasions through the medium of a historical figure."

This is concerned with the relationship of a message to its medium. Any message, when conveyed, should be consigned to a specific medium, and in accordance with the difference of the medium, the message manifests differently. In the case of Buddhism, if the message is the experience of the Buddha's perfect awakening, the medium is primarily the word uttered by a person in history.[7]

3. Divergence of the Teaching

Given the relationship between the message and the medium of Buddhism, the two distinctive characteristics of Buddhist truth, one relating to the fluidity of a Buddhist text, and the other to the peculiarity of the form are brought to our attention.

First, as long as the word of the Buddha is involved in history, it cannot but to lose its effect as time passes, and has to be re-verbalized by a new expression more suitable for new historical situations. Sacred texts in Buddhism, in fact, continued to be retold, rewritten and expanded as history went on. The enormous amount of the Buddha's teachings known as "eighty-four thousand entrances to the teaching" would be an ideal example for this Buddhist view of the relation of the truth to the word. The

7. The abovementioned "formula" of Buddhism concerning the relationship between the medium and the message is in stark contrast with that of the Veda, the orthodoxy of Indian religions. The Veda regards the words of scriptures as "something to hear through inspiration *śruti*" by "religious poets *ṛṣis*." The word in the Veda, transcendent of historical restrictions, is, in principle, an entity in itself to be equated with gods, truths, or worlds, and not a tool to convey anything other than what the word presents. In the Veda, as compared to Buddhism, the distinction between the message and the medium is by far obscure. In addition, in this religion, since the persons as medium concerned with the truth are limited to those of the clergy called Brahmin, the event of "god Brahmā's entreaty," which claims the presence of a specific historical person, can never take place.

teaching developed not in a convergent way, but rather expansively.

Second, if the truth of Buddhism should be re-verbalized by a specific person in history, the truth will be most likely to overlap with the verbal mediator. In addition, since all of the Buddhist texts were transmitted orally for at least two to three hundred years since the time of the Buddha's disappearance, texts during that period existed only in an anthropomorphic manner, and, in that system, those who utter the truth and the truth uttered by them inevitably coalesced.

These two characteristics of Buddhism, that is, the divergence of the teaching and the overlap of the teaching with a verbal mediator, invite the following two questions: first, didn't Buddhist teachings disperse unlimitedly to the extent that we cannot go back to the teaching of Śākyamuni Buddha? Second, given that Buddhist texts continue to be retold by a person in a specific historical period, how can we be assured of the authenticity of Buddhist texts?

This concern would be increased when the following well-known teaching is taken into account. The Buddha, as a reply to a question of what language should be used in preaching, replies that they should preach "in their own language" (*sakāya niruttiyā*).[8] This answer seems to have had significant influence in the multi-lingual situation in India. If transmission through different languages were allowed in this environment, Buddhist communities would disperse into different groups with the increase of the use of different languages, and then the members of the communities would become unable to communicate with each other. This, as a consequence, would lead to the eventual disappearance of the teaching.

The unification of language for the dissemination of a religion is usually thought to be at vital necessity for the following three reasons: first, for the purpose of protecting the teaching from chaotic infusion, then, to establish the authorization of the transmission, and at last, for preserving the identity of the religion. The Qur'an, the holy words of which are regarded as invalid when translated, meets this requirement in the simplest form. The Buddha, however, was never concerned about this.

---

8. *anujānāmi bhikkhave sakāya niruttiyā buddhavacanaṃ pariyāpuṇituṃ* (Vin. ii 139.14–16). Cf. Brough [1980]. Here I tentatively follow a frequently adopted interpretation of this term. However, as Ruegg pertinently discusses in his paper (Ruegg [2000]), the term *nirutti* does not appear usually to mean "language" in Pāli (nor does *nirukti* in Sanskrit), and this meaning does not seem to be required in the context of the passage. We may take this phrase, accepting his understanding, as "verbal delivery" and "intonation (a suprasegmental or prosody)."

4. Convergence of the Teaching: Secrecy to Publicity

Contrary to this pessimistic expectation, the teaching of the Buddha in fact did not disperse without limit, but was preserved in a relatively coherent system of dissemination. Setting aside the untiring efforts by the disciples to establish the system for transmission after the death of their teacher, the following situation that prevented the teaching from dispersing must be noted.

According to several materials dealing with the history of the development of Buddhist communities, it was Mahākāśyapa, the disciple that some sources regard as the first heir to the Buddha, who summoned the monks to the first meeting of collaborative recitation known as *saṃgīti*. The Buddha's teaching retained in the memories of each disciple was, thus, confirmed in the presence of the other members of the Buddhist community.[9] Leaving aside the matter of whether this so-called first conference took place exactly as related in traditional sources, some sort of assembles that conformed the ritual meetings such as *uposatha* or *varṣavāsa* that had been conducted during the lifetime of the Buddha, were most likely to function as this kind of conference to confirm the teaching of the Buddha.[10]

This confirmation through collaborative activities presumably served, first of all, as a significant occasion for the collection and continuation of his teaching. This activity, at the same time, was most likely to be effective in protecting the teaching from the possible danger of disappearance in terms that the transmission was conducted in the dimension of orality. In a community with a firmly established system of oral transmission, the core of the teaching is rarely modified for the reason that the preservation of the contents has to be consigned to the memory of the members in a coherently organized group and the rewriting or abolishing of a text, more likely to occur in the case of a written one, rarely takes place. Seen from the relationship between the truth and the word in Buddhism, as has been discussed in the previous chapter, the teaching of the Buddha may

---

9. As for the studies on the first conference, see Shimoda [1997]. Regarding Mahākāśyapa, see: Hecker [1987]; Lamotte [1962].
10. As some sources show, some of the Buddha's disciples were from the family of *brāhmaṇa*, well versed in transmitting orally the words of the Veda; another group of people called *śramaṇa*, who were related to the tradition of world-renouncers and sometimes familiar with the passing down of epic poems, also composed a certain Buddhist group. Owing a great deal to the knowledge and technique of the people of these two strands, the preservation and dissemination of Buddha's teachings was made possible.

seem to expand and spread without limit. But this, in fact, did not take place due to the restriction brought by this feature of the technique of oral transmission.

The event of collaborative recitation (*saṃgīti*) has another important aspect; this activity was an occasion for each of the disciples to express *in public* the teaching of the Buddha that he had kept privately inside himself, and thereby to have his personal memory publicly authorized by the community. In other words, that was an attempt to bring the word of the Buddha hidden inside as an individual's experience out in public into a community called the Saṃgha; this activity, in terms that something hidden in one's own experience becomes manifest to others, corresponds exactly to the event of "the god Brahmā's entreaty of the Buddha to teach." As the Buddha revealed his experience to others when he came back to this world of verbal expression from his experience of meditation, so his disciples, at the time the Buddha passed away from this verbal world, revealed the word of the Buddha in public to others. As the moment the Buddha disclosed his experience through the medium of word, the medium, the word of the Buddha, started to exist "between the Buddha and his disciples," so the instant the disciples publicized the Buddha's word, the word began to exist "among the disciples."

The disappearance of the Buddha's corporeal existence led his disciples to the venture of collaborative recitation, and the circumstances in which the word of the Buddha was embedded shifted from "between the Buddha and his disciples" to "among the disciples." Those who had become ordained during the time of the physical absence of the Buddha were able to hear the word of the Buddha through the medium of his disciples, and there was no other way for them to encounter the Buddha than hearing the voice of the Saṃgha. By the disappearance of the Buddha's physical existence, the significance of the Saṃgha was absolutely enhanced as from a community of collegial practitioners to the matrix from which the word of the Buddha is generated and to which it is ascribed. As a result, the endeavor of collaborative recitation, by means of making the word of the Buddha public and authoritative, established the legitimacy of the teaching of the Buddha during the time of the Buddha's absence. This was an important step to the "canonization" of the word of the Buddha.

5. Introduction of the Technique of Writing: More Developed Canonization

Several hundred years after the Buddha's *parinirvāṇa*, a significant change took place in the history of the transmission of the teaching: the redaction of the teaching to written texts. According to the *Dīpavaṃsa*, a Pāli chronicle passed down in Sri Lanka, the technology of writing redaction of teaching was introduced in the first century BCE in the wake of an order-splitting controversy between the two camps, one holding in high esteem the individual practice of meditation and the other paying more attention to establishing a system for the transmission of teaching, again the same sort of conflict between "experience vs. word." In this case as well, Buddhist monks declared the winner on the side of the word, and, during the reign of King Vaṭṭhagāmanī Abhaya, the monks finally agreed to adopt writing to protect the teaching from the danger of decay caused by calamities such as famines, deluges, wars, and the like.[11]

So long as no evidence, immediate or circumstantial, is available that supports the details of the condition for the redaction of the oral teaching to written texts as described in the Pāli chronicles, whether these accounts can be a reflection of historical reality in Sri Lanka may be open to question, and we should not be so careless to regard the accounts in the Pāli literature as descriptions of actual events that took place in India. The diffusion of written words by the King Aśoka in the first half of the third century BCE through his edicts all over the subcontinent allude to the assumption that the redaction to written texts in India should date back far earlier than in Sri Lanka, and probably was conducted in rather different cultural environments by those who were much accustomed to the usage of written words. In this case, unlike the accounts given in the Pāli chronicles, the redaction was likely to be gradually disseminated.[12]

Although the scarcity of historical sources prevents us from specifying with certainty both the date and the manner of the transition from oral to writing that developed in the Buddhist transmission system, there is no doubt that this redaction made a major impact on the dissemination system of Buddhist teachings, such that it must have revised the history of Buddhism. Among several important changes assumed to have been caused by the adoption of writing redaction, three aspects are particularly

11. *Dīpavaṃsa*, xx. 20–21; *Mahāvaṃsa*, xxxiii 100–101. Regarding the recent products of Buddhist studies on the topic of orality, see: Shimoda [2002].
12. As for the use of writings in the Indian subcontinent, see: Falk [1993].

worthy of attention. First, the change in form of the teaching from spoken words to written scriptures must have drastically revolutionized the way of seeing the world. Second, the alteration of the medium of dissemination is likely to have changed the concept of the "validity" or "authority" of the teaching. Third, these two changes must have caused the consolidation of the different lineages of teaching, and served as foundations to bring out new Buddhist movements, culminating in the manifestation of the characteristics of the Mahāyāna.

First of all, the advent of written texts liberates people from the conditions of the consciousness oriented by auditory sense and the spoken word; the spoken word, transitory by nature, exists only for the duration of the speaker's utterance, and, as a consequence, the existence of aurally sensed objects are as much momentary. With the emergence of written words, however, words come to exist emancipated from the immediate situation of a speaker, and the word in written texts can exist much more liberated from the confine of time. Thus, the word in scriptures can go beyond the phenomenal dimension of a speaker, create their own autonomous cosmos, and come to invite people to a considerably different world of cognition. In this new world of consciousness, highly enhanced intellectual activities, such as abstraction, objectification, symbolization, or rationalization, can rapidly develop.[13]

Second, this change in the medium from orality to literacy had considerable influence on "the sense of authority" of Buddhist teachings.[14] The appearance of the new technology of written texts, which drastically expands the range of intellectual activities, can surpass the significance of the original validity of oral distribution, and eventually establish a new authority in the lineage of transmission. Just as the endeavor of the collaborative recitation "*saṃgīti*" relocated the dimensions of the word of the Buddha from individual to communal, the advent of written redaction changed the dimension of transmission from the (oral) community to written texts.

Third, and finally, the emergence of written texts is most likely to have promoted the integration or assimilation of different teachings in the hands of different lineages. Oral transmission, dependent solely on person-to-person communication, makes each of the communities individually coherent, but

13. Ong [1982].
14. Lopez [1995] dealing with this topic from a different perspective of this paper gives valuable suggestions in observing the influence the technique of the writing redaction might well have had on the compilers of the Mahāyāna *sūtras*.

nonetheless independent of each other. In this stage, assimilation of different lines of teachings is unlikely to take place. However, once the teachings of different lineages that have been heretofore confined in their own tradition are redacted into the medium of written texts, they become liberated to a new dimension in which they can be compared simultaneously, and can even merge.

6. Characteristic of Mahāyāna Sūtras

Although almost all the Buddhist communities must have eventually adopted writing system, there seems to have been a difference among them in terms of the speed in which the change in the medium took root in each community. Some groups that had firmly established the system of oral transmission did not make the transition easily, and even if they introduced the new technology of writing, they may have felt no need to use written texts other than as subsidiary materials. The role of written scriptures in this context is limited to the use of text as a source for accumulating information. Those who continued in this approach are unlikely to have imagined that different lineages of transmissions could be consolidated into a new single text. It may be the case that those who retained the original system of transmission did not cease to place priority on "hearing" the voice of a teacher. They are worthy of the name *śrāvaka*, or "hearers."

However, as we have seen, the advent of written texts removes the restrictions inherent in an oral transmission system, and provides an ideal medium that can reflect a far broader range of teachings. In this situation, we may guess that in some circles this new technology was readily accepted. Thus they incorporated into one and the same scripture a variety of teachings, including philosophy, disciplinary rules, literature, and exegesis, which had been transmitted as separate traditions.

Furthermore, since written words can do a good turn to transcending the limitations of time and space, and thereby bring the past into the present, those who read scriptures dealing with the events during the lifetime of the Buddha may well have recognized themselves to be in the presence of the Buddha and his teaching. Both an awareness of different lineages of transmission and the conviction of the transcendence of temporal restriction brought about by the use of written texts seem most likely to have inspired the redactors to maintain the intention of establishing a more comprehensive tradition of Buddhism.

One end result of this new activity was, in all likelihood, the composition of Mahāyāna *sūtras*, which exhibit the following three significant traits: first, they regard *sūtras* in the form of scripture as the Buddha himself and a *stūpa/caitya* itself. Second, these *sūtras* dedicate an assiduous effort to harmonize various sorts of conflicting events in the history of Buddhism. Finally, these *sūtras* shift the context in which to locate technical terms from the context of the practice of meditation to a verbal dimension.

All these features are consonant with the distinct character that will appear when several sorts of elements separated from each other at the time of oral transmission become integrated by the redaction of teachings into one and the same scripture. In fact, we find no difficulty in acknowledging among the compilers of Mahāyāna *sūtras* "the intention" of reconciling the different constructs of Buddhist traditions by employing hermeneutical strategy represented by the word "*saṃdhābhāṣa.*"[15] This hermeneutical effort brings their consciousness back to the origin of Buddhism, where they recognize themselves to be those who are being engaged in the activity of the Buddha. In this respect, they are worthy of the name "*bodhisattva.*" This endeavor to recollect and unify a variety of constructs once divided into pieces at the time of oral transmission is in good harmony with the name of a single path, "*ekayāna*," or a great path, "*mahāyāna.*"

Although the concept of *bodhisattva*, one of the core elements of the Mahāyāna, is confirmed in some *sūtras* at an early stage of mainstream Buddhism, we cannot reduce the characteristics of *bodhisattvas* as found in Mahāyāna *sūtras* to the linear and continual development of the earlier concept of *bodhisattva*. Mahāyāna *sūtras* contain in them a various kinds of subjects, such as doctrinal ideas common to the *sūtras* of the non-Mahāyāna, motifs and narratives abstracted from the Buddha's biographies, discussions of disciplinary rules and rituals, and so on. We find no essential connection between the wealth of topics found in Mahāyāna *sūtras* and the ideal of *bodhisattva* common to almost all of the Buddhist scriptures. To unify a variety of topics surrounding the Buddha would require a huge screen on which to project them all at once.

This requirement cannot be fulfilled in the dimension of oral transmission, but when a text in a written form is available, this material, able to continue to exist beyond temporal limitation, can serve as this huge screen. A *bodhisattva* who appears on this new screen will be embellished with the characters and virtues appropriate for this backdrop, and will be

15. Regarding this theme, see Ruegg [1990].

worthy of a new hero.[16]

7. Development of the Mahāyāna

The release of the restrictions inherent in oral transmission by the appearance of written texts provided ideal conditions for realizing the original attitude of the Buddha toward his teaching; since the word is no more than the medium of conveying the contents of experience, the teaching must be repeatedly revised to fit ever-changing situations. New teachings, thus, continued to be added to the former through the history of Buddhism, which resulted in an enormous number of collections of words, both in the Pāli canon and in the Mahāyāna.

When we compare these two categories of *sūtras*, however, we cannot but notice a conspicuous point of difference. In the Pāli canon, it seems that the compilation of *sūtras* in the category of Tripiṭaka was first completed, followed by the continuous addition and accumulation of *Abhidharma* literature. In Mahāyāna Buddhism, on the other hand, *sūtras* themselves were extended in content and increased in number. As a consequence, Buddhism in the Pāli canon has a limited number of *sūtras* along with an enormous number of *Abhidharma* texts, whereas Mahāyāna Buddhism retains numerous *sūtras* having extended content.[17]

Regarding this difference between these two systems of *sūtras*, not a few scholars have been possessed with a peculiar notion that Buddhism in the Pāli canon has acknowledged only the historical Buddha, and has stuck to his teachings, whereas Mahāyāna Buddhism has fabricated a number of Buddhas and *sūtras* on their own accord. This presumption, however, is in sheer contradiction to what is indicated by existing literary and non-literary sources of Buddhism.

First of all, Buddhism in the Pāli canon does not consider *sūtras* as the

---

16. Gombrich [1990] would be the first work to discuss the possibility for the introduction of writings to be the origin of the Mahāyāna. His discussion, however, is oriented by the preconception that the Mahāyāna was an individual invention by using this new technology. Viewed from the studies on the oral aspect of religions, this presumption is unacceptable. See, for example, Graham [1987]. Harrison [2003], which describes the harmony of the writing and reading texts with the practice of meditation in the Mahāyāna, seems to have the same position as Graham does. As for the variety of topics in discussing the origin or the characteristics of the Mahāyāna, see Ruegg [2004].

17. I have discussed several occasions this topic using as an ideal example the *Mahāparinirvāṇasūtra*. Shimoda [2000].

record of the word of the historica Buddha and shows no hesitation in incorporating the words of disciples and of non-humans into the body of a *sūtra*. In addition, due to the limitations of oral dissemination, wordings or phrasings of a *sūtra* were assimilated to the forms that had been preserved in the tradition of epic literature and in that of the Vedic religion. Furthermore, since the system of oral transmission gives no other option to the followers than to accept the teaching of the Buddha through the medium of a person, and since there is no objective criterion by which to judge whether the teaching at issue originates in the historical Buddha, it would make the most sense to assume that Buddhists of later generations accepted the word of the Buddha solely on the basis of the trust in the person who transmitted the word.

In transmitting the teaching of the Buddha formulated by these characteristics, the concept of the "historical Buddha" in the word can not properly function. The redaction of teachings from oral to written texts can make a clear distinction between the word of the Buddha and the word of commentary on them. It is not far from the point to conjecture that the collection of words that had been passed down before the introduction of writing system were categorized as *sūtras*, whereas the teachings added thereafter were classified as commentaries. In reality, regardless of the name of the category of a text, commentaries and sub-commentaries of a *sūtra* were used as foundations on which one understands the *sūtra* at issue, and in this respect, the expansion of commentaries is virtually equal to the expansion of a *sūtra* itself. A need for revising the word of the Buddha to adjust for a new historical situation was no doubt envisaged in the Pāli canon as well.

A clear division made between *sūtras* and commentaries as found in the Pāli canon was most probably caused by the method of editing scriptures at an initial stage, and not by a philosophical or doctrinal understanding of the distinction between the *Dharma* and the *Abhidharma*. If the redaction of oral teachings into written texts was completed at a certain time, as in the way stated in the *Dīpavaṃsa*, there would emerge a collection of Buddhist texts in which two layers are clearly distinct between the previously transmitted texts and later added commentaries.

In contrast to this process of editing the Pāli canon, the formation process of Mahāyāna *sūtras* seems to stay quite opposite: Mahāyāna *sūtras* do not seem to have experienced a drastic shift from oral to writing as the Pāli canon did, and the writing system was gradually introduced into the Buddhist communities. In this case, the change of dissemination took root step by step, and, as a result, the effort to orally transmit teachings and the attempt to redact them into scriptures coexist in producing sūtras. In the case of the Mahāyāna, since there is no essential distinction between a *sūtra* transmitted from the previous generations and a commentary added later, the result is, no doubt, the gradual extension of a *sūtra* itself.

8. Impact of Editing Techniques on the Consciousness of Readers

The difference in editing methods found between the *sūtras* in the Pāli canon and those of the Mahāyāna seemed to have brought a significant difference in the consciousness of those who followed each of these two systems. The disciples who based their thought and practice on the Pāli canon, who inherited *sūtras* that had been preserved virtually untouched since the introduction of the system of writing redaction, allocated themselves as commentators on the transmitted *sūtras*, and continued to remain outside the *sūtras*.

By contrast, in the case of the compilers of Mahāyāna *sūtras*, their consciousness resided, as it were, inside a written text and, when they added a new interpretation to a transmitted *sūtra*, they had new words reborn in the same *sūtra*, instead of adding them from outside a text as commentarial words. These compilers, in contrast to those who came in contact with the words of the Buddha through oral transmission, must have been convinced that they could directly encounter the Buddha inside the written texts passed on beyond generations.

If the activity conducted by those "hearers" who inherited a *sūtra* in the Pāli canon is regarded as a commentary from outside a text, the activity of "*bodhisattvas*" who succeeded to Mahāyāna *sūtras* can be seen as a dialogue taking place inside the *sūtra*. Bodhisattvas, who believed themselves to be able to communicate inside a text with the word of the Buddha and to redevelop the correspondence to the words, were most likely to have an awareness of inheriting the whole history of Buddhism from the time of the Buddha Śākyamuni through to the present, and of re-expressing the history within the same history. In contrast to "a history of cumulative appearance" that characterizes Pāli Buddhism, in Mahāyāna Buddhism "a dialogical history" is shown, in which the constructs of a past and the present inseparably coalesce in one.

With the introduction of the redaction of the oral teachings to written texts, Buddhists gradually came to pursue two different paths in accordance with the form of different evaluations for the scriptures. The difference was primarily a matter of compiling and using scriptures, but eventually exerted a deep influence on the consciousness of those who were engaged in the written texts in a different manner. As a result, two distinct types of Buddhists, that is, those who endeavor to remain as *śrāvakas* separate in distance from the existence of the Buddha, and those who become *bodhisattvas*, capable of residing in the presence of the Buddha in the text, did appear.

9. Characteristics of the Buddhist Canon in East Asia as Compared to those of Pāli

In this section, we will digress for a while into the issue of distinctive features of Buddhist canon in East Asia, which characterize the Buddhism in China, Korea and Japan. We find an acute difference between the canonical scriptures of the Chinese and those of the Pāli traditions with regard to their treatment of the Mahāyāna: the former strongly reflects the influence of the Mahāyāna, whereas the latter leaves out the least remnants of the Mahāyāna from its canon. Apart from sporadic evidence for the process of the compilation of these cannons, we have almost no historical apparatus that can sufficiently bridge the gap between the two. There is no choice for us but to resort to an inference as reasonable as we can.

First of all, in addition to the different process by which these two canons were compiled, as has been discussed up to here, we should pay due attention to the totally different circumstances of culture and society in ancient China and Ceylon. In the case of Sri Lanka, Buddhism was introduced together with other cultural and political institutions from India, a far more developed country as compared to the island. What particularly draws our attention is the story that all the regalia necessary for a king's coronation were brought to Ceylon simultaneously with the introduction of Buddhism. In addition, given that the history of ancient Ceylon starts with the birth of the Buddha, the introduction of Buddhism into Ceylon was not merely the introduction of a religion but rather the emergence of revolutionary social changes. In ancient Sri Lanka, the unification of small, traditional communities into the island-sized state was likely to be realized through the power of King Aśoka. This is ideally exampled by a legend that shows the unification of various legends of regional gods into the stories of the Buddha during the reign of Aśoka. Buddhism, without doubt, functioned as a leading doctrine in both the religious and the worldly spheres in ancient South Asia.

If Buddhism in ancient Ceylon had these two inseparable aspects, religious and social, Buddhism in that island was strongly under the control of political conditions; if the society needs to be stable, it will show a strong inclination to make Buddhism conservative. When we take up a few examples in modern Theravada countries, we readily find that attempts to purify the Buddhist orders almost always have a strong connection with the reestablishment of a political system in the countries. Buddhist teachings in ancient Sri Lanka were unable to be free from political control, and accordingly, an attempt to reintroduce Buddhism was most probably conducted under political influence.

When China introduced Buddhism from India, however, the society and culture of the country had already attained to a surprisingly high level. In complete contrast to the case of Ceylon, there was no need for Chinese society to import cultural products or political institutions. There was no room for ancient China to accept a new national history oriented by the legend of the Buddha as did in Ceylon. Instead, what attracted the attention of the Chinese people most of all was the legendary stories of the Buddha and the content of his teaching itself. In these conditions, China introduced the Buddhism of rather purely idealistic aspects, separated from its substructure. The empire could not have accepted Buddhism if the people had not been allowed to abstract only the idealistic aspects from the entire body of Indian Buddhism, which was rooted in social and cultural elements peculiar to India, and completely alien to China. Buddhism brought into China was much less institutionalized as compared to that of Sri Lanka. The fact that the *vinaya* scriptures were introduced into China far later than the introduction of various *sūtras* is eloquent of the indifference of the Chinese to the institutional aspects of Buddhism.

Given both the astonishingly high level of Chinese literacy at that time and the stories concerning the earliest Buddhist transmission recorded by Chinese historiography, it seems most likely that Buddhism was accepted in an atmosphere of adopting a kind of romanticism, in which the Chinese people believed it possible to realize their ideal of Taoism, especially long-cherished dream of obtaining longevity. The early Buddhist texts translated into Chinese were mostly dependent on the terms of Taoism, which had been seeking for actual methods towards this goal. The texts most suited to this aim were, no doubt, the texts of the genre of the *sūtra*, particularly relating to the practice of mediation and belonging to the Mahāyāna, which contain the stories of modifying the world view, attaining eternal life and obtaining supernatural powers through ascetic practices or meditations.

Taoism shows close relations with the magico-ritual aspects of Buddhism, and this type of religion does not require a firmly established institutional system.

If it is possible to accept Buddhism only in the form of scriptures with no regard to institutions, it will be easier to introduce a new movement of Buddhism, for the task can be performed simply by introducing new scriptures. It is obvious from early historical records concerning Chinese translations of Buddhist texts that new Buddhist texts were brought into China continuously, alomost immediately after they had been produced in India. In this respect, Chinese translations can be regarded as more faithful reflection of the historical circumstances surrounding the production of texts in India than those of the southern tradition.

10. Four Great References

As the last subject of this paper, I will briefly mention an important discussion regarding a criterion for determining the word of the Buddha, evidenced in the Buddhist sources themselves, known as "the four great references *cattāro mahāpadesā*."[18] This discussion can be summarized as follows: when one hears a certain monk insisting that this should be the word of the Buddha since he has heard it from the Buddha himself, from elders in the community, from monks who have memorized the *sūtra*, the *vinaya* or the *abhidharma*, or from an religiously inspired monk, one should not accept, or reject, the word immediately, but should ascertain whether the word is incorporated in the *sūtra*, or attested to in the *vinaya*, and then accept or reject accordingly.[19]

This passage shows that the criterion for discerning the word of the Buddha consists not in the words of people, such as of the Buddha, of members of the community, of those who have memorized the *sūtra* or *vinaya*, or of an inspiring person, but lies in the word of the text of the *sūtra* or the *vinaya*. If this statement has actual significance, then the *sūtra* and the *vinaya* mentioned here must have existed independent of people, and, in all likelihood, in the form of written texts.

This discourse reveals the following three factors: first, the words acknowledged by a community, memorized by specialists or conveyed by influential practitioners, are regarded as equal to the words uttered

---

18. Regarding recent studies on this topic, see: An [1998], Fujita [1998].
19. For example, DN ii 123.29–124.20.

by the Buddha. Second, despite the possible presence of written texts, controversies are still initiated in the way of dealing with the words of people. Lastly, as the muteness of this passage regarding written texts alludes, Buddhists seem to raise no question about the authority of written texts.

In oral transmission, there is no objective testimony to verify the authenticity of the word of the Buddha. A certain teaching can be accepted as the word of the Buddha not because it is proved to be as such, but because it is being given by a reliable person. After the disappearance of the Buddha, those words uttered by a monk in authority in the community, by a specialist in the transmission of the teaching, or by a practitioner having spiritual influence, might have reasonably started to be regarded as equally authentic.

Once a written text appeared, this text may have made another authority independent of those people who have been engaged in the transmission of the word of the Buddha. Nevertheless, the emergence of scriptures separated from the medium of person was the birth of another world of the word, and Buddhists, instead of substituting the written texts for the oral texts, allowed these two sorts of text to coexist. Buddhists in this condition were compelled to work for these two different, independent worlds of the word. As a result, controversies were still initiated from the world of oral transmission in the presence of written texts.

This passage of "the four great references" is likely to reflect a complicated, confusing situation caused by the appearance of written texts. Those Buddhists who experienced the shift in the medium of transmission from orality to literacy, and those who eventually reached the conclusion that the ultimate criterion lay in written texts, might have regarded the written texts "as a whole" as authentic, for there was no objective criterion with them for discerning the inauthenticity. It is highly likely that all *sūtras* transmitted to Buddhists in India existed as a kind of "thesaurus," a store of wisdom, from which Buddhists freely draw necessary words, phrases, or sentences of teachings with the aim of re-creating new works to fit a new historical context within the confines of the world of the words.

The attitude of the theorists of the Mahāyāna, such as Sthiramati or Bhāviveka, who accept all the Mahāyāna *sūtras* as completely authentic, is an eloquent support for our argument. For them, who stand in front of already developed scriptures, the real question is not that they discern authentic *sūtras* from inauthentic ones, but how they reconcile conflicts or controversies found among these *sūtras*, and how they single out the most appropriate words, phrases, or texts for their own need.

Their effort may properly be termed "hermeneutics." Hermeneutics is an endeavor of interpretation concerned primarily with the realization of harmony in the diversities of texts, and not an attempt at the elimination of conflicting elements or texts from their consideration. If the corpus of the Mahāyāna *sūtras* is a sort of a store of knowledge, the venture to discern authentic from inauthentic in these scriptures would be no more absurd than an attempt to tell genuine, true words from invented, false words "in dictionaries."

11. Concluding Remarks

The Buddha's activities, starting with a hesitation about entrusting his experience to the word, came to bear fruit as the history of his discourse to disciples for all through forty-five years until his last moment. The word of the Buddha, a4t first individually and internally cherished by his disciples, became public in Buddhist communities after the master's absence from this world. His teaching, having long been transmitted orally as texts retained in the memory of disciples, was, at one time, consigned to the technology of writing. The word of the Buddha planted their seeds in the material called scriptures, and the seeds bloomed into flowers of new words in a variety of *sūtras* in the history of Buddhism.

This series of history, taking place in a time from two to five centuries after the Buddha's *parinirvāṇa*, shows that the effort to establish Buddhist canons formed a dialogical process throughout these years. The Buddha's personal experience, when revealed in his words, was received by his followers in their individual, inner world of experience. These words preserved in their memories were, at the time of the master's disappearance, again publicly opened for, and authorized by, the members of the Buddhist community. Later, when oral dissemination was challenged by the dissemination through the new medium of writing, a new context emerged between persons and scriptures.

These shifts of context of the word of the Buddha are likely to have proceeded not in a linear fashion as mutually exclusive alternatives come out one after another, but in such a complicated manner as preceding elements coalesce with those following on the one hand, and these two elements coexist on the other. Noteworthy in this respect is the fact that this process went on in essentially close relation to the changes in the consciousness of the readers and compilers of Buddhist scriptures who passed down the word of the Buddha to subsequent generations.

It seems high time we reconsidered the word "history" in its deeper sense. "Being historical" means being involved in the state of being transformed and developed in the course of time. As long as the message cannot be independent of the medium, and the medium is inevitably being transformed during the course of history, the message of Buddhism manifests differently in accordance with its development in history. The history of the formation process of Buddhist scriptures is consonant with the history of the transformative process of the experience of individuals who have encountered these scriptures. To rethink of the history of Buddhism from the viewpoint of "the dialogical approach," instead of reconstructing a history by dealing with scriptures merely as documents, is in urgent need to open up a new horizon in investigating into "the history" of formation process of Buddhist scriptures in India.

Selected Bibliography

Allon, Mark

1997 *Style and Function: A Study of the Dominant Stylistic Features of the Prose Portions of Pali Canonical Sutta Texts and Their Mnemonic Functions*, Tokyo: The International Institute for Buddhist Studies.

An, Yan-Gyu

1998 *Buddhology in the Mahāparinibbāna Suttanta and its Commentary*, D. Phil Thesis at University of Oxford, pp. 80–112.

Barthes, Roland

1977 *Image, Music, Text*, Noonday Press.

Bond, Gorge

1982 *The Word of the Buddha: The Tipitaka and Its Interpretation in the Theravada Buddhism*, Colombo: Gunasena.

Brough, John

1996 "Sakāya Niruttiyā: Cauld kale het," in H. Bechet (ed.), *The Language of Earliest Buddhist Tradition*, Göttingen, pp. 35–42.

Collins, Steven

1992 "Notes on Some Oral Aspects of Pali Literature," *Indo-Iranian Journal* 35: 121–135.

Cousins, Lance S.

1983 "Pali Oral Literature," in P. Denwood and A. Piatigorisky (eds.), *Buddhist Studies Ancient and Modern*, London: Curzon Press.

Edgerton, Franklin

1924 "The Meaning of Sāṃkhya and Yoga," *American Journal of Philology* 45 (1): 1–46.

Eliade, Mircea

1958 *Yoga: Immortality and Freedom*, translated from French by W.R. Trask, (2nd edn.), Princeton University Press.

Falk, H.

1993 *Schrift im alten Indien: Ein Forschungsbericht mit Anmerkungen*, Tübingen.

Fujita, Shodo

1998 "Butsugo no Teigi wo meguru Kōsatsu" (*On a Definition of the Word of the Buddha), *Indogaku Chibettogaku Kenkyū* 3: 1–51.

Gethin, Rupert

1992 "The Mātrikās: Memorization, Mindfulness, and the List," in J. Gyatso (ed.), *In the Mirror of Memory: Reflections on Mindfulness and Remembrance in Indian and Tibetan Buddhism*, New York: SUNY Press, pp. 149–172.

Gombrich, Richard F.

1990 "How the Mahāyāna Began," in T. Skorupski (ed.), *The Buddhist Forum*, Vol. 1, (London), pp. 21–30.

Graham, William A.

1987 *Beyond the Written Word: Oral Aspects of Scripture in the History of Religion*, Cambridge University Press.

Harrison, Paul

2001 "The Anatomy of Revelation: Rewriting the History of Mahāyāna Buddhism" (Paper prepared for the conference "Investigating the Early Mahāyāna" at Stanford University).

2003 "Mediums and Messages: Reflections on the Production of Mahāyāna Sūtras" (Paper prepared for the symposium: "Mahāyāna Reconsidered: On the Basis of Recent Controversies and Achievements," 48th International Conference of Eastern Studies, Tōhō gakkai, 16 May 2003).

Hecker, H.

1987 *Lives of the Disciple: Mahā kassapa, Father of the Saṅgha*, Kandy:

Buddhist Publication Society.

von Hinüber, Oskar
1989 *Der Beginn der Schrift und frühe Schriftlichkeit in Indien*, (Akademie der Wissenschaftlichen Klass, Jahrgang 1989, Nr. 11) 1990, (Cf. Review by M. Hara in *Indo-Iranian Journal* 38 (1): 71–76).
1993 "From Colloquial to Standard Language: The Oral Phrase in the Development of Pali," *Premier Colloque Etienne Lamotte*, Louvain-la-Neuve, pp. 101–113.
1994 *Untersuchungen zur Mündlichkeit früher mittelindischer Texte der Buddhisten* (Akademie der Wissenschaften und der Literatur, Meinz. Abhandlungen der Geistes-und Sozialwissenschaftlichen Klasse, Jahrgang 1994, Nr. 5), (Cf. Review by M. Hara in *Indo-Iranian Journal* 39, 1996: 163–168).

LaCapra, Dominic
1982 *Rethinking Intellectual History: Texts, Contents, Language*, Cornell University Press.

Lamotte, Étienne
1962 *L'enseignement de Vimalakīrti* (*Vimalakīrtinirdeśa*), Louvain.

Lopez, Donald Jr.
1995 "Authority and Orality in the Mahāyāna," *Numen* 4: 21–47.

Ong, Walter J.
1982 *Orality and Literacy: The Technologizing of the Word*, London/New York: Methuen.

Ruegg, David Seyfort
1989 "Allusiveness and Obliqueness in Buddhist Texts: Saṃdhā, Saṃdhāya and Abhisaṃdhi in Buddhist Texts," in C. Cailat (ed.), *Dialectes dans les littératures Indo-Aryennes*, Publications d'institut de civilisation indienne, fasc. 55.
2000 "On the Expressions *chandaso āropenta, āyataka gītassara, sarabhañña* and *ārṣa* as applied to the word of the Buddha," in R. Tsuchida and A. Wezler (eds.), *Harānandalahalī*, Reinbek, pp. 283–306.
2004 "Aspects of the Study of the (Earlier) Indian Mahāyāna," *Journal of the International Association of Buddhist Studies* 27 (1): 3–62.

Sakamoto (Goto), Junko
1992 "Bonten Kanjō no Genkei" (The Prototype of the Story "Brahmā's Request"), *Indogaku Bukkyōgaku Kenkyū* 41 (1): (62)–(72).

Schmithausen, Lambert

1981 "On Some Aspects of Descriptions or Theories of "Liberating Insight" and "Enlightenment" in Buddhism," in K. Bruhn und A. Wezler (hrsg.), *Studien zum Jainismus und Buddhismus*, Wiesbaden, pp. 199–250.

Shimoda, Masahiro

1996 "Satori to Sukui: Indobukkyō Ruikeiron Saikō" (Enlightenment and Salvation: Reconsideration of Typology of Indian Buddhism), *Shūkyō Kenkyū* 70 (1): 25–46.

1997 *Nehangyō no Kenkyū* (*A study on the Mahaparinirvāṇasūtra*), Tokyo: Shunjūsha, 1997.

2000 "Chūshakusho to shiteno Daijōnehangyō: Nikāya Attakatā to no Icchi ni miru Nehangyō no Tenkai Keitai" (*The Mahāyāna Mahāparinirvāṇasūtra as Auto-commentary: Development of the Mahāparinirvāṇa sūtra, Viewed from the Concordance with Aṭṭhakathā), *Abidaruma to Indo Shisō* (Abhidharma and Indian Thought: Essays in Honor of Professor Doctor Junsho Kato on His Sixtieth Birthday), Tokyo: Shunjusha, pp. 327–339.

2001 "Buddha within and beyond History: The Buddhology in the Saddharmapuṇḍarikasūtra in Connection with an Episode of 'God Brahman's Request for the Buddha's First Sermon,'" *An Anthology of East Asian Buddhism, A Commemorative Volume in Honor of Ven. Sheng-yen on His Seventieth Birthday*, Tokyo: Sankibō busshorin, pp. 93–114.

2002 "Kōtō Denshō kara mita Indo Bukkyō Seiten Kenkyū ni tsuite no Oboegaki" (*On the oral aspect of Buddhist literature in ancient India), *Indo Tetsugaku Bukkyōgaku* 17: 30–45.

2004a "God Brahmā's Entreaty to the Buddha to Teach: The Transmission of the Dharma Reflected in the Lotus Sutra," *The Middle Way: Journal of Buddhist Society*, London, 227–235.

2004b "Seinaru Shomotsu no kanata ni" (*Beyond Sacred Scriptures), *Gengo to Shintai: Seinarumono no Ba to Baitai* (*Language and Corpus: The Matrix and The Medium for Sacredness, Kōza shūkyō #5 (*Lectures on Religions), Tokyo: Iwanami shoten, pp. 25–52.

2006 "Mahāyānasūtra as Auto-commentary: As Evidenced in the Mahāparinirvāṇasūtra," Paper prepared for series of lectures at SOAS 2006.

de La Valée Poussin, Louis

1936/7 "Musīla et Nārada: le chemin du nirvāṇa," *Mélanges chinois et bouddhiques*, pp. 189–222.

Vetter, T.

1998 *The Ideas and Meditative Practices of Early Buddhism*, Leiden.

* This is a modified and extended version of my paper: Shimoda [2004b] and [2007]. I am grateful for Dr. Albert Charles Muller for his invaluable suggestions for improving English.

CHAPTER 3

THE GANDHĀRAN DISTURBANCE IN THE LATE 4TH CENTURY CE AS A *CONTEXT*: A NEW VIEWPOINT OF GANDHĀRAN BUDDHISM

Shigeru SAITO

Introduction

Northeast India was always one of the centers of Buddhist faith. Buddhism was brought there in the 3rd century BCE. The king Aśoka of Mauryans sent the Buddhist priest Madhyāntika there for preaching. In the Kushan era, Buddhist cultures flourished in Gandhāra under the protection of the kings. The reign of Kaniṣka I in the 2nd century CE was the golden age of the empire. He built the memorial tower of Buddhism in the capital Puruṣapura, which became the center of Gandhāran Buddhism. After the 1st century, from the reign of Vāsudeva, the Kushan Empire was on the decline.

The purpose here is to explore further into Gandhāran Buddhism based on *Text* and *Context*. First section surveys Gandhāran Buddhism in 402 CE with special emphasis on passages of Fa xian's (法顯) record, the *Gao seng fa xian zhuan* (高僧法顯傳). Second section analyzes the *Context* of Gandhāran Buddhism after establishing the *Text* from a passage in the *Gao seng fa xian zhuan* (高僧法顯傳). Third section attempts to demonstrate the problems of Indian Buddhism in the *Da tang xi yu ji* (大唐西域記) by making use of this *Context*. Furthermore, in fourth section demonstration of the problems of Chinese Buddhism in the *Gao seng zhuan* (高僧傳) by use of this *Context* is also attempted.

1. Gandhāran Buddhism in 402 CE

Fa xian (法顯) is one of the famous Chinese priests who traveled to India. He left Chang an (長安) in 399 CE and arrived at North India via Xi yu (西

域) and Cong ling (葱嶺). After visiting many sacred places of Buddhist interest in India, he returned to Jian kang (建康) in 413 CE by sea. The *Gao seng fa xian zhuan* (高僧法顯傳), which is his record of travels in India, is a certain text for understanding the Buddhist state in Central Asia and India of the 5th century CE.

In 402 CE Fa xian (法顯) visited the Gandhāran region, Su he duo (宿呵多, Skt. *Suhata), Jian tuo wei (犍陀衛, Skt. Gandhāvatī), Zhu cha shi luo (竺刹尸羅, Skt. Takṣaśilā) and Fu lou sha (弗樓沙, Skt. Puruṣapura).[1] Buddhism in the region was recorded in the *Gao seng fa xian zhuan* (高僧法顯傳). First, they had four Buddhist towers commemorating the Buddha's feats in previous birth as a Bodhisattva.[2] The four towers are the one in *Suhata (宿呵多) that commemorates a Bodhisattva who cut off pieces of his flesh to save a dove,[3] the one in Gandhāvatī (犍陀衛) that commemorates a Bodhisattva who sacrificed his eyes for a blind person[4] and the two in Takṣaśilā (竺刹尸羅) that commemorates a Bodhisattva who sacrificed his head for a person and his body for a hungry tiger.[5] Second, there are two towers in Puruṣapura (弗樓沙), which is now called Peshawar in northern Pakistan. One tower was built by Kaniṣka I. The other was built for storing Buddha's bowl, which remained authoritative in Gandhāran Buddhism.[6] A temple was also built and housed about 700 Buddhist monks for the protection of the bowl.[7]

It should be clear, from what has been said above, that Gandhāran Buddhism existed in 402 CE when Fa xian (法顯) stayed there, and its main characteristic was the pilgrimage to sacred places of Buddhist interest. Furthermore, there were about 700 monks at the Buddha's bowl temple in Puruṣapura. In connection to this, Fa xian did not refer to the number of temples or monks in *Suhata (宿呵多), Gandhāvatī (犍陀衛) or Takṣaśilā (竺刹尸羅).

---

1. On the Sanskrit words of places in India, see Deeg [2005].
2. 高僧法顯傳, 858a–b. Beal [2005 (1869): 29–33]. Nagasawa [1996: 28–32]. Deeg [2005: 226–231] / [2005: 521–522].
3. 高僧法顯傳, 858a–b: 昔天帝釋試菩薩化作鷹鴿割肉貿鴿處. 佛既成道與諸弟子遊行. 語云. 此本是吾割肉貿鴿處. 國人由是得知. 於此處起塔金銀挍飾.
4. 高僧法顯傳, 858b: 佛爲菩薩時. 亦於此國以眼施人. 其處亦起大塔金銀挍飾.
5. 高僧法顯傳, 858b: 竺刹尸羅漢言截頭也. 佛爲菩薩時. 於此處以頭施人. 故因以爲名. 復東行二日至投身餵餓虎處. 此二處亦起大塔. 皆衆寶挍飾.
6. 高僧法顯傳, 858b.
7. 高僧法顯傳, 858b: 於此處起塔及僧伽藍. 并留鎭守種種供養. 可有七百餘僧.

2. *Text* and *Context* of Gandhāran Buddhism

In the preceding section I pointed out the number of temples and monks in Puruṣapura when Fa xian (法顯) visited Gandhāra. This section concentrates on those numbers. Below is a table illustrating the number of temples and monks in Puruṣapura and *Mo tou luo* (摩頭羅, Skt. Mathurā) from the *Gao seng fa xian zhuan* (高僧法顯傳).[8]

Table 1: The number of temples and monks in Puruṣapura and Mathurā.

	Puruṣapura	Mathurā
The number of Temples	1	20
The number of Monks	ca. 700	3000

As this table indicates, there are not many temples and monks in Puruṣapura compared with those in Mathurā. Chinese monk Xuan zang (玄奘), who visited Puruṣapura in ca. 630 CE, recorded that there were 1000 temples (which is now considered to be only 10 temples)[9] in Puruṣapura. Some temples that were referred to by Xuan zang (玄奘) in the early 7th century CE must also have stood there in 402 CE although the number of temples cannot be clearly defined. It is a fact that the number of monks was decreasing when Fa xian (法顯) stayed at Puruṣapura. This is another characteristic of Gandhāran Buddhism in 402 CE, although little attention has been given to this point. From this viewpoint, one may say that there were few monks studying dogma in the temples.

In this paper, I will use the passage below concerning Puruṣapura in the *Gao seng fa xian zhuan* (高僧法顯傳) as a *Text* according to *Text Science*. The *Text* shows the conditions of Gandhāran Buddhism of the 5th century CE.

> *Text*: [King] built a tower and a temple here [where the Buddha's bowl exists]. [He] protected them and held many memorial services for them. The temple has about 700 monks.[10]

---

8. 高僧法顯傳, 859a: 國名摩頭羅. 又經蒱那河. 河邊左右有二十僧伽藍. 可有三千僧. Beal [2005 (1869): 53]. Nagasawa [1996: 44]. Deeg [2005: 528].
9. 大唐西域記, 879c: 僧伽藍千餘所. 摧殘荒廢蕪漫蕭條. Beal [1981 (1884): 98], Watters [2004 (1904–1905): 202], Mizutani [1971: 81]. Ji [2000: 233] doubts the letter '千(1000)' concerning the number of temples in the *Da tang xi yu ji* (大唐西域記). It regards '千 (1000)' as '十 (10)'.
10. 高僧法顯傳, 858b: 於此處起塔及僧伽藍. 并留鎮守種種供養. 可有七百餘僧. Beal [2005 (1869): 29–33]. Nagasawa [1996: 32–36]. Deeg [2005: 523].

Now that we have defined the *Text*, the next step is to provide a *Context* about the *Text*. In inquiring into the *Context*, the rulers in Puruṣapura before 402 CE need to be established. Puruṣapura became the Kushan Empire capital during the reign of king Kaniṣka I in the 2nd century CE. After the 1st century, the Kushan Empire was on the decline. The cause of its decline was mainly the war against the Sasanian Persian empire from Iran.

During the reign of Sapur I (240–272), the Sasanids increased their territory. The *Inscription of Shapur I at Naqsh-i Rustam* indicates the territory under their rule. Consider the following quotation.[11]

> 1 ... Persis, Parthia, Khuzistan, Mesene, Assyria, Adiabene, Arabia, Azerbaijan, Armenia, 2. Georgia, Segan [Makhelonia = Mingrelia], Arran [Albania], Balasakan, up to the Caucasus mountains and the Gates of Albania, and all of the mountain chain of Pareshwar, Media, Gurgan, Merv, Herat and all of Aparshahr, Kerman, Seistan, Turan, Makuran, Paradene, Hindustan [India = Sind], the Kushanshahr up to Peshawar, and up to Kashgar, Sogdiana and to the mountains of Tashkent, and on the other side of the sea, Oman. And we have given to a village district the name Peroz- Shapur and we made Hormizd-Ardashir by name Shapur.

What is immediately apparent in this quotation is that Sapur I conquered Peshawar (Puruṣapura).[12] He defeated the Kushan and obtained northwest India (Gandhāra) for its silk trade. The Sasanian rulers governed Gandhāra from that point and issued the coins engraved with 'the King of the Kushans (*kûŝân ŝâh*)' or 'the King of the Kings of the Kushans (*kûŝân ŝâhânŝâh*)'.[13] Yet little is known of how they governed there.

Under the reign of Sapur II (309–379), the Sasanian movements in northwest India became more active because of conflicts with the eastern nations. Roman historian Ammianus Marcellinus wrote of Sapur II making expeditions into the east in the *Rerum Gestarum Libri* XVI, 9–4 as follows:

> A long time elapsed before this message reached the territory of the Chionitae and Euseni, where Sapor was spending the winter.[14]

---

11. Frye [1984: 371].
12. '*Pshkbwr*' in the inscription has often been identified with Puruṣapura in Sanskrit such as in Henning [1947: 53–54]. But, according to Vogelsang [2002: 160–161], the identification could be a conjecture.
13. See Herzfeld [1930].
14. Hamilton [2004 (1986): 99]. Cf. Rolfe [1971 (1935): 243].

The above passage is a record in 356 CE. According to Marcellinus's record, Sapur II fought to exclude the Chionitae and the Euseni from his territory. At this time, Sapur II ruled the land of the Chionitae and the Euseni, where he was spending the winter. The word 'Chionitae' is translated from the Latin '*Chionitas*' and the word 'Euseni' is translated from the Latin '*Eusenos*'.[15] The Chionitae is defined as the Hun, while the Euseni is identified as the Cuseni in Marshall [1975 (1951): 73], Frye [1984: 311] or Harmatta [1990: 93], and defined as the Kushan. Furthermore, there was a petition by Kabul's judge in the Persepolis Inscription. He hopes that Shapur II, the King of Kings will return to Kabul safely in the petition.[16] In regards to the petition in the inscription, Marshall [1975 (1951): 73] sees this as Shapur II retuning after the war against the Chionitae and the Euseni. According to Marshall [1975 (1951): 73], this war went on between 350 and 358 CE. Otherwise, Harmatta [1990: 97] indicates three Chionitae Wars: the First Chionitae War between 350 and 359 CE, the Second Chionitae War between 367 and 370 CE, and the Third Chionitae War between 376 and 377 CE. There are no materials that depict the circumstances of Puruṣapura during these wars although Shapur II made Kabul his base of operations against Gandhāra and Panjāb in Marshall [1975 (1951): 73]. All these facts make it clear that Shapur II, the Huns, and the Kushans involved the people of Puruṣapura in the wars.

Peace in Puruṣapura came under the dynasty of Kidāra which took over the Kushan in Gandhāra. The Chinese historical record, the *Wei shu* (魏書), includes Kidāra in a passage concerning Da rou zhi guo (大月氏國) as follows:

> King Ji duo lo (寄多羅, Skt. Kidāra) is brave. [He] took command of his army, crossed over the great mountains southernly and conquered northern India. All five kingdoms to the north of Gan tuo luo (乾陁羅, Skt. Gandhāra) submitted to him. During in the reign of Shi zu (世祖 423–452), a man from the empire did business in Jing shi (京師, Chang an).[17]

In addition to this, the *Wei shu* (魏書) includes Kidāra in the passage concerning Xiao rou zhi guo (小月氏國) as follows:

---

15. *Rerum Gestarum Libri*, XVI, 9–4. See Rolfe [1971 (1935): 242].
16. Frye [1966: 87].
17. 魏書 vol. 102. 西域傳, 2275: 北王寄多羅勇武, 遂興師越大山, 南侵北天竺, 自乾陁羅以北五國盡服屬之. 世祖時其國人商販京師. See Marshall [1975 (1951): 74].

> The capital of Xiao rou zhi guo (小月氏國) was the Fu lou sha (富樓沙, Skt. Puruṣapura) castle. The king was the son of king Ji duo lo (寄多羅, Skt. Kidāra) in Da rou zhi (大月氏).[18]

According to Matsuda [1937:42–43], the above passages of the *Wei shu* (魏書)show the circumstances in ca. 437 CE, when the Kidāra conquered the Gandhāra region. Furthermore, Enoki [1958: 42] states that Kidāra unified the south and north side of the Hindu Kush Mountain between 412 and 437 CE based on Chinese materials.[19] Because there is not a trace of Kidāra in the *Gao seng fa xian zhuan* (高僧法顯傳), the time when Fa xian visited Puruṣapura is between Sapur II's expedition to the east and Kidāra's unification.

Judging from the above, the *Context* about the *Text* mentioning the number of temples and monks in the *Gao seng fa xian zhuan* (高僧法顯傳) is the Gandhāran Disturbance between Sapur II's expedition to the east and Kidāra's unification. This is between ca. 350 and ca. 410 CE. During the the Gandhāran Disturbance between ca. 350 and ca. 410 CE, many monks had to leave Puruṣapura in order to avoid it. As a result, the number of temples and monks in Puruṣapura decreased and the monks' function became only to protect.

3. A New Interpretation of Indian Buddhism

This paper sets the *Context* as the Gandhāran Disturbance between ca. 350 and ca. 410 CE. Next, I try to interpret one of the problems in Indian Buddhism, that of Asaṅga and Vasubandhu, both of whom came from Puruṣapura. Consider the following quotation concerning Puruṣapura in the *Da tang xi yu ji* (大唐西域記):

> Na luo yan tian (那羅延天, Skt. Nārāyaṇadeva), Wu zhuo pu sa (無著菩薩, Skt. Bodhisattva Asaṅga), Shin qin pu sa (世親菩薩, Skt. Bodhisattva Vasubandhu), Fa jiu (法救, Skt. Dharmatrāta), Ru yi (如意, Skt. Manorātha) and Lei zun zhe (脇尊者, Skt. Badhanta Pārśva) are Śāstra masters. [They] are from [Puruṣapura].[20]

---

18. 魏書 vol. 102, 西域傳, 2277: 小月氏國、都富樓沙城. 其王本大月氏王寄多羅子也.
19. In Odani [1996: 111–112], Kidāra's unification is in ca. 380 CE established by coins issued by Kidāra. And, according to Gandhāran art, Takada [1983 (1967): 256] makes Kidāra's conquest as being at the end of the 4th century CE.
20. 大唐西域記, 879c: 作論諸師則有那羅延天. 無著菩薩. 世親菩薩. 法救. 如意.

Asaṅga and Vasubandhu are brothers and are outstanding in the scholarship of the Yogacara School. The following is their work records. This paper regards these records as the *Text*s of *Text Science*.

3.1. Asaṅga

A. Ayodhyā

Text 1: There is an old temple in a large mango forest 5 or 6 li (里) to the southwest of the castle. Although A seng ga (阿僧伽, Asaṅga) is notated as Wu zhuo (無著) in the *Tang* (唐) representation, the Bodhisattva [Asaṅga] studied and guided people at the [temple]. Every night Bodhisattva Asaṅga went up to the Tuśita Palace and taught the *Yu jia shi di lun* (瑜伽師地論, Skt. *Yogācārabhūmi*), the *Zhuang yan da cheng jing lun* (莊嚴大乘經論, Skt. *Mahāyānasūtrālaṅkāra*), the *Zhoug bian fen bie lun* (中邊分別論, Skt. *Madhyāntavibhāga*) etc. of Maitreya Bodhisattva. Every day [he] lectured for the crowd.[21]

B. Kauśāmbī

Text 2: There is a deserted building in a mango forest to the east of the temple, where Wu zhuo pu sa (無著菩薩, Bodhisattva Asaṅga) wrote the *Xian yang sheng jiao lun* (顯揚聖教論).[22]

3.2. Vasubandhu

A. Puruṣapura

Text 3: There is an old room to the east of Lei zun zhe (脇尊者, Badhanta Pārśva)'s room. Shin qin pu sa (世親菩薩, Bodhisattva Vasubandhu) wrote the *A pi da mo ju she lun* (阿毘達磨俱舍論, Skt.

脇尊者等. 本生處也. Beal [1981 (1884): 98], Watters [2004 (1904–1905): 202], Mizutani [1971: 81], Ji [2000: 233–234]. Cf. 大唐大慈恩寺三藏法師傳, 230a. Takada [1987 (1940): 48], Beal [1976 (1911): 63], Nagasawa [1998: 93].

21. 大唐西域記, 896b: 城西南五六里. 大菴沒羅林中有故伽藍. 是阿僧伽唐言無著菩薩請益導凡之處. 無著菩薩夜昇天宮於慈氏菩薩所受瑜伽師地論莊嚴大乘經論中邊分別論等. 晝爲大衆講宣妙理. Beal [1981 (1884): 226], Watters [2004 (1904–1905): 355–356], Mizutani [1971: 172], Ji [2000: 452]. Cf. 大唐大慈恩寺三藏法師傳, 233c. Takada [1987 (1940): 68], Beal [1976 (1911): 85], Nagasawa [1998: 127].

22. 大唐西域記, 898b: 伽藍東菴沒羅林中有故基. 是無著菩薩. 於此作顯揚聖教論. Beal [1981 (1884): 236–237], Watter [2004 (1904–1905): 371], Mizutani [1971: 180], Ji [2000: 471]. Cf. 大唐大慈恩寺三藏法師傳, 234c. Takada [1987 (1940): 71], Beal [1976 (1911): 91], Nagasawa [1998: 132].

Abhidharmakośabhāṣya) there.[23]

B. Śākala Castle in Ṭakka

Text 4: There is a temple in the old castle of She jie luo (奢羯羅, Skt. Śākala). The temple housed about 100 monks that all studied Hinayana Buddhism. Shin qin pu sa (世親菩薩, Bodhisattva Vasubandhu) wrote the *Sheng yi di lun* (勝義諦論) there.[24]
Text 5: At this time Shin qin (世親, Vasubndhu) was at the Śākala Castle in Zhe jia (磔迦, Skt. Ṭakka) and heard that Zhong xian (衆賢, Skt. Saṃghabhadra) would arrive there from a far distance.[25]

C. Ayodhyā

Text 6: There is an old temple in the large castle. Although Fa su pan du pu sa (伐蘇畔度菩薩, Skt. Bodhisattva Vasubandhu) is noted as Shin qin (世親) in the Tang (唐) representation and as Po sou pan dou (婆藪盤豆) in the old [translation], he is translated as Tian qin (天親). [He] wrote various Mahayana and Hinayana books there over several decades.[26]
Text 7: There is an old temple to 40 *li* (里) to the northwest from Asaṅga's deserted hall. [The temple] is bounded on the north by the Ganges and has a tower (Stūpa) made of brick, which is about 100 *chi* (尺) in height. There, Shin qin pu sa (世親菩薩, Bodhisattva Vasubandhu) converted Mahayana [Buddhism].[27]

---

23. 大唐西域記, 880c: 脇尊者室東有故房. 世親菩薩於此製阿毘達磨俱舍論. Beal [1981 (1884): 105], Watters [2004 (1904–1905): 210], Mizutani [1971: 88], Ji [2000: 246–247].
24. 大唐西域記, 889b: 奢羯羅故城中有一伽藍. 僧徒百餘人. 並學小乘法. 世親菩薩昔於此中製勝義諦論. Beal [1981 (1884): 172], Watters [2004 (1904–1905): 291], Mizutani [1971: 140], Ji [2000: 364]. Cf. 大唐大慈恩寺三藏法師傳, 231c. Takada [1987 (1940): 54–55], Beal [1976 (1911): 73], Nagasawa [1998: 103].
25. 大唐西域記, 891c: 世親是時在磔迦國奢羯羅城. 遠傳聲問衆賢當至. Beal [1981 (1884): 193], Watters [2004 (1904–1905): 325], Mizutani [1971: 140], Ji [2000: 400].
26. 大唐西域記, 896b: 大城中有故伽藍. 是伐蘇畔度菩薩, 唐言世親, 舊日婆藪盤豆譯曰天親訛謬也, 數十年中於此製作大小乘諸異論. Beal [1981 (1884): 225], Watters [2004 (1904–1905): 355], Mizutani [1971: 171], Ji [2000: 450–451]. Cf. 大唐大慈恩寺三藏法師傳, 233c. Takada [1987 (1940): 68], Beal [1976 (1911): 85], Nagasawa [1998: 126].
27. 大唐西域記, 896c: 無著講堂故基西北四十餘里至故伽藍. 北臨殑伽河. 中有塼窣堵波. 高百餘尺. 世親菩薩初發大乘心處. Beal [1981 (1884): 228], Watters [2004 (1904–1905): 358], Mizutani [1971: 173], Ji [2000: 455].

D. Kauśāmbī

Text 8: Shin qin pu sa (世親菩薩, Bodhisattva Vasubandhu) lived in this [room], wrote the Wei shi lun (唯識論), refuted Hinayana Buddhism and confuted the non-Buddhist.[28]

As mentioned above, the eight *Texts* show the areas in which Asaṅga and Vasubandhu did their preaching activity. Although a large number of studies have been made on their theories, little attention has been given to their geographical areas. Most of the *Texts* show their activities in Puruṣapura, with the exception of his *Abhidharmakośabhāṣya* (阿毘達磨俱舍論) writing in *Text* A. These *Texts* from in the *Da tang xi yu ji* (大唐西域記) make it clear that their birthplaces are different from their place of activity. With this we can understand the differences in those two places by the Gandhāran Disturbance in between ca. 350 and ca. 410 CE as the *Context* in this paper. Asaṅga and Vasubandhu left Puruṣapura, which they were from, and moved to the east so as to avoid the Gandhāran Disturbance.

Furthermore, this *Context* clearly defines when Asaṅga and Vasubandhu lived. Some attempts have been made by scholars to set their dates. Ui [1982 (1935): 414] supposed that Asaṅga lived in 310–390 CE and Vasubandhu lived in 320–400 CE, based on the date when their works were translated into Chinese. Furthermore, Hikata [1954] supposed that Asaṅga lived in 395–470 CE and Vasubandhu lived in 400–480 CE, based on the *Po sou pan dou fa shi zhuan* (婆藪槃豆法師傳). The reason for this supposition is the passage of Ayodhyā king Bi ke luo mo a zhi duo (馝柯羅摩阿袟多, Skt. Vikramāditya) and prince Po luo zhi di (婆羅袟底, Skt. Bālāditya),[29] who lived at the same time as Vasubandhu. Hikata [1954] identified Bi ke luo mo a zhi duo (馝柯羅摩阿袟多, Skt. Vikramāditya) as the Guptan emperor Puragupta-Vikramāditya and prince Po luo zhi di (婆羅袟底, Skt. Bālāditya) as Puragupta's son Narasimhagupta-Bālāditya. Because Puragupta-Vikramāditya succeeded the throne in ca. 486 CE, Hikata [1954] supposed these dates. Moreover, Kato [1989: 58–68] supposed that Vasubandhu lived in 350–430 CE, based on the dates of Abhidharma Masters.

The Context in this paper is the Gandhāran Disturbance between ca. 350

28. 大唐西域記, 898a: 世親菩薩嘗住此中作唯識論破斥小乘難諸外道. Beal [1981 (1884): 235], Watters [2004 (1904–1905): 370], Mizutani [1971: 180], Ji [2000: 471]. Cf. 大唐大慈恩寺三藏法師傳, 234c. Takada [1987 (1940): 71], Beal [1976 (1911): 91], Nagasawa [1998: 132].

29. 婆藪槃豆法師傳, 189c: 國王馝柯羅摩阿袟多. 譯爲正勤日. 婆藪槃豆法師傳, 190b: 正勤日王太子名婆羅袟底也. 婆羅譯爲新.

and ca. 410 CE. This is from Sapur II's expedition to the east and Kidāra's unification. In this paper, I supposed that Asaṅga and Vasubandhu left Puruṣapura and moved to the east so as to avoid the Gandhāran Disturbance. Now I will expand the *Context* into the dates of Asaṅga and Vasubandhu. According to the *Context*, the dates in which Asaṅga and Vasubandhu flourished must be between ca. 350 and ca. 410 CE.

4. A New Interpretation of Chinese Buddhism

This paper sets a *Context*, which is the Gandhāran Disturbance between ca. 350 and ca. 410 CE. Next, I try to interpret another problem in Chinese Buddhism, the translators of the Chinese texts. Consider the 35 translators in the following table based on the *Gao seng zhuan* (高僧傳):

Table 2: Translators in Yi jing zhuan (訳経傳)

The *Gao seng zhuan*	Translators
vol. 1	1. 攝摩騰 2. 竺法蘭 3. 安清 4. 支樓迦讖 5. 曇柯迦羅 6. 康僧會 7. 維祇難 8. 竺曇摩羅刹 9. 帛遠 10. 帛尸梨密 11. 僧伽跋澄 12. 曇摩難提 13. 僧伽提婆 14. 竺佛念 15. 曇摩耶舍
vol. 2	1. 鳩摩羅什 2. 弗若多羅 3. 曇摩流支 4. 卑摩羅叉 5. 佛陀耶舎 6.佛馱跋陀羅 7. 曇無讖
vol. 3	1. 釋法顯 2. 釋曇無竭 3. 佛馱什 4. 浮陀跋摩 5. 釋智嚴 6. 釋寶雲 7. 求那跋摩 8. 僧伽跋摩 9. 曇摩密多 10. 釋智猛 11. 畺良耶舎 12. 求那跋陀羅 13. 求那毘地

Most of them are priests from India or Central Asia. Especially, there are nine priests from Ji bin (罽賓). Although some attempts by scholars to locate Ji bin (罽賓) have been made,[30] it is only clear that the word '*Ji bin* (罽賓)' indicates Gandhāra, Kaśmīr or widely northwest India. Information

30. Shiratori [1970 (1917): 358–359] shows that the region of Ji bin (罽賓) was different depending on the era. According to his research, the word of Ji bin (罽賓) indicated the Gandhāra region between Qian han (前漢) and Jin (晉), the Kaśmīr region in ca. 400 CE and Kapisa in Sui (隋) or Tang (唐). Otherwise, Kuwayama [1990: 43–59] supposes the word of Ji bin (罽賓) in the *Chu san zang ji ji* (出三藏記集) and the *Gao seng zhuan* (高僧傳) can indicate Gandhāra region based on Buddha's bowl in Puruṣapura. Moreover, Enomoto [1993] showed that the word Ji bin (罽賓) in the Buddhist literature from 4th to 6th century CE meant north or northwest India including Gandhāra, Kaśmīr, or Tokhara. Depending on the usage it represented a particular region in north or northwest India.

of the priests from Ji bin (罽賓) is as follows:

Table 3: The nine priests from Ji bin (罽賓)

Name	Route from Ji bin (罽賓)	The Date[1]
僧伽跋澄 (Seng ga ba cheng)[2]	罽賓→関中	建元17年 (381 CE)
僧伽提婆 (Seng ga ti po)[3]	罽賓→長安	建元 (365–385 CE)
曇摩耶舎 (Tan mo ye she)[4]	罽賓→廣州	隆安 (397–401 CE)
弗若多羅 (Fu ruo duo luo)[5]	罽賓→長安	弘始 (399–415 CE)
卑摩羅又 (Bi mo luo you)[6]	罽賓→亀茲→関中	弘始 8 年 (406 CE)
佛陀耶舎 (Fo tuo ye she)[7]	罽賓→沙勒→亀茲→長安	弘始12年 (410 CE)
佛駄什 (Fo tuo shi)[8]	罽賓→揚州	景平元年 (423 CE)
求那跋摩 (Qiu na ba mo)[9]	罽賓→師子國→闍婆→南海	元嘉元年 (424 CE)
曇摩密多 (Tan mo mi duo)[10]	罽賓→諸國→亀茲→敦煌	元嘉元年 (424 CE)

1. The dates in the Table 3 are when their earliest stays were confirmed.
2. 高僧傳, 328a–b.
3. 高僧傳, 328c–329a.
4. 高僧傳, 329b–c.
5. 高僧傳, 333a.
6. 高僧傳, 333c.
7. 高僧傳, 333c–334b.
8. 高僧傳, 339a.
9. 高僧傳, 340a–342b.
10. 高僧傳, 342c–343a.

According to the table, nine priests from Ji bin (罽賓) arrived in China between ca. 380 and ca. 420 CE. Some of them visited China after they stayed in Central Asia (西域). Because all nine priests accomplished translations in China, their activities were admired in Chinese Buddhist history. Or, to put it another way, their movements are the leaving of Ji bin (罽賓), which suggests there was a specific reason for their parting from Ji bin (罽賓).

Here the word '*Ji bin* (罽賓)' becomes a *Text* in this paper. It has not ever been clear why Nine priests from '*Ji bin* (罽賓)' visited China in this era. Now, I would like to emphasize the *Context* in this paper. The *Context* is the Gandhāran Disturbance between Sapur II's expedition to the east and Kidāra's unification. This is between ca. 350 and ca. 410 CE. The *Context* can be expanded into the *Text* of '*Ji bin* (罽賓)'. The Gandhāran Disturbance nearly concurs with the dates when the nine priests came to

China. According to the *Context*, it can be interpreted that some of the priests from '*Ji bin* (罽賓)' moved to China so as to avoid the Gandhāran Disturbance.

5. Conclusion

This paper explored further into Gandhāran Buddhism based on *Text* and *Context*. I have come to the following conclusion:

1. According to the *Gao seng fa xian zhuan* (高僧法顯傳), the Gandhāran people's faith was focused on towers in 402 CE, although the number of temples and monks had decreased.

2. This paper fixed a passage about the number of temples and monks in Puruṣapura as a *Text* in *Text Science*.

3. The *Text*, which indicates a decrease of monks in Puruṣapura, was fixed as the *Context*, the Gandhāran Disturbance between Sapur II's expedition to the east and Kidāra's unification. This is between ca. 350 and ca. 410 CE.

4. I showed a new interpretation of Indian Buddhism by the *Context*: It was in order to avoid the Gandhāran Disturbance that Asaṅga and Vasubandhu from Puruṣapura moved to the east in the *Da tang xi yu ji* (大唐西域記). According to my opinion, the dates in which Asaṅga and Vasubandhu flourished must be between ca. 350 and ca. 410.

5. I showed a new interpretation of Chinese Buddhism by the *Context*: It was also in order to avoid the Gandhāran Disturbance that the nine priests from Ji bin (罽賓) went to China to translate texts into Chinese.

References

Primary Sources

Rerum Gestarum Libri, Ammianus Marcellinus. *Ammianus Marcellinus*, 3 vols., with an English Translation by John C. Rolfe, London: William Heinemann Ltd / Cambridge: Harvard University Press, 1971–1972 (1935, 1939, 1940). (Reprint)

Po sou pan dou fa shi zhuan (婆藪槃豆法師傳), trans. Zhe di (真諦), *Taisho shinshu daizokyo* (大正新脩大蔵経), vol. 50, No. 2049.

Gao seng zhuan (高僧傳), Hui jiao (慧皎), *Taisho shinshu daizokyo* (大正新脩大蔵経) vol. 50, No. 2059.

Da tang xi yu ji (大唐西域記), Xuan zang (玄奘) / Bian ji (辯機), *Taisho shinshu daizokyo* (大正新脩大蔵経), vol. 51, No. 2087.

Da tang ci en si sang zang fa shi zhuan (大唐大慈恩寺三蔵法師傳), Hui li (慧立) / Yan cong jian (彦悰). *Taisho shinshu daizokyo* (大正新脩大蔵経), vol. 50, No. 2053.

Gao seng fa xian zhuan (高僧法顯傳), Fa xian (法顯), *Taisho shinshu daizokyo* (大正新脩大蔵経), vol. 51. No. 2085.

Wei shu (魏書), Wei Shou (魏収), 6 vols., Beijing: 中華書局.

Secondary Sources

Beal, Samuel

2005 (1869) *Travels of Fah-hian and Sung-yun: Buddhist Pilgrims, from China to India* (400 A.D. and 518 A.D.), Delhi: Low Price Publication. (Reprint)

1976 (1911) *The Life of Hiuen-Tsiang by the Shaman Hwui Li; With an Introduction Containing an Account of the Works of I-Tsing*, San Francisco: Chinese Materials Center. (Reprint)

Deeg, Max

2005 *Das Gaoseng-Faxian-Zhuan als Religionsgeshichiche Quelle*, Wisebaden: Harrassowitz Verlag.

Enoki, Kazuo (榎 一雄)

1958 "The Dates Kidârites (キダーラ王朝の年代について)," *Toyo Gakuho* (東洋学報), 41–3: 1–52.

Enomoto, Fumio (榎本 文雄)

1993 "Ji-bin, the Location of a Center of Indian Buddhism (罽賓――インド仏教の一中心地の所在)," in *Encounter of Wisdom between Buddhism and Science: Essays in Honour of Professor Keishō Tsukamoto on His Sixtieth Anniversary* (塚本啓祥教授還暦記念論文集 知の邂逅――仏教と科学), Tokyo: Kosei Publishing, pp. 259–269.

Frye, Richard N.

1966 "The Persepolis Middle Persian Inscriptions from the Time of Shapur II," *Acta Orientalia*, vol. 30: 81–93.

1984 *The History of Ancient Iran*, München: C.H. Beck.

Hamilton, Walter

2004 (1986) *Ammianus Marcellinus: the Later Roman Empire* (A.D. 354–378), Selected and translated by Walter Hamilton with an Introduction and Notes by Andrew Wallage-Hadrill, . London: Penguin Books Ltd. (Reprint)

Harmatta, J.

1990 "Chionitae, Euseni, Gelani," in J. Harmatta (ed.), *From Alexander the Great to Kül Tegin: Studies in Bactrian, Pahlavi, Sanscrit, Arabic, Aramaic, Armenian, Chinese, Türk, Greek and Latain Sourses for the History of Pre-Islamic Central Asia*, Budapest: Akadémiai Kiadó, pp. 89–97.

Henning, W.B.
1947 "Two Manichaean Magical Texts with an Excursus on the Parthian ending *-ēndēh*," *Bulletin of the School of Oriental and African Studies*, XII–1: 39–66.

Herzfeld, Ernst
1930 "Kushano-Sasanian Coins," *Memory of the Archæological Survey of India*, No. 38, Calcutta: Government of India Central Publication Branch.

Hikata, Ryusho (干潟 龍祥)
1954 "Sesin Nendai Saiko (世親年代再考)," in S. Hanayama, N. Tsuji, R. Yuki and H. Nakamura (eds.), *Miyamoto Shoson Kyoju Kanreki Kinen Ronbunshu Indogaku Bukkyogaku Ronshu* (宮本正尊教授還暦記念論文集　印度學佛教學論集), Tokyo: Sanseido Publishing, pp. 305–323.

Ji, Xian-lin (季 羡林)
2000 『大唐西域記校中 上』中外交通史籍叢刊 6, Beijing: 中華書局.

Kato, Junsho (加藤 純章)
1989 *Kyoryobu no Kenkyu* (経量部の研究), Tokyo: Shunjū-sha.

Kuwayama, Shoshin (桑山 正進)
1990 *Kapishi-Gandhara Shi Kenkyu* (カーピシー＝ガンダーラ史研究), Kyoto: Institute for Reserch in Humanities, Kyoto University.

Marshall, John
1975 (1953) *Taxila*, 3 vols., Varanasi: Bhartiya Publishing House. (Reprint)

Matsuda, Toshio (松田 壽男)
1937 "Kitaragetsushi ni tsuite no Ko (寄多羅月氏に就いての考)," *Kokushigaku* (國史學), 33: 28–56.

Mizutani, Shinjo (水谷 真成)
1971 *Daitosai'ikiki* (大唐西域記), Tokyo: Heibonsha.

Nagasawa, Kazutoshi (長澤 和俊)
1996 *Hokkenden Yakuchu Kaisetsu: Hokuso-bon, Nanso-bon, Korai Daizokyo-bon, Ishiyamadera-bon Shisyu Eiin to Sono Hikaku-kenkyu* (法顯傳訳注解説　北宋本・南宋本・高麗大蔵経本・石山

寺本四種影印とその比較研究), Tokyo: Yuzankaku.

1998 *Genjosanzo* (玄奘三蔵), Tokyo: Kodansha.

Rolfe, John C.

1971 (1935) See *Rerum Gestarum Libri* of Ammianus Marcellinus.

Shiratori, Kurakichi (白鳥 庫吉)

1970 (1917) "Keihinkoku Ko (罽賓國考)," *Shiratori Kurakichi Zenshu* (白鳥庫吉全集), vol. 6, Tokyo: Iwanami Shoten, pp. 295–359. (Reprint)

Takada, Osamu (高田 修)

1987 (1940) "Jionji Sanzohosshi Den (慈恩寺三蔵法師傳)," Kokuyaku Issaikyo Wakan Senjutsu-bu Shiden-bu (国譯一切經和漢撰述部 史傳部), vol. 11, Tokyo: Daito Publishing, pp. 1–242. (Reprint)

1983 (1967) *The Origin of Buddha Statues* (佛像の起源), Tokyo: Iwanami Shoten. (Reprint)

Odani, Nakao (小谷 仲男)

1996 *Gandhara Bijutsu to Kushan Ocho* (ガンダーラ美術とクシャン王朝), Kyoto: Dohosha.

Ui, Hakuju (宇井 伯壽)

1982 (1935) "Shitekijinbutsu toshite no Miroku Oyobi Mujaku no Chojutsu (史的人物としての彌勒及び無着の著述)," *Indotetsugaku Kenkyu* (印度哲学研究), vol. 1, Tokyo: Iwanami Shoten, pp. 355–414. (Reprint)

Vogelsang, Willem J.

2002 (1988) *The Afghans*, Oxford/Malden: Blackwell.

Watters, Thomas

2004 (1904–5) *On Yuan Chwang's Travels in India (A.D. 629–645) (two vols. bound in one)*, edited after his death by T. W. Rhys Davids and S. W. Bushell, with Two maps and Itinerary by Vincent A. Smith, Delhi: Low Price Publication. (Reprint)

* I would like to thank Robert King for his assistance in correcting my English.

III

VEDĀNTA, MĪMĀṂSĀ AND VYĀKARAṆA

CHAPTER 4

CONSUMING SCRIPTURE: PHILOSOPHICAL HERMENEUTICS IN CLASSICAL INDIA

Parimal G. PATIL

Introduction: Philosophical Hermeneutics

Hermeneutics—the study of methods for interpretation and the recovery of meaning—is among the most neglected subject areas in the study of Indian philosophy.[1] This is surprising given the commentarial orientation of Sanskrit philosophers and philosophical literature. Unlike many contemporary philosophers, Sanskrit philosophers often identify themselves with specific text traditions and develop their own philosophical positions by "commenting" on texts that their traditions take to be foundational.[2] Hermeneutics is thus inherent in (and so essential to) the practice of philosophy in classical India.

---

1. Very briefly: Although hermeneutics can be traced back to classical Greece (and especially to the Stoics), it is often said that hermeneutics proper originated with the attempt to develop theoretical frameworks for biblical exegesis (e.g., Philo of Alexandria, Origenes, Augustine, Spinoza). By the early 19th century, however, hermeneutics included textual interpretation in general (e.g., in the work of Schleirmacher) and by the early 20th century it came to be identified with methods for the recovery of meaning within the historical sciences (*Geisteswissenschaften* e.g., in the work of Dilthey). Later still, hermeneutics was transformed, and came to be understood as what makes possible the self-disclosure of the structure of understanding as such (e.g., in the work of Heidegger and Gadamer). I am using the term "hermeneutics" as it was used in its earlier history. For a brief, but helpful, historical discussion of philosophical hermeneutics see Ramberg and Gjesdal [2005], and for a more extensive account see Grondin [1994].
2. It is important to note that there are many kinds of commentaries and many examples of quasi-commentarial literature. By the term "commentaries" I mean those texts that are explicitly identified as such e.g., *Śabarabhāṣya, Nyāyavārttika, Tattvasaṃgrahapañjikā*, etc. For a very interesting and comparative discussion of commentarial literature see Griffiths [1999].

Among Sanskrit philosophers, the standards for philosophical hermeneutics were set by those who followed the text traditions defined by Jaimini's *Mīmāṃsā-sūtras*. Later philosophers and theologians, such as those who followed the text traditions defined by Bādarāyaṇa's *Vedānta-sūtras*, developed their hermeneutics in close and critical conversation with the practices of the Mīmāṃsakas.[3] An essential feature of both of these text traditions is their commitment to Veda, the paradigmatic category of Hindu scripture and the definitive source for knowledge of *dharma*.[4] The commitment of Mīmāṃsā and Vedānta to Veda is such that, to a significant degree, the philosophical projects of many Mīmāṃsakas and Vedāntins can be understood as attempts at recovering and systematizing the meaning of Vedic texts and practices. For many Mīmāṃsakas and Vedāntins, therefore, it is with Vedic exegesis and hermeneutics that philosophical theology must begin.[5]

As a way of addressing the issue of texts and contexts in Indian philosophy, I want to focus on how Vedic texts were used in an intellectual context, defined by the work of a remarkable philosophical theologian, the Mīmāṃsaka, Kumārilabhaṭṭa (ca. 7th CE). Although the term "context" is usually used to refer to the cultural, social, and political "outsides" of texts, it is important to keep in mind that the "outside" of a particular text (or group of texts) also includes other texts. In my view, Kumārila's work can itself provide an important context in which to understand Veda. In fact, in his view, it is the only legitimate context in which to understand it. In this paper, I want to discuss Kumārila's approach to Vedic hermeneutics in order to discover what it can teach us about texts and contexts in Indian philosophy, and what we can learn from him about scripture, its authoritative status, and what it means to properly understand it.

---

3. See Halbfass [1991], where the relationships between these two text traditions are discussed. Also see Parpola [1981] and Parpola [1994], where the dating of the foundational texts of these traditions is discussed.
4. See Halbfass [1991: Chapters 2 and 3] for an accessible, yet learned, introduction to this issue.
5. By the term "exegesis," I mean the practice—rather than the theory—of interpretation and the recovery of meaning. In the work of Kumārila (and the Vedāntins, Śaṅkara and Rāmānuja) exegesis and hermeneutics are often inextricably linked. On my use of the term, "theology" refers to an intellectual practice and a sub-discipline of the study of religion, as it is constituted in the North American academy. This use of the term goes well-beyond its etymological meaning. For a discussion of "theology" along the lines in which I am using it, see Clooney [1993: 4–15], Jackson and Makransky [2000: 1–52], and Patil [2001].

I will organize my remarks around the following three questions and will try and explain how Kumārila would answer each of them. The questions that I want to ask are: (1) What counts as scripture? (2) Wherein lies its authority? (3) What can be said about philosophical theology on the basis of scripture and how can this be justified through exegesis, and other commentarial and "quasi-commentarial" practices?[6] I hope that by seeking answers to these questions we will be able to better understand the role that Veda played in intellectual and philosophical contexts, and perhaps discover something about the relationship between hermeneutics and philosophical theology in classical India.

Kumārila's Mīmāṃsā: A Theology of Ritual

Part 1. What Counts As Scripture and Wherein Lies Its Authority

According to Mīmāṃsakas such as Kumārila, "Veda" is the paradigmatic category of scripture. This is because the texts that belong to this category are taken to be the uniquely authoritative foundation for our knowledge of *dharma*—that is, our knowledge of what we should and should not do if we want to get certain things that we believe will contribute to our satisfaction in this life and beyond.[7] It is in how to acquire a wide variety of things such as cows, rain, sons, yogic powers, revenge, and heaven through processes such as ritual, whose workings we cannot explain empirically, that is the domain of *dharma*.[8] In these matters, Veda is taken to be uniquely authoritative since it is the only infallible source for our knowledge of this trans-empirical domain, and the trans-empirical processes that are essential to it.[9] Like the universe itself, Veda is eternal and, as a result, is said to be authorless (*apauruṣeya*), and therefore free from the kinds of errors that plague both human and divine compositions. It is uniquely foundational

---

6. By "quasi-commentarial literature" I am referring to texts that do not comment on a single text from beginning to end, but that largely consist in the interpretation and elaboration of statements that are drawn from foundational or canonical texts of a particular tradition. Examples include the *Nyāyabhūṣaṇa*, *Naiṣkarmyasiddhi*, *Tattvabindu*, etc.
7. For a brief discussion of the differences between Kumārila's "hypothetical" interpretation of injunctions and his rival Prabhākara's "categorical" interpretation, see Halbfass [1988: 326] and Halbfass [1991: 68].
8. For a relatively detailed and yet accessible survey of this concept in "traditional Hinduism" see Halbfass [1988: Chapter 17]. I will be using the term "Veda" to refer to both the category and the texts that belong to it.
9. Halbfass [1988: 282].

in that without Veda there would be no way of knowing *dharma*: The domain of *dharma* is inaccessible to all ordinary and extraordinary ways of knowing. Veda is, therefore, understood to be the unique, uncreated, timeless, and infallible "testimony of *dharma*" itself.[10] While the basis for our knowledge of *dharma* is Veda, our awareness of this fact is based on reason (*nyāyamūla*). Thus, important parts of Kumārila's work are devoted to demonstrating, rationally, that our knowledge of *dharma* must be based on Veda (*vedamūla*).[11] It may be helpful to think of this as Kumārila's "philosophical" project, in order to distinguish it from his more "theological" project of providing a framework within which to understand Veda and, therefore, *dharma*.

Śruti: Veda

According to Mīmāṃsakas such as Kumārila, "Veda" is restricted to the texts of the Ṛk, Yajus, and Sāma Vedas. For them the status of the Atharvaveda corpus is more problematic, and it may not be Vedic at all.[12] Even within the texts that define the category of "Veda" there is a difference in the authoritative status of the different kinds of linguistic expressions found in them e.g., injunctions (*vidhi*), on the one hand, and liturgical utterances (*mantra*), recommending narratives (*arthavāda*), and names (*nāmadheya*), on the other.[13]

Injunctions (*vidhi*), such as the statement, "Someone who seeks heaven should perform the *Agniṣṭoma* ritual,"[14] stipulate what one who seeks certain things should do (and what one who seeks to avoid certain things should not do). They define *dharma*, and so are, by definition, authoritative. According to Kumārila, the Vedic injunction to study the Veda (*svādhyāyo 'dhyetavyaḥ*) implies that each and every statement in the Veda must be attended to, since each serves a purpose that is relevant for our knowledge of *dharma*.[15] The ways in which these statements are relevant can almost always be traced to how they are related to specific injunctions.[16]

---

10. Halbfass [1988: 282]. "The Veda stands and speaks for itself as the timeless and uncreated testimony of *dharma*. It does not have an author; for this very reason, it has no room for error and deception."
11. Most notably his *Ślokavārttika* (ŚV).
12. Halbfass [1991: 4].
13. See Halbfass [1991: 4 n. 9]—for references to primary sources. This issue is discussed in great detail in Jha [1964: 147–224].
14. *jyotiṣṭomena svargakāmo yajeta*, ĀŚSū 10.2.1.
15. *Arthavādādhikaraṇa*, TV 1.2.7, especially pp. 47–48.
16. See *Balābalādhikaraṇa*, TV 3.3.14.

For example, liturgical utterances (*mantra*) such as the statement, "I offer the leftovers to Agni,"[17] contribute to *dharma* because when uttered during the performance of a ritual they typically bring to mind specific things that are necessary for the enjoined ritual action to be successful, such as the name of the deity to whom one is making the offering.[18] In effect, liturgical utterances trigger one's memory (*smāraka*) about things that are relevant for the performance of a particular enjoined act. Since such statements are a part of Veda, they are authoritative. But, in so far as their only function is to trigger one's memory, like a mnemonic, their authority extends only to the linguistic form of the utterance itself.[19]

Recommending narratives (*arthavāda*) are also authoritative in that they are a part of Veda. The nature of their authority, however, is rather different from that of liturgical utterances.[20] Recommending narratives, such as the statement, "Vāyu is the fastest of divine beings,"[21] are correlated with specific injunctions and support the injunctions with which they are correlated. By implying, for example, that an offering to the "fastest of divine beings" will lead to the fastest results, the statement, "Vāyu is the fastest of divine beings," supports an injunction by motivating a person to perform a ritual to Vāyu.[22] It is important to note that, according to Kumārila, recommending narratives neither tell us what we should want (they do not prompt us to desire certain things) nor do they tell us anything about what the world is like (they do not have any factual or informational content). Rather, they are merely instrumental—they make use of convenient fictions to motivate us to undertake certain enjoined acts. They are authoritative only with respect to the positive or negative advice they provide about the best way to bring about a particular result.

The privileged status of Veda itself does not mean, however, that there are no other sources that can be used for learning about *dharma*. In fact, there are numerous other textual sources that are said to be authoritative, though

17. *agnāye juṣṭaṃ nirvapāmi*.

18. TV 1.2.31–1.2.53, especially p. 206, *Mantrāvidhāyakatvādhikaraṇa*, TV 2.1.31, and *Mantralakṣaṇādhikaraṇa*, TV 2.1.32, especially pp. 481–482. The example is quoted from *Amantrādhikaraṇa*, TV 2.1.34, where it is cited in a discussion of "modification" (*ūha*).

19. It is through implication that we come to know to which injunction a particular liturgical utterance applies. See *Holakādhikaraṇa*, TV 1.3.1.

20. See *Arthavādādhikaraṇa*, *Audumburādhikaraṇa*, and *Nigadādhikaraṇa*, TV 1.2.1–1.2.30, especially p. 46.

21. *vāyur vai kṣepiṣṭhā devatā*, TS 2.1.1.1.

22. This example is discussed at *Arthavādādhikaraṇa*, TV 1.2.7, p. 49.

not foundational. These texts are not strictly speaking Veda, rather, they are Vedic, or based on/derived from Veda. In addition, there are also non-textual sources such as the behavior of good, learned people (*sadācāra*). To better understand the scope the category of scripture and the ways in which Vedic texts and practices are also authoritative, it will be helpful to consider why Kumārila takes the Sanskrit Epics and the Dharma-text of Manu (*mānavadharmaśāstra*), and also the behavior of good, learned people (*sadācāra*) to be authoritative with respect to *dharma*.

Smṛti: Epics (Itihāsa) and Dharma-texts (Dharmaśāstra)

According to Kumārila, the Sanskrit epics—the *Mahābhārata* and the *Rāmāyaṇa*—were composed by Vyāsa (*dvaipāyana*) and Vālmīki in strict accordance with Veda.[23] They are, therefore, completely consistent with it. Each contains injunctions and an incredible number of purely narrative episodes. Both epics are also said by Kumārila to be universally studied and accepted by the learned, and to be relevant for nearly everyone.[24] Kumārila explains that many of the injunctions found in the epics are directly based on those found in the Veda and so are absolutely authoritative with respect to *dharma*. The epics are so consistent with Veda that Kumārila says that we can even reason that the epic injunctions that are not found in Veda itself are still authoritative, since they must be based on Vedic statements that were known to the learned authors of the epics but are no longer extant and so no longer known to us.[25]

For Kumārila, of the numerous Dharma-texts, only the Dharma-text of Manu (*mānavadharmaśāstra*) is authoritative. He says that unlike the other well known texts of *dharma*, it alone is applicable throughout *Āryavarta* and universally accepted by the learned.[26] Kumārila also notes that many of the injunctions found in it are also found in Veda and that, in fact, there is only one injunction that is not entirely consistent with Veda.[27] On the basis of these observable facts, Kumārila concludes that Manu constructed his text to be in strict accordance with Veda and, therefore, that any injunction

---

23. ŚV, *Sambandhākṣepaparihāra* v. 64–65; *Arthavādādhikaraṇa*, TV 1.2.7, especially pp. 50–51.
24. *Holākādhikaraṇa*, TV 1.3.15–23, especially p. 87. It is worth noting that Kumārila excludes those who are blind, deaf, dumb, and mentally impaired from this group.
25. *Arthavādādhikaraṇa*, TV 1.2.7, especially p. 51.
26. *Smṛtyadhikaraṇa*, TV 1.3.2.
27. *Śiṣṭākopādhikaraṇa*, TV 1.3.4.

in Manu's text that is not found in Veda itself must be based on a Vedic text that is no longer available to us, either because the text itself is no longer extant or because it is extant but "lost."[28] Kumārila argues that the assumption of a Vedic source for these injunctions is the simplest (and only) way to account for the recognized excellence of Manu's text and the confidence that generations of learned people have had in it.[29]

In contrast to Veda itself (*śruti*), Vedic texts (*smṛti*) are those that are no longer still heard in their original form and are based on only an imperfect 'memory' of the original.[30] There is always a human hand in their composition and the texts are, therefore, in principle, fallible.[31] Where they are found to be incompatible with Veda, their authority is always trumped by Veda itself.[32] In addition, if any such texts are discovered to be based on personal experiences, the testimony of others, or to be intentionally misleading, they cannot be authoritative and so cannot be Vedic. Actual Vedic texts, such as the Sanskrit epics and the Dharma-text of Manu, are authoritative because they are based on Veda. Their authoritative status is evident since throughout *Āryavarta* these texts are accepted by learned men belonging to the three classes (*śiṣṭatrivarṇakadṛdhaparigraha*).[33] And the simplest way to account for this incontrovertible and observable fact is to assume that these texts are based on sections of Veda that are no longer available or on those that are available but can no longer be found, either because those who preserve them live in very remote places or because those portions of Veda that support a particular Vedic statement are scattered throughout the Veda and cannot be easily located and collated.[34]

Ācāra: Practices of Good People (sadācāra)

In addition to authoritative textual sources for *dharma*, Kumārila argues

---

28. *Smṛtyadhikaraṇa*, TV 1.3.2. Also see *Śiṣṭākopādhikaraṇa*, TV 1.3.4.
29. *Smṛtyadhikaraṇa*, TV 1.3.1–2. Also see *Virodhādhikaraṇa*, TV 1.3.3. Liturgical utterances are the basis for inferring an injunction that was never uttered, but *smṛtis* like Manu's Dharma-text are a basis for inferring Vedic texts that were once uttered but now are no longer known.
30. "The very idea of *smṛti*, for instance, or so I have suggested, originated with Mīmāṃsā—as a Vedic text no longer extant, no longer actually still being 'heard' (*śruti*) in its original wording during recitation, but existing only as a 'memory' (*smṛti*) of the original, and in new wording ..." Pollock [2004: 773].
31. *Smṛtyadhikaraṇa*, TV 1.3.1.
32. *Virodhādhikaraṇa*, TV 1.3.3.
33. "the learned of the three *varṇas* accept them (*śiṣṭatrivarṇakadṛdhaparigraha*)." See TV 1:.76.12 and Pollock [1997: 414].
34. *Smṛtyadhikaraṇa*, TV 1.3.2.

that many of the practices of good, learned people are also authoritative.[35] Those practices that are simply for the purpose of maintaining oneself, pleasure, or material gain, however, are generally not taken to be so.[36] This is because such practices are common to everyone and are usually based on discernable motives and observable results. For Kumārila, only those practices that are unique to good, learned people are authoritative with respect to *dharma*. What these practices are authoritative about is the connection between the observable behavior of good, learned people and certain generally desirable results such as heaven etc.[37] According to Kumārila, "good, learned people" are those among the inhabitants of *Āryavarta* whose conduct is observed to be in strict accordance with Veda. When such people are observed to do things that are not prohibited by Veda, but for which there is no textual support in Veda, it may be presumed that they are based on Vedic texts that are "lost". Otherwise, why would good, learned people do them? In addition, the Dharma-text of Manu clearly states that "The practices of good, learned men are authoritative with respect to *dharma*."[38] And so, since the Dharma-text of Manu is authoritative, the practices of good, learned people must be too. The practices of good, learned people are therefore authoritative in that they are, for the most part, based either on Veda itself or Vedic texts.[39]

Conclusion to Part 1

For Kumārila, the category of scripture includes an obviously (and perhaps surprisingly) broad range of texts and practices. These texts and practices can be legitimately classified as "scripture" because they are the only authoritative resources for our knowledge of *dharma*. Thus, not only Veda itself (*śruti*), but also texts that are Vedic (*smṛti*)—like the epics and the Dharma-text of Manu—and practices that are determined to be Vedic—like the example set by good learned people (*sadācāra*)—are resources that we

35. *Sadācāraprāmāṇyādhikaraṇa*, TV 1.3.7, *Holākādhikaraṇa*, 1.3.15–23.
36. *Sadācāraprāmāṇyādhikaraṇa*, TV 1.3.7, especially p. 363.
37. *Sadācāraprāmāṇyādhikaraṇa*, TV 1.3.7.
38. MDhŚ 2.6.
39. It is worth noting that, according to Kumārila, many of these good, learned people are so immersed in Veda, and are so committed to acting in a manner sanctioned by Vedic texts, that they are unable to have any ideas contrary to Veda. In fact, their intuitions are thoroughly conditioned by Veda and they themselves are only satisfied (*ātmatuṣṭi*) by what is in strict accordance with Veda. Thus, whatever such a person says and does really has its source in the impressions left by Veda and thus is Vedic, and as Kumārila says, is as authoritative as Veda itself.

may draw upon for learning about what we should and should not do if we want to get certain things that we believe will contribute to our satisfaction in this life and beyond. While Veda itself is independently authoritative, the epics, the dharma-text of Manu, and the practices of good, learned people are only authoritative by association with Veda. What counts as scripture for Kumārila, then, is any text or practice that is not contradicted by Veda and can, in principle, be shown to be directly or indirectly based on either a known or unknown text of Veda. The variety of ways in which this "can be shown" is what allows for scripture to be such a broad and seemingly open category.

For Kumārila, however, the category of scripture is also rather narrow in the sense that, according to him, Veda is the only legitimate basis for the authority of the range of texts and practices that actually do contribute to our knowledge of *dharma*. Thus, Buddhist and Jaina texts, and also those of the "Hindu" Pāñcarātrins and Pāśupatas, are not scriptural and therefore are illegitimate resources for our knowledge of *dharma*. Even the supposedly "orthodox" text traditions of Sāṃkhya and Yoga, and the philosophical and theological frameworks that are based on them, are deemed non-Vedic by him.[40]

Part 2. What has been said about theology on the basis of scripture, and how has this been justified through commentarial and "quasi-commentarial" practices?

For Kumārila, determining what counts as scripture enables one to identify the only legitimate resources for learning about *dharma*. Understanding the different ways in which these resources are authoritative enables one to learn how they are related to one another, wherein their authority lies, and for which dimensions of *dharma* they are authoritative. Much of this, however, is preliminary to what Kumārila thinks can actually be said on the basis of these resources about "theological (or *dharma*-logical)" matters and why he thinks that what he says about "theology" is sanctioned by Veda.

For Kumārila, philosophical theology is the attempt to provide a meaningful and defensible framework within which to think about *dharma*. Given his view of the relationship between *dharma* and Veda, theology amounts to providing a framework within which to properly interpret

40. *Śiṣṭākopādhikaraṇa*, TV 1.3.4, Pollock [1989: 21 n. 12]. For an excellent discussion of this issue see Halbfass [1991: Chapter 3].

and understand Veda. For Kumārila, then, philosophical theology is inextricably linked with Vedic hermeneutics. Kumārila's position on the status of Veda is such that it requires him to be able to account for each and every expression found in Veda, and to interpret and understand Veda from within a framework that is entirely consistent with it and the other sources that he says are authoritative in matters of *dharma*. Kumārila is also committed to working within the text tradition defined by Jaimini's *Mīmāṃsā-sūtras* and with its philosophical and theological principles. His understanding of scripture and his commitment to the text tradition based on Jaimini's *Mīmāṃsā-sūtras* thus provide the boundaries within which Kumārila practices philosophical theology.

In what follows, I want to discuss three specific examples of how Kumārila relates scripture and theology, with the hope of beginning to discover what he thinks it means to interpret scripture properly and to properly learn from and understand it.

Example #1: Divinities (Devatā-s)

It is commonplace that when rituals are described in Veda, various gods are invoked and named. Veda states, for example, "It is to Viṣṇu that one must offer the *Upāṃśu* ritual" and "Being pleased, Indra satisfies him with children and cattle."[41] What is not explained, however, is to what the names "Viṣṇu" and "Indra" refer: Are they real embodied beings who actually participate in the ritual?[42] Is their presence necessary for the efficacy of rituals? Are they the recipients of sacrificial offerings?[43] A common-sense reading of the texts in question suggests that the various deities referred to are in fact real participants in the sacrifice and that they may even be the primary objects of ritual activity. Such a reading is also confirmed by over a century of scholarship on Veda and Vedic religion.[44] According to Kumārila, however, this is not at all a proper interpretation of these statements.

Kumārila argues that in injunctive statements such as "It is to Viṣṇu that one must offer the *Upāmśu* ritual" the name "Viṣṇu" is subordinate to the action expressed by the injunction: It serves a syntactic role by indicating

41. *Anuṣṭhānādhikaraṇa*, Ṭu 9.1.6.
42. *Anuṣṭhānādhikaraṇa*, Ṭu 9.1.6–10, *Uccāraṇaniyamādhikaraṇa*, Ṭu 10.4.23.
43. *Upāṃśūyājādhikaraṇa*, TV 2.2.9–2.2.12.
44. For an excellent discussion of Vedic religion see Jamison and Witzel [1992] and Witzel [2003].

a grammatical, rather than an actual, recipient of the sacrifice.[45] On this line of reasoning, the names "Viṣṇu" and "Indra" are necessary, but for practical reasons. For the one who is performing the ritual, Viṣṇu is (the one) in whose name the offering is being made. Viṣṇu is not literally the one to whom the offering is being made. Thus, the statement "It is to Viṣṇu that one must offer the *Upāṃśu* ritual" does not mean that Viṣṇu is literally a recipient of the offerings, like someone who receives a gift might be. Kumārila also argues, however, that names such as "Viṣṇu" and "Indra" are not just the sounds Vi-ṣ-ṇu and In-dr-a but, in fact, are proper names that do refer to something. Although he is clear that this something is not an embodied being, he does not discuss in any detail to what such names refer. Given his other philosophical views, we can infer that they refer to the concepts "Viṣṇu" and "Indra" which, since time immemorial, come to mind when Vedic statements in which these names appear are recited during the performance of a ritual.

According to common sense interpretations of these statements, and those based on historical and text-critical methods, Kumārila's explanation will seem fanciful and fantastic. What I am interested in thinking about, however, is according to what kind of hermeneutics Kumārila's interpretation makes sense. Let us consider two more examples before attempting to answer this question.

Example #2: Liberation (Mokṣa), Knowledge (Jñāna), and the Self (Ātman)

In Veda, there are passages in which the goal of liberation (*mokṣa*) is mentioned, and knowledge of *brahman* and/or the self is enjoined, seemingly for the purposes of liberation. Famous examples include statements such as "It is he that Brahmins seek to know by means of Vedic recitation, sacrifice, gift-giving, austerity, and fasting. It is he, on knowing whom a man becomes a sage",[46] "A man who knows *brahman* knows the highest (that) there is",[47] "I, myself, am *brahman*",[48] "Only when a man knows him does he pass beyond death; there is no other path for getting

---

45. *Upāṃśūyājādhikaraṇa*, TV 2.2.9–12; *Devatādhikaraṇa*, Ṭu 6.3.17–18; *Anuṣṭhānādhikaraṇa*, Ṭu 9.1 6–10; *Uccāraṇaniyamādhikaraṇa*, Ṭu 10.4.23, discussed in Clooney [1985], Clooney [1997]. For the point that I am making here see Clooney [1997: 341–342].
46. BĀU 4.4.22, text and translation in Olivelle [1998: 124–125].
47. TU 1.2, text and translation in Olivelle [1998: 300–301].
48. BĀU 1.4.10, text and translation in Olivelle [1998: 48–49].

there",[49] "It is the self that is to be known",[50] "One should investigate the self, one should seek to know it",[51] and "It is through knowledge that one becomes free from death".[52]

As with the statements from Veda cited earlier, text-critical scholarship supports a rather straightforward reading of these statements, which leads one to suppose that liberation is important and that it is only through knowledge of *brahman* and/or the self that one can become a sage or achieve freedom from death. According to Kumārila, however, things like heaven, and not liberation, are enjoined, and action, not knowledge, is of primary importance in bringing about such results.[53] How then does Kumārila interpret and explain these passages?

Kumārila admits that there are Vedic injunctions to "know thyself"[54] and argues that they serve two purposes, neither of which is accurately captured by the "straightforward reading."[55] He says, for example, that knowing something about the self e.g., that it survives the death of the body, is related to ritual activity since it helps to explain why one would undertake lengthy Vedic rituals whose results (e.g., heaven) could only be enjoyed in a future life.[56] Knowing that the self survives the body seems to be necessary if one is actually going to undertake such complicated, lengthy, and expensive rituals.[57] Against what seems to be a straightforward reading of the above passages, Kumārila also argues that such injunctions do not support the interpretation that knowledge of the self brings about liberation (*mokṣa*).[58] He explains that statements in which "liberation" is mentioned as a desirable result are not really injunctive. Rather, they are recommending narratives (*arthavāda*) that help to motivate a person to

---

49. ŚU 6.15, text and translation in Olivelle [1998: 432–433].
50. This is cited in ŚV, *Sambandhākṣepaparihāra* v. 103.
51. ChU 8.7.1, text and translation in Olivelle [1998: 278–279]. Cited by Kumārila in *Vyākaraṇādhikaraṇa*, TV 1.3.27.
52. ĪU 11, text and translation in Olivelle [1998: 408–409].
53. ŚV, *Sambandhākṣepaparihāra* vs. 103–105, 108–110, *Vyākaraṇādhikaraṇa*, TV 1.3.27, and BṬ fragments from the *Nyāyakaṇḍalī* and *Nyāyasudhā*, quoted in Taber (forthcoming).
54. See ŚV, *Sambandhākṣepaparihāra* v. 103 and *Vyākaraṇādhikaraṇa*, TV MS 1.3.27 where Kumārila cites ChU 7.1.3 and ChU 8.7.1, among others. Mesquita [1994], Taber (forthcoming).
55. This is explicitly stated in the *Vyākaraṇādhikaraṇa*, TV 1.3.27.
56. ŚV, *Sambandhākṣepaparihāra* v. 103 and *Vyākaraṇādhikaraṇa*, TV 1.3.27 discussed in Mesquita [1994] and Taber (forthcoming).
57. This is also stated in *Vyākaraṇādhikaraṇa*, TV 1.3.27.
58. ŚV, *Sambandhākṣepaparihāra* v. 102, Mesquita [1994], Taber (forthcoming).

undertake lengthy Vedic rituals that will result, not in liberation, but in heaven etc.[59] In addition, if liberation is supposed to be an eternal state beyond pleasure and pain, Kumārila concludes that it cannot be brought about by any kind of practice. This conclusion is based on the philosophical principle that anything that can be caused can only endure for a limited period of time. Kumārila argues, therefore, that if liberation is something that can be brought about it must be a type of cessation that is brought about by the elimination of its cause. Thus, whatever liberation is, it cannot be the kind of thing that is brought about by knowledge of the self.[60]

Even though seeking liberation is not enjoined, Kumārila recognizes that there may be people who still want to be liberated. For such people, he provides an explanation of what liberation could be and how one could attain it. He points out that liberation cannot consist in the enjoyment of pleasures (*sukhopabhoga*) since then it would just be equivalent to heaven (*svarga*). On the basis of this, he argues that liberation must simply be the absence of rebirth,[61] and that if one were interested in liberation, it could not be through knowledge, but through action, that it could even be attained. More specifically, Kumārila says that this sort of liberation can be attained only by exhausting all of one's previous *karma* and avoiding any future *karma*. He explains that one is able to exhaust one's previous *karma* by experiencing its positive and negative effects and that one can avoid any further *karma* by performing obligatory ritual acts (*nitya-naimittika*) and by not doing anything that has been characterized as either optional (*kāmya*) or prohibited (*niṣedha*).[62] He qualifies this latter point by explaining that the performance of obligatory ritual acts is neutral only if they are undertaken without any desire for their results. And it is this sense of detachment, he says, that is the result of knowing the self.[63] It is worth noting that according to Kumārila, attaining liberation by exhausting one's accumulated *karma* etc. could take millions of years.[64]

---

59. ŚV, *Sambandhākṣepaparihāra* v. 104, Mesquita [1994], Taber (forthcoming).
60. ŚV, *Sambandhākṣepaparihāra* v. 105d–107.
61. ŚV, *Sambandhākṣepaparihāra* v. 108cd–109.
62. ŚV, *Sambandhākṣepaparihāra* v. 110.
63. ŚV, *Sambandhākṣepaparihāra* v. 111, Also see Kumārila's verse from the Bṛhaṭṭīkā quoted in the *Nyāyakandalī*, in Mesquita [1994: 465–467] and Taber [forthcoming: 23–24], as fragments #1, 2, 3, 6.
64. See Kumārila's verse from the Bṛhaṭṭīkā quoted in the *Nyāyakandalī*, in Mesquita [1994: 465–467] and Taber [forthcoming: 23], as fragment #4, where the complex question of how what Kumārila says about *mokṣa* in the ŚV relates to what he says in the TV and the Bṛhaṭṭīkā.

Again, the question that I want us to keep in mind is: According to what kind of hermeneutics would Kumārila's interpretation make sense?

Example # 3: Apūrva

Vedic sacrifices are extremely complex ritual processes that can last for days (e.g., the *Darśapūrṇamāsa*).[65] Even the simpler rituals are composed of a seemingly innumerable number of ritual acts, each of which is enjoined by Veda and which together bring about a desired result, even in the distant future. What is not explained in great detail in Veda itself, however, is how this works. As a part of his overall philosophical and theological project to explain and defend the significance and efficacy of Vedic rituals, Kumārila provides an explanation.[66]

According to Kumārila, each ritual act leaves or creates in the soul of the performer a disposition (*saṃskāra/śakti*) to produce a specified effect.[67] These "dispositions" accumulate until at the completion of the ritual they combine with each other to leave in the soul a final, composite disposition which endures, and in due time, either in this life or the next, produces its specified result. Kumārila helpfully uses the examples of farming and studying to explain how the accumulated effect of many actions can lead to a desired future result.[68] He refers to this change in the self or soul of a person who correctly performs a Vedic ritual as (being due to) "*apūrva*."[69] It may be helpful to think of *apūrva* as what connects an act to its result.

---

65. This example is discussed by Kumārila in the *Apūrvādhikaraṇa*, TV 2.1.5, p. 365.
66. Kumārila's explanation is found in the *Apūrvādhikaraṇa*, TV 2.1.5. For an accessible discussion of this section see Halbfass [1991: 300–311]. Also see *Teṣāmarthādhikaraṇa*, TV 3.1.8. For a wonderful example of how Kumārila defends the efficacy of a particular sacrifice—the *citrā* ritual, whose result is supposed to be cattle—see the *Citrākṣepavāda* and *Citrākṣepaparihāra* section of his ŚV at ŚV: 349–352 and ŚV: 483–488. For his brief treatment in the ŚV, see ŚV, *Codanāsūtra* v. 199 and ŚV, *Citrākṣepaparihāra* v. 8–9ab.
67. *Apūrvādhikaraṇa*, TV 2.1.5, Yoshimizu [2000: 163 n. 28].
68. TV 2: 365.15–17. Halbfass [1991: 303 n. 50], Yoshimizu [2000: 151]. It is worth noting that these are just examples and that, for Kumārila, *apūrva* is the unique result of Vedic rituals.
69. TV2: 369.8. In the ŚV, however, Kumārila briefly discusses the idea that *apūrva* is a kind of potentiality (*śakti*) that belongs to the self (*ātman*), and says that there is only one such potentiality of the self, namely, the capacity for knowledge. As Yoshimizu [2000: 154] has pointed out, however, in verse 199 of the *Codanāsūtra* of ŚV he also suggests that it might be a capacity of sacrificial acts themselves or perhaps the results of a sacrifice. For an excellent discussion of this issue see Yoshimizu [2000: 163 n. 28].

Since neither the term, nor Kumārila's concept of *apūrva*, can be found in a single authoritative text, (in addition to the philosophical problem of defending his theory of *apūrva*), Kumārila must explain how and why it can have such a central role in his theology. In order to do so, Kumārila appeals to an epistemological and hermeneutical principle known as "indispensable implication" (*arthāpatti*) through which one can learn about certain things in virtue of those things being necessarily implied either by some observed fact (*dṛṣṭārthāpatti*) or by known Vedic words or statements (*śrutārthāpatti*).[70] Since, according to Kumārila, *apūrva* is implied by Veda, his use and interpretation of it is thus sanctioned by scripture and is, in fact, scriptural.[71]

Not only does Kumārila's hermeneutics allow him to interpret Veda in seemingly fanciful and fantastic ways, but, as his treatment of *apūrva* shows, it also allows him to attribute to Veda concepts that are not at all present in it.[72] In concluding this paper, I want to finally address the question of according to what kind of hermeneutics any of this makes sense.

Conclusion: Principled Consumerism

The range of texts and practices that Kumārila includes in the category of "scripture" provides him with a variety of resources with which to develop his philosophical theology, and to which it must also be entirely responsible. Without scripture there could not be theology—that is, any

---

70. There are numerous places in the ŚV where Kumārila argues that we can come to know the presence of a capacity (*śakti*) on the basis of "indispensable implication" (*arthāpatti*). See Yoshimizu [2000: 163 n. 28] for a list of references and a very helpful discussion of the differences between the two kinds of indispensable implication.
71. His use of the term is, it seems, sanctioned by *śrutārthāpatti* since it functions in the realm of language (*śabdagocara*), while his interpretation of it as a capacity that inheres in the self seems to be justified by *dṛṣṭārthāpatti*, which has to do with 'things' (*arthagocara*). Something like this is also suggested by Yoshimizu [2000: 163 n. 28] who, more specifically, suggests that Kumārila's view on how we know that there is *apūrva* might be influenced by Sāṃkhya argument for *śakti*.
72. The extent to which Mīmāṃsā theologians were able to modify the system from within is perhaps most evident in what seems to be a very late and localized development. Āpadeva, his son Anantadeva, and nephew Bābādeva assert that in order to be liberated one should dedicate the accumulated *apūrva* to God (Govinda, Kṛṣṇa) who, in exchange, will grant you liberation. For Āpadeva's views see *Mīmāṃsānyāyaprakāśa* pp. 393, 394–397, and Abhyankar's commentary. I owe these references to Lawrence J. McCrea.

legitimate reflection on *dharma*—and thus scripture is the only possible basis for theology and the ultimate source of its authority and legitimacy. In order to learn from scripture and practice theology, however, it is necessary to properly interpret and understand it. Although some of the hermeneutical principles that Kumārila relies on to understand scripture may be present in scripture itself, Kumārila clearly draws upon the resources of his text-tradition and his own philosophical and theological creativity.[73] In his work, he thus balances and integrates his commitments to scripture, the philosophical and theological principles of his text-tradition, and his own sense of what is right.

One of the most striking features of Kumārila's approach to Veda is his decision to not attend to historical contexts or to intra- and inter-textual contexts in a manner familiar to us from more contemporary forms of text-criticism.[74] The reason for the first decision is relatively clear since, for Kumārila at least, Veda itself is not historical—it is authorless and eternal. And although other texts and practices that have scriptural content are historical, their scriptural content is not. For Kumārila, then, there is no historical world in which Veda itself was produced and so attention to its "history" is impossible. And while Kumārila would agree that some Vedic texts (such as the epics and Dharma-text of Manu) and Vedic practices (such as the conduct of good, learned people) are historical—in that they are the products of specific times and places—he argues that their scriptural content is not. Thus, when compared to Veda itself, historical context is irrelevant, even though it may be relevant for understanding other aspects of Vedic texts and practices.

Kumārila's treatment of intra- and inter-textual contexts is also striking. It is important, for example, that Kumārila never comments on an "entire text" (e.g., the hymns of a particular Veda or a single Upaniṣad) and does not privilege textual "proximity" in anything like the way that we generally do. Intra-textual contexts defined by single texts are, therefore, less significant for him than the inter-textual context of scripture as a whole. Even Kumārila's reliance on this inter-textual context, however, is more about individual sentences than about sentences in the context of paragraphs, chapters, or whole texts. For Kumārila, the context that is most relevant for interpreting and understanding a specific Vedic sentence is

73. For a discussion of this issue see Bronkhorst [1997].

74. The qualification "in a manner familiar to us from more contemporary forms of text-criticism" is important since Kumārila often appeals to intra- and inter-textual contexts when discussing a particular Vedic text.

defined by the textual world that is constructed around the injunction with which the sentence in question can be most closely associated. Thus, an injunction serves as the focal point for the construction of a textual world that is made up of all of those sentences in scripture that can be determined to be relevant to the sacrifice referred to in that particular injunction. It is through a set of principles for determining subordination, and especially subordination to an injunction, that the relevant textual world is defined.[75] It is important to remember that this textual world can be constructed even around a focal point that is no longer available! Very few of the principles that are used to construct this world, however, are internal to the world itself, and most are brought to it and defended on more philosophical grounds.

For Kumārila, then, if neither historical nor intra- or inter-textual contexts are of primary importance for properly interpreting and understanding scripture, what kind of context is? I want to suggest that the most important context for Kumārila is an intellectual one, defined by his commitments to what scripture is and why it is authoritative; his commitments to his text-tradition and its philosophical and theological principles; and his commitment to what he thinks is right. These three sets of commitments are all defended by independent philosophical arguments. They also support and inform one another, and it would be a mistake to see any one of them as primary or foundational. Each is in a kind of reflective equilibrium with the others.[76] When taken together, these commitments constitute the intellectual framework that is his philosophical theology. Even though an account of scripture and its authoritative status is itself a part of this framework, in my view, it is the entire framework that is the primary context within which scriptural statements are supposed to be properly interpreted and understood. In an important sense, Kumārila reverses the familiar order of moving from scripture to theology by bringing his theology to scripture. I want to refer to this approach to scripture as a hermeneutics of principled consumerism.

According to this hermeneutic model, what it means to properly interpret

---

75. This is extensively discussed in *Balābalādhikaraṇa*, TV 3.3.1–3.8.44. The principles of subordination are listed at MS 3.3.14. They are direct declaration (*śruti*), implication (*liṅga*), sentential connection (*vākya*), contextual connection (*prakaraṇa*), position (*sthāna*), and connections based on a name (*nāma*). For a very clear discussion of *Balābalādhikaraṇa*, TV 3.3.14, see McCrea [2003].

76. This term has been used in the context of Indian philosophy in Ganeri [2001: Chapter 5].

and understand scripture is just to make good use of it. To consume it, if you will, in accordance with one's own interests as a way of showing one's commitment to it; as a way of being faithful to it; and in recognition of its uniquely authoritative status.[77] That a scriptural statement has been properly interpreted and correctly understood can only be determined, according to this model, within the context of the intellectual framework that is one's philosophical theology. More specifically, the success of one's interpretation is directly related to the success of this framework. As I read Kumārila, then, it is because his framework can explain how and why Vedic rituals and practices are effective, and because it cannot be defeated by any known philosophical arguments that it properly interprets scripture and exemplifies a correct understanding of it. For Kumārila, what Vedic statements are really about is what his philosophical theology says they are.

The metaphor of theology as a renovation project may be helpful for thinking about the ways in which this consumerist hermeneutics is also principled. For Kumārila, the challenge is to take an existing framework—defined by the philosophical theology of his text tradition—and renovate it according to a strict set of rules. Some of these rules have to do with the resources that one may use in the renovation while others have to do with the ways in which they may be used. According to Kumārila, one may only use materials from a certain source (Veda and what is sanctioned by Veda) and must use these materials in accordance with the way they are classified. Doing otherwise would be misusing the materials. In addition, for Kumārila, there can be no unused pieces in the structure that is being renovated or in the materials that one is using for the renovation. Each and every piece must be accounted for. What counts as success is creating, in accordance with these rules, the best structure that one can from the pieces that one has. On this model, this is just what it means to make good and proper use of both the material that one is committed to using (Veda and what is sanctioned by Veda) and the original structure that one is committed to renovating (the philosophical theology of one's text tradition). What is principled about Kumārila's consumerism is that there are very strict rules on what you can use for your renovation and in how you can use those materials. What is consumerist about his work is that Kumārila already has a plan for what his finished structure will look like. On this model,

77. In the context of such a hermeneutics, our notions of "commitment" and "being faithful" may have to take on new meanings.

questions about the legitimate use, purpose, or value of a piece of building material can only be determined in the light of the structure as a whole and the rules of renovation. Similarly, for Kumārila, it is not possible to understand the meaning of scripture without understanding its role in the theological framework that gives it meaning.

To be genuinely open to what Hindu philosophers and theologians have to say about scripture, hermeneutics, and the relationship between texts and contexts, we must be open to radically revising not only our understanding of the basic concepts with which we think about these issues, but also our standards for evaluation. Although Kumārila's interpretations of Veda may still seem fanciful and fantastic, I hope that I have been able to explain, at least in a preliminary fashion, why Kumārila (and nearly everyone else in classical India) did not think that a consumerist approach to scripture was problematic, and why they did think that intellectual contexts provided the most important context for understanding Veda. When we take Kumārila's work seriously we are also able to see how deep commitments to scripture and text-tradition in fact made possible much of the creativity and innovation that is so characteristic of Hindu philosophical theology.

In conclusion, I want to end with a Sanskrit verse that touches on theme of the colloquium, and the issue of traditionalism and innovation.

api sphuṭati vindhyādrau
vāti vā pralayānile |
guruśāstrānugo mārgaḥ
parityājyo na dhimatā ||

Even if the Vindhyā mountains begin to crumble |
and the winds that bring about the destruction of the world begin to blow |
the path of one's teacher and text tradition |
is never to be abandoned by those who truly wise ||[78]

Abbreviations

ĀŚSū	Āpastamba-śrautasūtra
BĀU	Bṛhadāraṇyaka Upaniṣad in Olivelle [1998].
ChU	Chāndogya Upaniṣad in Olivelle [1998].
ĪU	Īśa Upaniṣad in Olivelle [1998].
MDhŚ	Mānavadharmaśāstra in Olivelle [2005].

78. *Laghuyogavāsiṣṭha* 6.5.45, cited by Pollock [1989].

MNP	Mīmāṃsānyāyaprakāśa in Abhyankar [1972].
MS	Mīmāṃsāsūtra in Abhyankar and Joshi [1980–94].
ŚU	Śvetaśvatara Upaniṣad in Olivelle [1998].
ŚV	Ślokavārttika in Ray [1993].
Ṭu	Ṭuptika in Abhyankar and Joshi [1980–94].
TS	Taittirīyasaṃhitā
TU	Taittirīya Upaniṣad in Olivelle [1998].
TV	Tantravārttika in Goswami [1984].
TV 1, 2	Tantravārttika in Abhyankar and Joshi [1980–94].

Bibliography

Abhyankar, K.V.

1972 *Mīmāṃsānyāyaprakāśa* by Āpadeva, Poona: Bhandarkar Oriental Research Institute.

Abhyankar, K.V. and G. Joshi

1980–1994 *Mīmāṃsādarśanam*, 3rd edn., vols. 2–7, 4th edn., vol. 1, Pune: Ānandāśrama Press.

Bronkhorst, Johannes

1997 "Philosophy and Vedic Exegesis in the Mīmāṃsā," in E. Franco and K. Preisandanz (eds.), *Beyond Orientalism: The Work of Wilhelm Halbfass and its Impact on Indian and Cross Cultural Studies*, Ponzan Studies in the Philosophy of the Sciences and the Humanities, vol. 59, Amsterdam: Rodopoi, pp. 359–372.

Clooney, Francis X.

1985 "The Concept of Dharma in the Mīmāṃsā Sūtras of Jaimini," in S. S. Janaki (ed.), *Mm. Professor Kuppuswami Sastri Birth Centenary Commemoration Volume, part 2*, Madras: Kuppuswami Sastri Research Institute, pp. 175–187.

1988 "*Devatādhikaraṇa*: A Theological Debate in the Mīmāṃsā Vedāntā Tradition," *Journal of Indian Philosophy* 16: 277–298.

1993 *Theology After Vedanta: An Experiment in Comparative Theology*, Albany: SUNY.

1997 "What's a god? The quest for the right understanding of *devatā* in Brāhmaṇical ritual theory (*mīmāṃsā*)," *International Journal of Hindu Studies* 1 (2): 337–385.

Ganeri, Jonardon

2001 *Philosophy in Classical India: The Proper Work of Reason*, Routledge.

Goswami, Mahaprabhulal
1984 *Mīmāṃsādarśanam*, vols. 1–4, Varanasi: Tara Book Agency.

Griffiths, Paul J.
1999 *Religious Reading: The Place of Reading in the Practice of Religion*, Oxford.

Grondin, Jean
1994 *Introduction to Philosophical Hermeneutics*, New Haven: Yale University Press.

Halbfass, Wilhelm
1988 *India and Europe: An Essay in Understanding*, Albany: SUNY.
1991 *Tradition and Reflection: Exploration in Indian Thought*, Albany: SUNY.

Jackson, Roger and John Makransky
2000 (eds.) *Buddhist Theology: Critical Reflections by Contemporary Buddhist Scholars*, Surrey: Curzon.

Jamison, Stephanie and Michael Witzel
1992 *Vedic Hinduism*, unpublished manuscript.

Jha, Ganganatha
1964 *Pūrva-Mīmāṃsā In Its Sources*, Varanasi: Banaras Hindu University Press.

McCrea, Lawrence J.
2003 "Interpretive Economy and Ideal Readers in Classical Indian Hermeneutical Theory," unpublished manuscript.

Mesquita, Roque
1994 "Der Idee der Erlòsung bei Kumārilabhaṭṭa," *Wiener Zeitschrift für die Kunde Südasiens* 38: 451–484.

Olivelle, Patrick
1998 *The Early Upaniṣads: Annotated Text and Translation*, New York: Oxford University Press.
2005 *Manu's Code of Law: A Critical Edition and Translation of the Mānava-Dharmaśāstra*, New York: Oxford University Press.

Parpola, Asko
1981 "On the Formation of the Mīmāṃsā and the Problems Concerning Jaimini, with Particular Reference to the Teacher Quotations and the Vedic Schools," [Part I], *Wiener Zeitschrift für die Kunde Südasiens und Archiv für indische Philosophie* 25: 145–177.
1994 "On the Formation of the Mīmāṃsā and the Problems Concerning

Jaimini, with Particular Reference to the Teacher Quotations and the Vedic Schools," [Part II], *Wiener Zeitschrift für die Kunde Südasiens und Archiv für indische Philosophie* 38: 293–308.

Patil, Parimal G.

2001 "A Prolegomenon to 'Christian God, Hindu God'," in Francis X. Clooney (ed.), *Hindu God, Christian God: How Reason Helps Break Down the Boundaries between Religions*, New York: Oxford University Press, pp. 185–195.

Pollock, Sheldon I.

1997 "'Tradition' as 'Revelation': *Śruti*, *Smṛti*, and the Sanskrit Discourse of Power," in S. Lienhard and I. Piovono (eds.), *Lex et Litterae: Essays on Ancient Indian Law and Literature in Honor of Oscar Botto*, Turin: Edizioni dell'Orso, pp. 395–417.

1989 "The Idea of Śāstra in Traditional India," in A. L. Dallapiccola (ed.), *Shastric Tradition in Indian Arts*, Stuttgart: Steiner Verlag, pp. 17–26.

2004 "The Meaning of *Dharma* and the Relationship of the Two Mīmāṃsās: Appaya Dīkṣita's 'Discourse on the Refutation of a Unified Knowledge-System of *Pūrvamīmāṃsā* and *Uttaramīmāṃsā*'," *Journal of Indian Philosophy* 32: 769–811.

Ramberg, Bjorn and Kristin Gjesdal

1995 "Hermeneutics," In Edward N. Zalta (ed.), *Stanford Encyclopedia of Philosophy*, URL=<http://plato.stanford.edu/archives/win2005/entries/ hermeneutics/>

Ray, Gangasagar

1993 *Ślokavārttikam*, Varanasi: Ratna Publications.

Taber, John

1989 "Are Mantras Speech Acts? The Mīmāṃsā Point of View," in H. Alper (ed.), *Mantra*, Albany: SUNY.

forthcoming "Kumārila the Vedāntin?" Unpublished Manuscript.

Witzel, Michael

2003 "Vedas and Upaniṣads," in Gavin Flood (ed.), *The Blackwell Companion to Hinduism*, Oxford: Blackwell Publishing, pp. 68–101.

Yoshimizu, Kiyotaka

2000 "Change of View of *apūrva* from Śabarasvāmin to Kumārila," in S. Mayeda, Y. Matsunami, M. Tokunaga and H. Marui (eds.), *The*

Way To Liberation: Indological Studies in Japan, Delhi: Manohar.

2004 "Notes on Kumārila's Approach to Ritual Scripture," in S. Hino and T. Wada (eds.), *Three Mountains and Seven Rivers: Prof. Musashi Tachikawa's Felicitation Volume*, Delhi: Motilal Banarsidass.

* In writing this essay, I have benefited from numerous conversations with my colleague Lawrence J. McCrea, and constructive comments by participants in the colloquium at Nagoya University.

CHAPTER 5

THE BEGINNINGS OF *BHAKTI*'S INFLUENCE ON ADVAITA DOCTRINE: THE TEACHINGS OF MADHUSŪDANA SARASVATĪ

Shoun HINO

Madhusūdana Sarasvatī was an Advaita Master who lived around 1500 CE in Bengal. Many books are ascribed to him,[1] but his *magnum opus* was *Advaita Siddhi*. This is one of four Siddhi works in the tradition of Advaita Vedānta, and is recognized as one of the most influential books. Moreover some maintain that Madhusūdana was the first ever Advaita Master to introduce the idea of *bhakti* into the tradition of the Advaita Vedānta school. This was a profound impact on the history of Advaita philosophy. The concept of *bhakti* had never been accessible in Advaita doctrine since Śaṅkara's foundation of the School.

Yet despite being an Advaita Master, Madhusūdana did refer to *bhakti*. He could have ignored it as his predecessors had done. We could assume that this was because of the time when he lived and the religious circumstances under which he propagated his Advaita School. In 16th century Bengal, the *bhakti* movements of Vaiṣṇava were prevalent and Islamic Sufism had a growing influence on Hinduism, so under such circumstances it would have been hardly possible to ignore *bhakti*.[2]

According to the Gupta's (1977) account of his influences

> 'He left home and stayed in Navadwip reading Nyāya (Logic) under the great contemporary masters. The floodgates of Śrī Caitanya's cult of love and devotion had just been opened and the entire country was submerged by the torrent. Young Madhusūdana came under the effective influence of this religious fervour. He intended to put this cult

1. Dasgupta [1973: 225]; Karmarkar [1962: xiii–xiv].
2. Mayeda [1982: 467–472].

on a firm metaphysical basis....'[3]

For Madhusūdana, a faithful Advaitin and an ardent bhakta, philosophical and religious thought should have gone hand in hand.[4] We could assume that he had an inner struggle between his philosophy and his (religious) mind resulting from surrounding influences.

Before entering into Madhusūdana's idea of *bhakti*, it would be profitable to take a glance at Hindu religious history, particularly on Advaita doctrine and *bhakti* or the *bhakti* movement between Śaṅkara (8th century) and Madhusūdana (16th century).

The Advaita teaching of the Brahman is one of the most fundamental aspects of Indian spirituality. The truth of mysticism, i.e., that the Brahman only is real, is a pan-Hindu thought. The history of Hindu religions comprises the Hindu orthodoxy of this Brahman-monism as its trunk and the two doctrines of *bhakti* and Tantrism as its branches and leaves.

The Vedic gods and others found in two epics, namely the *Mahābhārata* and the *Rāmāyaṇa*, in *Purāṇa* literature and in indigenous folklore—many gods were worshipped over the course of time, and this god-worship type of religion took its form in Hindu religion. *Bhakti* is a religious act of worshipping a confronting god. Irrespective of Śiva and Viṣṇu worships, *bhakti* has overwhelmingly prevailed in Hindu religiosity.

Bhakti is different from Śaṅkara's self-reliant meditation type of religion, and is a grace (of god) type. It maintains a god confronting a bhakta. Here a god is a personified transcendent, and there is a personified relationship between a god and a bhakta, the bhakta feeling as if he/she were confronting the god. This is done as an act of love and belief toward the confronting god.

The sacred Brahman is the absolute and abstract principle, but on the contrary, there must be an object to which the act of *bhakti* is dedicated. Consequently, the sacred is personified. For Rāmānuja (12th century) and Madhva (13th century) the object was a personified, transcendental Viṣṇu.

As a result of the influence of Rāmānuja's Viśiṣṭādvaita school of Vedānta, Madhusūdana's discussion of knowledge and *bhakti* is quite

3. Gupta [1977: xii].
4. Cf. Dasgupta [1973: 226]; in which he says, 'though he was such a confirmed monist in his philosophy, he was a theist in his religion and followed the path of *bhakti* ...'. And also cf. Mayeda [1980: 49]; in which he says that Madhusūdana introduced *bhakti* and tried to assimilate it into the system of Advaita. J. Gonda [1977: 261] uses the word 'reconcile' saying '... reconcile Advaita metaphysics with the devotion to a personal deity...'.

similar to the philosophical underpinnings of the aforementioned school. Madhva established the Dvaita school of Vedānta and this doctrine itself was criticized by Madhusūdana in the above-mentioned *Advaitasiddhi*.

After the times of Rāmānuja and Madhva, Viṣṇu worship was prevalent mainly in the form of both Kṛṣṇa and Rāma. In the 15th century, Rāmānanda, who was in the line of Rāmānuja, was active in Varanasi, and worshipped Rāma. He propagated the worship of Rāma-Śītā by way of *kīrtana* and *bhajan* in Hindi. *Rāmcaritmānas* of Tulsidās was in this school, which resulted in the explosive spreading of Rāma-worship in the north India.

Kabir, a disciple of Rāmānanda, criticized Hindu manners and customs due to the influence of Islamic Sufism. He later claimed that Rāma, Viṣṇu, Kṛṣṇa and Allah were all the ultimate reality and identical, and that therefore there was no distinction between Hinduism and Islam. Interestingly although Kabir was influenced by Islamic Sufism, much of the teaching of Nanak, a founder of the Sikh, can be traced back to Kabir.

The center of Kṛṣṇa-worship was Mathura and the worship spread in the Bengal and other areas. Apart from the *Bhāgavata Purāṇa*, Jayadeva's *Gītāgovinda* spurred Rādhā-worship. Viṣṇusvāmin and Nimbārka lived there; the latter in particular was in the line of the Rāmānuja school and wrote a *Brahmasūtrabhāṣya*. This is one of five commentaries on the *Brahmasūtra*.

The thought of *preman-prapatti* found in the *Bhāgavata Purāṇa* succeeded Vallabha and Caitanya. The ardent *bhakti* movement advocated by Caitanya was popular in east India, Bengal in particular resulting in its recognition as Bengal Vaiṣṇava or Gauḍīya Vaiṣṇava.

In the 16th century Vallabha founded a school in Vṛndāvan and Caitanya advocated Rādhā-Kṛṣṇa worship. Both, unlike Advaita Vedānta, stood for the affirmation of the world. Vallabha held the view that Brahman and Kṛṣṇa were identical and that the world created from the personified god Kṛṣṇa was real. This phenomenal world manifested from the eternal Kṛṣṇa was pure and absolute. Secular life was supreme. Vallabha affirmed the feelings and desires which inevitably followed, and encouraged the pleasures of a worldly life.

Viraha bhakti and *tāntric bhakti* are common in that both maintain the savior god and the affirmation of the world created by Him. For laymen who are not eligible and therefore not initiated into the disciplined monastery life, only liberation through God's grace is only possible, though members of a religious elite like Madhusūdana may take the way of self-reliant meditation through stage-theory. The Brahman is identified with God, the confronting god who gives grace, and is understood as the hidden god. 'All is the Brahman' is justified in the Hindu religious world.

Caitanya took recourse to *bhakti* and the *sādhana* of Tantrism. He emphasizes *kīrtana* among the nine forms of *bhakti*. *Kīrtana* is nothing but *bajan*, and chanting songs in praise of the Lord Kṛṣṇa to the accompaniment of drums and stringed instruments. Gatherings at temples generally comprise bajan and preaching, rather like programs of service at Christian churches. Caitanya emphasized this *kīrtana* and introduced dancing in addition to chanting. Jīvagosvāmin preached liberation by means of calling the name of the Lord Kṛṣṇa and chanting Kṛṣṇa songs, that is, by means of *kīrtana*. During *kīrtana* many a bhakta calls the name of Kṛṣṇa and chants a song of Kṛṣṇa. *Kīrtana* is nothing but *bhakti*. In the ecstatic excitement, the significance of the spiritual training of incessantly picturing Kṛṣṇa is achieved.

In the *kīrtana* form of *bhakti*, through dancing and singing, which are positive acts reminiscent of the power of *sādhana*, the *bhakta* is obsessed by the god. That is not by surrendering oneself and being filled with the god as in the case of *viraha bhakti*, but by the independent act of filling oneself with the god in oneself. Though it is nothing but an act of *bhakti* Caitanya enhanced the act of *kīrtana* into *sādhana*. *Bhakti* becomes *sādhanabhakti*. Both Vallabha and Caitanya, who were Vedāntins and also Madhusūdana's contemporaries, established more *bhakti*-based doctrines, and eventually both became charismatic religionists. Here we pay more attention to Caitanya, partly because he was from Bengal.

Both Vedāntas are laymen's religions, where Kṛṣṇa is a savior and *bhakti* towards Him is the sole means of liberation. Though Madhusūdana was an ardent devotee he was an eligible Advaitin and able to take the Advaitic way of meditation-based passage towards liberation. At this point, we should point out that he had three separate but inter-related views regarding liberation:

- Liberation through the Advaitic way
- Liberation through *bhakti*
- Liberation through Advaita supported by *bhakti*.

Liberation: The Advaitic Way

It is known that Advaita Vedānta, in the post-Śaṅkara period, diverged into the school of Bhāmatī and that of Vivaraṇa, and both schools developed different theories about various metaphysical problems. There is yet another standpoint of Advaita doctrine, that being Sureśvara's. Sureśvara was one of the disciples of Śaṅkara and his doctrine of Advaita does not follow either school but occupies an important part in the history of Advaita Vedānta as a Vārttikakāra.[5] As a matter of course Madhusūdana follows Sureśvara as far as Advaita doctrine is concerned. This is known from the following facts. On the initial page of his *Vedāntakalpalatikā*[6] he declares the affiliation of his thought saying "this book is to clarify the intention shown by Vyāsa, Śaṅkara, Sureśvara...." Also at several places in *Gūḍhārthadīpikā*,[7] he cites and takes recourse to Sureśvara's *Bṛhadāraṇya kopaniṣadbhāṣyavārttika* and develops his own ideas.

Liberation: The Bhakti Way

What performances are actually meant by the word *bhakti*? Madhusūdana enumerates nine acts of *bhakti*, citing *Bhāgavatapurāṇa* 7.5.23–24.[8] These are:

(1) *śravaṇa* 'hearing'
(2) *kīrtana* 'praising'
(3) *smaraṇa* 'remembrance'
(4) *pādasevana* 'the respectful bow to the foot of God'
(5) *arcana* 'worship'
(6) *vandana* 'expressing respect'
(7) *dāsya* 'the service to God'
(8) *sakhya* 'being a companion'
(9) *ātmanivedana* 'the homage to the Ātman'

This nine-fold *bhakti*, i.e., the religious acts of paying homage to and worshipping the god, is in another words said to be '*bhakti* as a means [to liberation]' (*sādhanabhakti*).

In the self-reliant type of religion, *bhakti* is a supplementary aid to the religious performance to reach the sacred, or to obtain liberation, and remains an idea adopted from the *Bhāgavatapurāṇa*. *Bhakti* is the means to liberation in the grace type of religion. When it is introduced into the self-

5. Hino [1982: 8].
6. *Vedāntakalpalatikā*, p. 2 (see note 1).
7. 2.40; 3.21; 3.37; 12.20; 18.2 etc.; and also cf. *Bhaktirasāyana* 1.23 (p. 56).
8. *śravaṇaṃ kīrtanaṃ viṣṇoḥ smaraṇaṃ pāda-sevanam /*
arcanaṃ vandanaṃ dāsyaṃ sakhyam ātma-nivedanam //23//

reliant type of religion, it does not have such a unique function.

Madhusūdana describes eleven stages of *bhakti* in *Bhaktirasāyana* 1.34–36.[9] These are derived from *Bhāgavatapurāṇa* 3.25.25[10] and are not his Advaitic ideas.

Among the eleven stages, the 1st – 4th are naturally the means to the 5th, *ratyaṅkurotpatti* 'the generation of the seed of love'. The *bhakti* of this 5th stage is nothing but the definition of *bhakti* at *Bhaktirasāyana* 1.3.[11] This is also due to *Bhāgavatapurāṇa* 2.29.11–12.[12]

The features of *bhakti*: (1) *bhakti* constitutes nine-fold acts and is itself *sādhanabhakti*, (2) there are eleven stages in *bhakti*, (3) *bhakti* is incessant mind-working to the god. All of these features are taken over from the *Bhāgavatapurāṇa*.

Madhusūdana clearly states that a detailed discussion is already done in the *Bhaktirasāyana* at various places in the *Gūḍhārthadīpikā* (7.16, 18.66). It is a matter of discussion how this should be estimated. From his formidable years he had known that *bhakti* was something respectful and effective for laymen not eligible for the Advaita way of quest for liberation. In addition to writing the *Bhaktirasāyana*, he composed two *stotras* (hymns), *Harilīlā* and *Ānandamandākinī*. Dasgupta actually states: 'he was a theist in his religion and followed the path of *bhakti*, or the *bhakti* as is evidenced by his numerous works promulgating the *bhakti* creed.'

Madhusūdana held the Advaita doctrine of liberation and knew that it was meant for eligible people (*adhikārin*) and not for laymen, in other words, all those who are not considered eligible. He showed laymen the way to liberation through Kṛṣṇa *bhakti*. Since childhood he had paid homage to Kṛṣṇa and did not hesitate to do so. His philosophical and *bhakti*-based book, *Bhaktirasāyana*, was a derivative of the *Bhāgavatapurāṇa*. While

---

9. *prathamam mahatma sevā tad-dayāpatratā tataḥ /*
śraddhā 'rtha tgeṣāṃ dharmeṣu tato hari-guṇa-śrutiḥ //34//
ṭato raty-aṅkurotpattiḥ svarūpādhigatis tataḥ /
prema-vṛddhiḥ parānande tasyātha sphuraṇaṃ tataḥ //35//
bhagavad-dharma-niṣṭhā 'tas svamiṃs tad-guṇa-śālitā /
premṇo 'tha paramā kāṣṭhety uditā bhakti-bhūmikāḥ //36//

10. *satāṃ prasaṅgām mama vīrya-saṃvido bhavanti hṛt-karṇa-rasāyanāḥ kathāḥ /*
taj-joṣaṇādāśv apavarga –vartmani śraddhā ratir bhaktir anukramiṣyati //

11. *drutasya bhagavad-dharmād dhārāvāhikatāṃ gatā /*
sarveśe manaso vṛttir bhaktir ity abhidhīyate //

12. *mad-guṇa-śrutimātreṇa mayi sarva-guhāśaye /*
manogatir avichinnā yathā gaṅgāmbhaso 'mbudhau //11//
lakṣaṇaṃ bhakti-yogasya nirguṇasya hy udāhṛtam /
ahaitukya-vyavahitā yā bhaktiḥ puruṣottame //12//

writing the book, he intended to justify *bhakti* as a means but strayed from following the teaching of Caitanya.

Liberation: Advaita Supported by *bhakti*

Madhusūdana Sarasvatī discusses the stages of liberation in the introductory part of *Gūḍhārthadīpikā* and others.[13] It shows parallels to what Madhusūdana described in his *Naiṣkarmyasiddhi* etc.[14] He clearly follows the line of thought of Sureśvara. I would like to first compare the stage-theory for liberation of both Masters and see how Madhusūdana understands *bhakti* regarding the stage-theory for liberation. Sureśvara's stage-theory for liberation has been discussed in detail elsewhere,[15] but we enumerate it here.

[1] *nityakarmānuṣṭhāna* 'the performance of the daily ritual'
[2] *dharmotpatti* 'giving rise to *dharma*'
[3] *pāpahāni* 'the annihilation of evil acts'
[4] *cittaśuddhi* 'purifying the mind' [= one of four *adhikāras* in Advaita]
[5] *saṃsārayāthātmyāvabodha* 'recognizing the true nature of the transmigratory existence' [= one of four *adhikāras* in Advaita; *nityānityavastuviveka* 'discriminatory knowledge between the eternal and the non-eternal' according to Śaṅkara]
[6] *vairāgya* 'abandonment' [= one of four *adhikāras* in Advaita; *ihāmutrārthaphalabhogavirāga* 'giving up the enjoying the fruit of wealth here and there' according to Śaṅkara]
[7] *mumukṣutva* 'cherished longing for liberation' [= one of four *adhikāras* in Advaita]
[8] *tadupāyaparyeṣaṇa* 'pursuing the means to liberation'
[9] *sarvakarmatatsādhanasaṃnyāsa* 'renunciation of all the acts and their means'
[10] *yogābhyāsa* 'the repeated practice of *yoga*' [*śamadamādisādhanasaṃpat* 'the obtainment of means like calmness, self-restraint']
[11] *cittasya pratyakpravaṇatā* 'internal observation of mind'

---

13. *Gūḍhārthadīpikā* 3.1; 6.43; 7.3 etc. which are not so elaborate as in the introduction, though.
14. *Bṛhadāraṇyakopaniṣadbhāṣyavārtika* 2.4.2–5.
15. S. Hino, *op. cit.*, pp. 13ff.

[12] *tattvamasyādivākyarthaprarijñāna* 'understanding the meaning of the sentence *tat tvam asi* etc.'

[13] *avidyoccheda* 'the annihilation of ignorance' [*jīvanmukti* 'liberation while being alive']

[14] *svātmany evāvasthāna* 'firmly staying in the Ātman' [*videhamukti* 'liberation when being dead']

On the other hand, Madhusūdana's stage-theory is as follows. This is taken from the introduction of *Gūḍhārthadīpikā*.

(1) *niṣkāmakarmānuṣṭhāna* 'the performance of obligatory acts' [= [1] of Sureśvara]

(2) *paramo dharmaḥ* 'the supreme dharma' [= [2] of Sureśvara]

(3) *japastutyādikam hareḥ* '*japa*, praise etc. for Viṣṇu'

(4) *kṣīṇapāpa* 'the annihilation of evil acts' [= [3] of Sureśvara]

(5) *cittasya viveke yogyatā* 'the application to the discriminatory knowledge of mind' [= [4] of Sureśvara]

(6) *nityānityaviveka* 'discriminatory knowledge between the eternal and the non-eternal' [= [5] of Sureśvara]

(7) *ihāmutrārthavairāgya/Vaśīkara* 'indifference to profits here and there called *Vaśīkara*' [= [6] of Sureśvara]

(8) *śamadamādisampatti* 'the obtainment of means like calmness, self-restraint'

(9) *saṃnyāsa/sarvaparityāga* 'renunciation of all'

(10) *mumukṣu* 'being desirous of getting liberated' [= [7] of Sureśvara]

(11) *gurūpasādanam upadeśagraha* 'attending to teachers and understanding their teachings'

(12) *vedāntaśravaṇādikam* 'hearing etc. of Upaniṣad'

(13) *tatparipākeṇa nididhyāsananiṣṭhatā* 'firmly staying at meditation through the completion of hearing etc.'

(14) *vākyāt tattvamasi(jñāna)/śabdāt sākṣātkāro nirvikalpaḥ* '(obtaining the knowledge of) *tat tvam asi* from the sentence itself' 'direct experience of the intuitive knowledge from the sentence'

(15) *avidyānivṛtti* 'the annihilation of ignorance' [= [13] of Sureśvara; 'the state of liberation while being alive']

After the annihilation of ignorance (=*jīvanmukti*), Sureśvara put the 14th stage (= *videhamukti*) while Madhusūdana has 16th up to 27th stages,[16] all

16. They are: *bhramasaṃśayau kṣīyate* (16th), *anārabdani karmāṇi naśyanti* /

of which show aspects of *jīvanmukti*. The similarity between the Masters seems obvious. It strongly suggests that Madhusūdana's stage-theory for liberation follows that of Sureśvara. Taking into consideration the fact that Sureśvara was a faithful disciple to Śaṅkara, it may be correct to state that as far as soteriology is concerned, Madhusūdana faithfully and rigidly observes the tradition of Advaita Vedānta beginning with Śaṅkara.

The above-stated stage-theory for liberation is discussed in the introduction of *Gūḍhārthadīpikā* in the 12th and 29th stanzas. The relationship of the stage-theory for liberation to *bhakti* is discussed in the 30th and 39th stanzas.

Bhakti is a driving force which leads one from a stage to next stage without delay. The absence of *bhakti* would make the progressions through the stages an impossibility. (33rd stanza) Even after being benefited by the god due to the performance of *bhakti* in the past life, it would be totally impossible to proceed through many stages or any at all. (35th stanza) Thus, *bhakti* is helpful to the progression through stages towards liberation, or is considered to be a promoting force. The act of *bhakti* with its use of body, mouth and mind is, in this sense, regarded as the most efficient cause. (31st stanza) An ardent *bhakti* devotee is ever becoming one with the absolute, and at the same time one who has dedicated his or her *bhakti* only to the god. (39th stanza) In this sense, *bhakti* accompanied by love (*preman*) is supposed to be the supreme means to liberation.

The stage-theory for liberation becomes available when the profane man wishes to be liberated or to become holy. In the pursuit of the usefulness of *bhakti* in the stage-theory, Madhusūdana recognized it as the driving power for proceeding from stage to stage. Here *bhakti* does not have the implication of being a quest for liberation by grace of the personified god. This *bhakti* is supplementary to back up the religious acts done by the profane.

Further, Madhusūdana interprets the word *bhakti* in a different way from his description in *Gūḍhārthadīpikā*. He uses the word *bhakti* as the specific contents of an idea in the discussion of the 12th –14th stages in his stage-theory for liberation outlined above.

āgaminī na jāyante (17th), *prārabdhakarmavikṣepād vāsanā na naśyati* (18th), *saṃyamenopaśāmyati* (19th), *īśvarapranidhānād samādhi* (20th), *manonāśo vāsanākṣaya eva ca* (21st), *tritayābhyāsaj jīvanmukti* [*tritaya* = *tattvajñāna, manonaśa, vāsanākṣaya*] (22nd), *savikalpasamādhi* (23rd), *nirvikalpasamādhi* (24th), *brahmavādin* (25th), *sthitaprajño viṣṇubhaktaś ca* (26th), *jīvanmukta ātmaratis* (27th).

He states in *Gūḍhārthadīpikā* 18.55 "... by means of *bhakti* which is of the nature of meditation (*nididhyāsana*) ...." The 12th – 14th stages (viz. hearing and reflection → meditation → the true knowledge → elimination of ignorance) are likewise mentioned in *Gūḍhārthadīpikā* 11.54 thus: the completion of hearing and reflection and meditation → obtainment of one's own nature → the elimination of ignorance. As for the relationship between hearing, reflection and meditation, he says in the introduction of *Gūḍhārthadīpikā* that meditation is the result of hearing and pondering, or the fruit of repetition of hearing and reflection (*abhyāsaphala* at 18.54). This meditation, which is the stage before liberation while being alive (*jīvanmukti*), or the manifestation of the true knowledge or the annihilation of ignorance (*avidyānivṛtti*), is identified with *bhakti*.

This *nididhyāsana-bhakti* equation reminds us of Rāmanuja's idea of *bhakti* in relation to *nididhyāsana*. According to him, *bhakti* is special knowledge (*jñānaviśeṣa*) which is full of love of God and absorbing oneself, and something depriving one's interest in others. Knowledge is defined as meditation which has reached the state of *bhakti*. It is the ultimate mode of meditation and is nothing but *bhakti*. This ultimate mode of meditation means the meditation which is most earnest, incessant, surpassing, beloved, and viewing God in the flesh and vividly. 'Most earnest and incessant' meditation is described as to meditate on God most earnestly and incessantly like the flow of oil. In this light, knowledge, the ultimate mode of meditation and a specific phase of *bhakti* are equated. He calls it *bhakti* or meditation which has reached the mode of *bhakti*. On the other hand, Madhusūdana says that *bhakti* is the culmination of knowledge, the culmination of continuous meditation. It is the incessant *bhakti* like the flow of oil. These words are as if borrowed from Rāmānuja, though they worshipped different Gods, Nārāyaṇa and Kṛṣṇa. Madhusūdana holds to the significance of knowledge and meditation, but he did not employ nine-fold *bhakti*. He believed in the God Kṛṣṇa.

Conclusion

Madhusūdana was a renowned and influential Advaitin in his day, and from his early years worshipped Kṛṣṇa. He might have worshipped Kṛṣṇa as a *grāmadevatā*, but he was not inclined to the *bhakti* cult founded by Caitanya, though it was quite prevalent and popular. I can assume a few reasons for this. Madhusūdana was a speculative boy and not convinced of Kṛṣṇa. On the contrary Caitanya's doctrine was based on a theistic Kṛṣṇa and did not require any metaphysical demonstration. Thus, though he was willing to respect Kṛṣṇa, he must have thought that Caitanya's *bhakti* was not for him.

After being initiated into the Advaita school of Vedānta, in the course of his disciplined monastery and worldly life, while devoting himself into the Advaita tradition, he must have pondered over Kṛṣṇa *bhakti* and how both Advaita and *bhakti* could meet together, if that was at all possible. He himself observed many a Kṛṣṇa bhakta and realized the effectiveness of that *bhakti* as a means to liberation. He also recognized that the Advaita doctrine is available only to *adhikāriṇ*s while Kṛṣṇa *bhakti* is available to both *adhikārin*s and non-*adhikārin*s. Under such circumstances Madhusūdana expresses his ideas and thoughts on Kṛṣṇa *bhakti* in various ways and at various places.

In his *Vedāntakalpalatikā* he ignores *bhakti* and observes his stance in the traditional doctrine of Advaita Vedānta. In this book he refutes the thought of liberation through the systems of other philosophical schools and follows the traditional Advaita way of liberation, without referring to *bhakti*. Insofar as he was a traditional and faithful Advaitin, there was no room for Kṛṣṇa *bhakti* to be brought in.

He held the Advaita doctrine of liberation and knew that it was meant for the eligible people (*adhikārin*). He must have known that for lay people there was only the way of liberation through Kṛṣṇa *bhakti*. He himself paid homage to Kṛṣṇa like lay people constituted majority.

While writing he did not follow Caitanya, but he composed two hymns and *Bhaktirasāyana* in keeping with *Bhāgavatapurāṇa*.

The following phases are his incorporation of *bhakti* into the Advaita doctrine in two ways. This is a matter of the effectiveness of *bhakti* for an *adhikārin*.

Firstly, he points out the significance of *bhakti* as a driving force for progressing in the stages of liberation. He even says that without it one could not proceed from one stage to another. One who had been favored by Kṛṣṇa in the past life could proceed. Such statements strongly suggest the existence of Kṛṣṇa and the effectiveness of *bhakti* even for *adhikārin*s. It is not that *bhakti* is not always necessary for Advaitins. It does not touch the Advaita doctrine but is added as if it were supplementary. He himself must have often experienced being favored by god's grace while progressing through the higher stages of liberation of the Advaita stage-theory.

Secondly, taking recourse to the *nididhyāsana*= *bhakti* equation, he presented another interpretation of *bhakti*. He intended to establish no alternative to Advaita by saying that the already established idea of *nididhyāsana* is in the end to be equated with *bhakti*. He did this from the Advaita standpoint while Rāmānuja did the same from *bhakti* thought.

Madhusūdana was a noted Advaitin but lived during the fervor of the *bhakti* movement, Caitanya's *bhakti* in particular. We have Dasgupta's words as a devotee of religion and an Advaitin as a philosopher,[17] but perhaps we may be allowed to state more specifically at the end of this paper that Madhusūdana was an ardent bhakta and through believing in it (as based on the existence of Kṛṣṇa, and therefore based on affirmation of the world) he interpreted the Advaita doctrine of liberation.

Bibliography

Primary Sources

Bhāgavata Mahāpurāṇa, in *Śrīmad Bhāgavata Mahāpurāṇa (with Sanskrit text and English translation)*, rendered into English by C.L. Goswami, 2 vols., Gorakhpur: the Gita Press, 1971.

Bhaktirasāyana, in *Śrībhagavadbhaktirasāyana*, edited with editor's commentary by Janardana Sastri Pandeya, Varanasi: Girijeśa Kumāra Pāṇḍeya, 1976.

Gūḍhārthadīpikā, in *Śrīmadbhagavadgītā with the commentaries Śrīmat-Śaṅkarabhāṣya with Ānandagiri; Nīlakaṇṭhī; Bhāṣyotkarṣadīpikā of Dhanapati; Śrīdharī; Gītārthasaṅgraha of Abhinavaguptācārya; Gūḍhārthadīpikā of Madhusūdana with Gūḍhārthatattvāloka of Śrīdharmadattaśarmā*, edited by Wasudev Laxman Pansikar Sastri, Bombay: Nirnaya Sagar Press, 1936.

Secondary Sources

Dasgupta, S.

1973 *A History of Indian Philosophy*, vol. 2, London: Cambridge University Press.

Gonda, J.

1977 *A History of Indian Literature*, Wiesbaden: Otto Harrassovitz.

Gupta, S.K.

1977 *Madhusūdana Sarasvatī on the Bhagavadgītā*, Delhi: Motilal Banarsidass.

Karmarkar, R.D.

1962 *Vedāntakalpalatikā*, Poona: BORI, Post-Graduate and Research Department Series No. 3.

---

17. See note 1.

Mayeda, Sengaku

1980 *The Philosophy of Vedānta with Special Reference to Śaṅkara*, Heirakuji-shoten, Sara-sosho 24.

1982 "Changes in the Advaita Vedānta in the 16th Century with Special Reference to Madhusūdana Sarasvatī" *The Commemoration Volume of Dr. Yoshirou Tamura's 60th Year: The Study of Buddhism*, Shunjusha.

Hino, Shoun

1982 *Sureśvara's Vārtika on Yājñavalkya-maitreyī Dialogue*, Delhi: Motilal Banarsidass.

CHAPTER 6

BHARTṚHARI ON TEXT AND CONTEXT

Toshiya UNEBE

1. Introduction

The cultural environment surrounding human beings consists of a complex of texts containing various types of signs and symbols. From the viewpoint of the *Text Science*, found in the title of this volume, every form of human expression—regardless of modalities such as language, image, or gesture—is considered to be a text as long as it serves the purpose of communicating ideas and information. This concept of a text was the subject of a project titled Studies for the Integrated Text Science conducted from 2002 to 2007 at the Graduate Schools of Letters, Nagoya University, under the 21st century COE program supported by the Japanese Ministry of Education, Culture, Sports, Science and Technology.

According to the results of the project summarized by Hirano [2007: 265–271], it was concluded that irrespective of the type of text, every text consists of two elements, namely, "explicit text" and "implicit text." A text explicitly communicates some meaning. This perceptible element of a text is called an explicit text. Every text is capable of communicating various non-explicit meanings that could be generated in the receiver's mind when the text is received. This imperceptible element of a text, which communicates some possible meaning, is called an implicit text. Further, these meanings of the text are generated through the understanding of the interaction with its context.

According to Hirano [2007: 269], this view is based on the so-called contextualism in the field of the philosophy of language. As opposed to literalism, Recanati [2004: 90], the most influential advocator of contextualism in recent times, states that "no proposition could be expressed without some unarticulated constituent being contextually provided."

According to him [2004: 83], "The debate between Literalism and Contextualism was at the forefront of attention in the philosophy of language of the middle of the twentieth century." However, if we examine ancient India, we may find that this issue was argued among the Indian grammarians and thinkers.[1] Although I am currently unable to present this argument in its entirety, in this paper, I would like to introduce the ancient Indian counterpart of modern contextualism by presenting how the fifth-century Indian grammarian/philosopher Bhartṛhari treats context in his linguistic theory, widely known as the theory of the indivisible sentence (*akhaṇḍa-vākya-vāda*). Scholars have clarified that Bhartṛhari considers a sentence (*vākya*) as the indivisible unit of speech and meaning of a sentence (*vākyārtha*) as something indivisibly and instantaneously perceived as a flash of understanding (*pratibhā*) by the listener of the speech.[2] However, the role of context in his theory has not been sufficiently explained thus far.

As the title of his *magnum opus*, the *Vākyapadīya* (VP), indicates, Bhartṛhari mainly argues about a sentence (*vākya*) in contrast with a word (*pada*). Therefore, he focuses on the significance of a sentence *vis-à-vis* the words that constitute it. Thus, there seems to be no independent section in Bhartṛhari's *Vākyapadīya* where he solely explains context. However, this still does not imply that he considers the issue to be an insignificant one. I hope that the idea of this ancient Indian grammarian will prove to be relevant even for the present *Text Science*.

2. Bhartṛhari's Theory of the Indivisible Sentence and its Understanding, *Pratibhā*

Before we examine Bhartṛhari's idea of context, we should briefly consider his basic standpoint, the theory of the indivisible sentence (*akhaṇḍa-vākya-vāda*).

As stated above, according to Bhartṛhari, a sentence is to be considered as an indivisible, integral unit, and words have no meaning of their own.[3]

---

1. Their discussion, as a matter of course, has its own background. The issues dealt with in this paper are originally argued in a highly technical context developed in the tradition of Sanskrit grammar (*vyākaraṇa*) and the hermeneutics of Vedic scriptures (*Mīmāṃsā*). Since the technical points have already been clarified by previous studies, I will list them as references in the footnotes.
2. See, for example, Palsule [1980] and Raja [1969: 224–227].
3. With regard to this point, we can find similar ideas in contemporary contextualism.

Words are recognized when they are abstracted from the indivisible sentence in the same manner that the components of a word such as the base and affix are abstracted for a grammatical explanation of the word. He states the following:

> Just as an explanation of a beautiful picture is given by presenting [partial] differences with individual features like blue color, an explanation of a sentence, that is independent (*nirākāṅkṣa*), is provided by other linguistic elements (namely, words (*pada*) constituting the sentence) that are interdependent (*sākāṅkṣa*). (VP 2.8–9)
>
> Just as bases (*prakṛti*), affixes (*pratyaya*), and so on are distinguished [from each other] in a word, the abstraction (*apoddhāra*) of words is brought about in a sentence. (VP 2.10)[4]

To enjoy a beautiful picture is, as a whole, a single experience. However, when we attempt to communicate it to others, we have to divide the communication into parts and describe the features of the picture by individually explaining each part. Without extracting the many partial features from one picture, we cannot express our appreciation of it. Similarly, although we analyze a sentence by dividing it into words in order to explain it, a sentence is fundamentally one single indivisible unit.

However, this type of abstraction and analysis does not occur in daily communication. Normally, we are able to understand what the speaker means without analyzing a sentence by dividing it into words. According to Bhartṛhari, the meaning of a sentence (*vākyārtha*) is not merely the sum total of meanings of its constituent words. A listener of the sentence understands the meaning of the whole sentence in its totality as a flash of

---

Recanati [2004: 189] states the following: "According to Contextualism, the meaning of words and/or phrases is not determinate enough to yield even a minimal proposition" and "One extreme position denies that words have meanings in anything like the traditional sense."

VPwr 38; VPII 8–9:
citrasyaikasya rūpasya yathā bhedanidarśanaiḥ /
nīlādibhiḥ samākhyānaṃ kriyate bhinnalakṣaṇaiḥ // VP 2.8
tathaivaikasya vākyasya nirākāṅkṣasya sarvataḥ /
śabdāntaraiḥ samākhyānaṃ sākāṅkṣair anugamyate // VP 2.9
yathā pade vibhajyante prakṛtipratyayādayaḥ /
apoddhāras tathā vākye padānām upapadyate // VP 2.10
*In this paper, I use VPwr as the source text. Although readings presented in VPII are occasionally different from those of VPwr, I mention here only the page numbers of VPII to avoid a digression from the main subject. When VPII assigns a different verse number, I will insert it after the page number.

understanding (*pratibhā*). Bhartṛhari's oft-cited verses on *pratibhā* are as follows:

> When meanings [of constituent words of a sentence] are understood separately, flash of understanding (*pratibhā*), which is totally different from [the meanings of the constituent words], takes place. They call it, that which is presented by the meanings of the words, the meaning of the sentence (*vākyārtha*). (VP 2.143)
> Without being tangibly perceived (*avicārita*), it (*pratibhā*) brings about something like an amalgam of meanings [of constituent words]. It becomes the object [of understanding] as if it is endowed with every character [of constituent words]. (VP 2.145)
> Whether it (*pratibhā*) is produced by a present linguistic expression or by following a latent power (*bhāvanā*) [implanted by previous linguistic experiences], nobody can exceed it with regard to "what should be done" (*itikartavyatā*). (VP 2.146)[5]

While *pratibhā* is a flash of understanding that occurs in the listener's mind when a sentence is heard, it is also described as the object of the understanding, namely, the meaning of a whole sentence that is different from the meanings of the constituent words. Since in this case, the object of understanding is not an external tangible object, it should be considered as the content of understanding rather than its object. There is no need to distinguish between the understanding and its content. In any case, *pratibhā* is the meaning of a sentence as a whole as well as its total intuitive understanding. Moreover, it informs human beings about "what should be done" (*itikartavyatā*). *Pratibhā* enables a person to understand what to do.

3. Context and Meanings of Words

Although *pratibhā* is a total indivisible understanding of the meaning of a sentence, if we attempt to reflect on it and explain it to others, the explanation inevitably becomes analytical, as in the case of the

---

5. VPwr 70–71; VPII 65–966:
vicchedagrahaṇe 'rthānāṃ pratibhānyaiva jāyate /
vākyārtha iti tām āhuḥ padārthair upapāditām // VP 2.143
upaśleṣam ivārthānāṃ sā karoty avicāritā /
sārvarūpyam ivāpannā viṣayatvena vartate // VP 2.145
sākśāc chabdena janitāṃ bhāvanānugamena vā /
itikartavyatāyāṃ tāṃ na kaś cid ativartate // VP 2.146

abovementioned example of the explanation of a picture. We must resort to the abstraction (*apoddhāra*) of the meanings of words from a sentence in order to explain it. Without a sentence, however, the meaning of an isolated word cannot be a valid means for communication. Bhartṛhari displays this with the following simple example of a negative sentence:

> In a way, one understands meaning, which is preceded by the grasping of a word. Then, in a sentence, one again understands that meaning differently. (VP 2.239)
>
> Even if many meanings are understood through many [constituent words], when a negation is made in the end, they cease [expressing the existence of the thing meant]. Therefore, one should not rely on them. (VP 2.240)[6]

Here, Bhartṛhari shows the relation between the meaning of a word and a sentence. According to him, the meaning of a sentence is, as a matter of course, ultimately predominant over the meanings of words. A lucid example of this is a negative sentence having a negation particle at the end of the sentence, because all the affirmative meanings expressed by the preceding words can be cancelled out by the last negation particle.

Even if we accept what Bhartṛhari says about the relation between the meaning of a word and a sentence, we usually consider a word in a sentence to be meaningful. When a certain word is abstracted from a sentence, it is considered to have its own meaning. However, the meaning of such an abstracted word is still highly dependent on the surrounding words or the context in which it is used.

We commonly experience situations where we cannot identify the intended meaning of a word in a sentence when the other elements of the sentence are not available due to some reason. Bhartṛhari examines the determinative factors for the meaning of an abstracted word, and provides a list of them in VP 2.314–317. He identified and collected fifteen factors, and suggested that there could be more.[7] Here, I will translate another verse

---

6. VPwr 80; VPII 98, 251:
anyathā pratipadyārthaṃ padagrahaṇapūrvakam /
punar vākye tam evārtham anyathā pratipadyate // VP 2.239
upāttā bahavo 'py arthā yeṣv ante pratiṣedhanam /
kriyate te nivartante tasmāt tāṃs tatra nāśrayet // VP 2.240

7. The last word of the list "... *svarādayaḥ*" (... accent *and so on*) found in VP 2.317 indicates that the list is not exhaustive. To understand Bhartṛhari's argument as a whole, Iyer's translation [1977: 135–138] and Aklujkar's summary [1990: 147] are informative. For a detailed study of these factors, see Raja [1969: 48–59].

referring to three of them.

> On account of the meaning (*artha*) [of other words] and situation (*prakaraṇa*) or connection (*yoga*) with another word, [a word] abandons simultaneity (*yaugapadya*) and settles itself in successiveness (*paryāya*). (VP 2.251)[8]

Three factors, namely, *artha*, *prakaraṇa*, and *yoga* are enumerated above. They restrict capacity of a word to express many meanings simultaneously, so that it conveys one meaning on a particular occasion. In the *Vṛtti* on the above verse,[9] Bhartṛhari illustrates the first factor—meaning of other words (*artha*)—with sentences such as "He offers oblation with cupped hands" (*añjalinā juhoti*), "He worships the sun joining his palms" (*añjalinā sūryam upatiṣṭhate*), and "With *cupped handful* as a measure, he provides a bowlful [of alms]." (*añjalinā pūrṇapātram upaharati*). The word *añjalinā* can be understood in three ways: (1) a cavity formed by both hands, (2) a gesture of salutation by hand, and (3) a certain measure. An example of the second factor—situation (*prakaraṇa*)—is the well-known phrase *saindhavam ānaya*. The word *saindhava* means both "salt" and "horse." If the sentence is used in the context of eating, it means "pass me the salt"; however, if it is used by a person who is about to go out, it should mean "fetch the horse." For the third one, connection (*yoga*) with another word, Bhartṛhari provides figurative sentences as examples: "The boy is [lively like] fire" (*agnir māṇavako*) and "The man from *Vāhīka* country is [dull like] an ox" (*gaur vāhīka*). Since the words "fire" and "ox" are associated with "boy" and *Vāhīka*, respectively, their literal meanings are discarded, and their figurative use and meanings are understood.

We can understand that these determinative factors are contextual. Whatever literal meanings (if any) the words have, in actual sentences,

---

8. VPwr 81; VPII 104, 255:
yaugapadyam atikramya paryāye vyavatiṣṭhate /
arthaprakaraṇābhyāṃ vā yogāc chabdāntareṇa vā // VP 2.251
Raja [1969: 48–49, 54] has pointed out that the first two factors are found in the MBh on P 6.1.84. They are also referred to in the MBh on P 1.1.23. There are many references and interpretations of these factors. In particular, *artha* is also interpreted as the purpose (*artha*) of the phrase. Although I present a different interpretation above, while doing so, I found it slightly difficult to distinguish between *artha* as the "meaning of other words" and as the "connection (*yoga*) with another word." See Iyer's translation of VP 2.251, 314 [1977: 109, 135–136], where he translates *artha* in both ways.
9. VPII 255. Most of the examples are also found in the *Vṛtti* on VP 2.314–317.

we can only understand the contextual meanings with the help of these factors.[10]

In the above examples, the first and third factors refer to the relation of the word in question with other words in the same sentence, as in the abovementioned case of a negative sentence. The second one, *prakaraṇa*, refers to the situations or circumstances that surround the sentence containing the relevant word.

Bhartṛhari illustrates *prakaraṇa* with another example. As shown in the following quotation, we should note that when one abstracts the meaning of a word from a text, he/she is resorting to its context, namely, the circumstances outside the text; therefore, even in the case of a text that only consists of one word, what is understood by its listener is not just the meaning of the word abstracted from the context.

> According to the situation (*prakaraṇa*), from the object (*karman*) [expressed] in the speech sound (*śruti*) of *dvāram* (door) [only], *badhāna* (*dvāraṃ badhāna*: Shut the door!) or *dehi* (*dvāraṃ dehi*: Give way!) is understood with the help of a means [other than the explicit expression]. (VP 2.335)[11]

What is understood by the listener of the text through words such as "door" is not just the literal meaning of the word found in dictionaries. When the text is heard, it is clear that the listener, depending on the context of the text—both the discourse and circumstances—instantaneously understands the proper sentential meaning (*vākyārtha*) as well. We may be able to assume that a text includes its context in itself and not vice versa.

Moreover, we should note that this type of intuitive understanding of the meaning of a sentence, which informs us what to do (namely, to open the door or to give way to the speaker), is called *pratibhā* by Bhartṛhari.

---

10. Since grammarians have compiled a list of the Sanskrit verbal roots (*dhātupāṭha*) and nouns (*padapāṭha*) with the definitions of their meanings, we may basically understand them from the point of view of literalism. However, as shown in fn. 8, Patañjali had already referred to *artha* and *prakaraṇa* in his MBh.

11. VPwr 89; VPII 137, 280 (VP 2.333):
yathāprakaraṇaṃ dvāram ity asyāṃ karmaṇaḥ śrutau /
badhāna dehi vety etad upāyād avagamyate // VP 2.335

4. Context as the Larger Textual Body Surrounding a Sentence

4.1. In the previous section, we examined the relation between the meaning of a word and its context. Although Bhartṛhari uses the term *prakaraṇa* to refer to the situation or circumstances where a speaker uses and listener receives a text, other factors he refers to (*artha* and *yoga*) are connected to the relation of the word to the sentence to which it belongs.

However, when we use the word "context," we usually consider a larger textual body than a single sentence. What is the relation between a sentence and its context in this sense?

In the tradition of Sanskrit grammar, this issue is discussed with respect to a text that contains multiple verbs. It appears that there had been two views on it:

> Even if there are many finite verb forms (*tiṅanta-s*) that are interdependent (*sākāṅkṣa*), there is single-sentence-ness (*ekavākyatā*) [of the passage that consists of those that respectively have finite verb forms]. In this way, the prohibition of the loss of an accent (*nighāta*) in the presence of a verb ending (*tiṄ*) after other verb endings, [which results from P 8.1.28 *tiṄ atiṄaḥ*], would be meaningful. (VP 2.447)
> However, for those [such as Kātyāyana] who hold that the fixed definition of *vākya* is a stretch that has a single verb ending (*ekatiṄ*) in the science of grammar, the term "after non verbal" (*atiṄaḥ*) [in P 8.1.28] would be meaningless because there would be different sentences [if there is more than one verb, and thus, a verb never comes after another verb in a sentence]. (VP 2.448)[12]

Although what is discussed in the above verses is a highly technical problem about the non-accentuation of verbs, the point of difference is rather simple: the first verse presents the view that a text, which consists of some parts that have a verb, should be treated as a single sentence if the parts are interdependent (*sākāṅkṣa*). The second verse presents the view that the same text should be treated as multiple sentences because a sentence is defined as a stretch that has a single verb ending (or a verb in a certain conjugation form).

---

12. VPwr 100; VPII 176, 315 (VP 2.442–443):
bahuśv api tiṅanteṣu sākāṅkṣeṣv ekavākyatā /
tiṅā tiṅbhyo nighātasya paryudāsas tathārthavān // VP 2.447
ekatiṅ yasya vākyaṃ tu śāstre niyatalakṣaṇam /
tasyātiṅgrahaṇenārtho vākyabhedān na vidyate // VP 2.448

As scholars have already clarified, it seems that the issue of non-accentuation (*nighāta*) was considerably important to the Grammarians and the Mīmāṃsakas because it is related to the definition of sentence (*vākya*).[13] Bhartṛhari actually deals with this issue at the very beginning of VP 2, immediately after introducing various views on the nature of *vākya* (VP 2.3–6). According to Kātyāyana, the author of the *Vārttika*, a sentence should be a stretch that has a single verb ending (*ekatiṄ*), as referred to in VP 2.448 above.[14] On the other hand, for the Mīmāṃsakas, a text with multiple verbs also can be a single sentence because a verb can qualify another verb.[15]

The single-sentence-ness (*ekavākyatā*) mentioned in the preceding VP 2.447 is also the topic of VP 2.348–353, where Bhartṛhari deals with the relation between general and exceptional rules.[16] There, he argues that because a certain general rule and its exception must be interdependent, there should be single-sentence-ness (*ekavākyatā*) even if they actually consist of many sentences. VP 2.447, after all, states that Pāṇini, the author of the *Sūtra*, holds that a text which consists of many sentences can be regarded as a single sentence in the case of the rules of verb accentuation also.[17]

Now, which of the two views does Bhartṛhari prefer? In fact, following the above verses, he merely states that both views are not firmly established:

---

13. Since many detailed studies on the technical aspect of this issue have already been conducted, hereafter, I will only limit myself to presenting a more general interpretation of this issue from the textual/contextual point of view. See Joshi [1968: 105–124], Raja [1976], Iyer [1977: 2–4, 191–193], and Cardona [1983: 117–132], and Akamatsu [1998: 11–12, 135–136, and 277–279] for Japanese readers.
14. Kātyāyana provides his definition of *vākya* in *Vārttika* 9 and 10 on P 2.1.1: "*ākhyātaṃ sāvyayakārakaviśeṣaṇam vākyam, sakriyāviśeṣaṇaṃ ca*" and "*ekatiṅ.*" In VP 2.448, the second definition is being referred to. For the text, translation and a detailed study on the section of the MBh including these *Vārttikas*, see Joshi [1968: 19–20, 105–124].
15. Cardona [1983: 121–122] and Raja [1969: 151–152] point out that the Mīmāṃsakas' definition of *vākya* appears in *Mīmāṃsāsūtra* P 2.1.46: "*arthaikatvāt ekaṃ vākyaṃ sākāṅkṣaṃ ced vibhāge syāt.*" Bhartṛhari, explaining the Mīmāṃsākas' point of view presented in VP 2.4, states that it is said that a verb form can be a qualifier of another verb form (VP 2.5 cd: *tiṅantaṃ tatrāhus tiṅantasya viśeṣakaṃ*).
16. See Iyer's translation [1977: 148–151] and Aklujkar's summary [1990: 148].
17. This interpretation of the *sūtra* is based on the idea of the Mīmāṃsakas, or it is their view. As shown in *Mīmāṃsāsūtra* 2.1.46 mentioned in the fn.15, the Mīmāṃsakas hold that a *vākya* is that which provides one meaning (*ekārtha*) and consists of parts that are interdependent (*sākāṅkṣam*). For *ākāṅkṣā*, see Raja [1969: 157–164].

> In case of [a phrase that contains two verbs, for instance] "Look, a deer is going!" whether (1) [the verb "look" is] connected to another verb ["is going" to form a single sentence such as "Look at the deer going!"] or (2) [the verb "look" is] again connected to [the noun "deer," which is already] connected [to another verb "is going" to form a second sentence "Look at a deer!" along with the first sentence "A deer is going."], both [of the views, namely, (2) "there are two] different [sentences"] (*bheda*) and (1) ["there is only] one [sentence"] (*abheda*) cannot be established. (VP 2.449)[18]

Thus, he does not display his preference for either of the views. The phrase that contains two verbs "Look, a deer is going" (*mṛgaḥ paśyata yāti*)[19] can be understood in two ways—as one sentence: "Look at the deer going!" and also, as two sentences: "Look at a deer!" and "A deer is going." If both are acceptable, it cannot be stated that both the ways are firmly established. Although Bhartṛhari does not explicitly deny this, he seems to be dissatisfied with Kātyāyana's formal definition. Moreover, he does not display any explicit support for it even in VP2.3–6 where he discusses the Mīmāṃsakas view, which was critical of Kātyāyana's view.

Following the above verse, Bhartṛhari argues about the issue from a different point of view:

> It is where "what should be done" (*itikartavyatā*) can be expected from the [syntactical and semantic] relation (*sāmarthya*) of its meaning that is said to be [a sentence], which is not dependent on any other linguistic element (*aśabdalakṣaṇākāṅkṣa*) and is endowed with the perfect meaning. (VP 2.450)
>
> Further, in addition to a mere statement of fact, some possible meaning is supplied. Even though nothing is used to express it, with the speech sound [uttered and heard], a sentence is completed. (VP 2.451)[20]

---

18. VPwr 100; VPII 176, 315 (VP 2.444):
tiṅantāntarayukteṣu yuktayukteṣu vā punaḥ /
mṛgaḥ paśyata yātīti bhedābhedau na tiṣṭhataḥ // VP 2.449

19. Raja [1990: 5], citing the same example with different wording *paśya mṛgo dhāvati*, states that "even later grammarians agreed that there can be simple sentences with more than one finite verb if other conditions are fulfilled." Since the word *paśya* is referred to in the P 8.1.39 itself as one of the rules for accentuation of verbs, it seems to be natural to claim as the VP 2.447 does with the very example. However, Bhartṛhari apparently has a different standpoint.

20. VPwr 100; VPII 177, 316 (VP 2.445–446):
itikartavyatārthasya sāmarthyād yatra kāṅkṣyate /

Although what is to be defined is not explicitly mentioned in the first verse, it appears that he modestly presents his own definition of a sentence (*vākya*). This definition states that a sentence is where the knowledge of "what should be done" (*itikartavyatā*) is obtained. This definition is in accordance with the explanation of the meaning of the sentence, *pratibhā*, which we examined in the second section of this paper. An instantaneous understanding of "what should be done" (*itikartavyatā*)[21] is nothing but *pratibhā*, the meaning of the sentence. Thus, it is appropriate to state that what is defined in the first verse is a sentence (*vākya*).[22]

The second verse states that it is not necessary to place together all the explicit expressions that literally refer to everything that needs to be expressed to complete a sentence. It is impossible to collect all literal counterpart expressions for the meaning expressed by a sentence.

In daily communication, we observe that the complete meaning of a sentence occurs like a flash of understanding on hearing the voice of the speaker; moreover, when it occurs, any linguistic defect, namely, phonetic, grammatical, or formal incompleteness, does not cause a problem. From the empirical point of view, Bhartṛhari defines a sentence (*vākya*) based on its meaning.

The view stated in VP 2.447, which refers to the single-sentence-ness (*ekavākyatā*), is also related to one whole sentence and its meaning. However, in this view, since the meanings of partial sentences are understood first, followed by the accumulation of these parts as one whole

---

aśabdalakṣaṇākāṅkṣaṃ samāptārthaṃ tad ucyate // VP 2.450
tattvānvākhyānamātre tu yāvān artho 'nuṣajyate /
vināpi tatprayogeṇa śruter vākyaṃ samāpyate // VP 2.451

21. It should be noted that in the ritual context, the term *itikartavyatā* has been understood as a certain ritual act enjoined by a Vedic injunction, which may consist of a few sentences. Thus, Bhartṛhari's statement here can be persuasive to the Mīmāṃsakas, and his terminology, including *ākāṅkṣā*, is consciously related to that of the Mīmāṃsakas. See Raja [1969: 159–162].

22. Bhartṛhari appears to evade a conflict with Kātyāyana's view. As Cardona [1983: 117–119] clarified, the term *vākya* is derived from √*vac* "speak" with the *kṛtya* suffix *ṆyaT*. The replacement of the *-k* for the *-c* of √*vac* is provided by P 7.3.52; however, with an exceptional rule P 7.3.67: *vaco 'śabdasaṃjñāyām*, the replacement does not occur if it does not mention any technical term for some linguistic unit. In this way, the word *vācya* and the technical term for the linguistic unit in question (i.e. sentence). *vākya* are derived. Since the formation process is the same, the meaning of the term *vākya* could be understood as that of *vācya* (to be spoken). Only the difference is that *vākya* is a term for a linguistic unit. In this respect, it seems that *vākya* is not necessarily a sentence and can be any form of speech. However, this type of interpretation is not explicitly expressed anywhere

sentence, it is totally different from the view stated here. According to the new definition, irrespective of whether a phrase contains one, many, or no verbs, as long as "what should be done" (*itikartavyatā*) is understood through the syntactic and semantic relation (*sāmarthya*)[23] as a whole, it should be regarded as a sentence.

4.2. The relation between a phrase or a passage with many verbs and a sentence within it is also explained in the sections where Bhartṛhari records various objections from those who consider a word (*pada*) to be the minimum linguistic unit (VP 2.61–87) and counters them (VP 2.88–115).

> [Objection:]
> When an assemblage of many sentences becomes a [passage] that consists of many parts that are interdependent (*sākāṅkṣāvayava*), in order to establish one meaning, the sentences would have no meaning [since they are parts of the larger passage, even if it can be grammatically regarded as a sentence.] (VP 2.76)
> [Reply:]
> [Through abstraction,] many sentences, which are similar to words [abstracted from a sentence], can be brought about as something different from [the whole passage]. In the same way, [only] when [the partial sentences are] not with other sentences [through abstraction], they can be regarded as having a different meaning [from that of the whole passage]. (VP 2.112)[24]

As we have observed in the second section of this paper, Bhartṛhari does not regard a word as a meaningful linguistic unit when it is counterposed to the sentence that contains it. The opponents of this view state the following: if so, when a sentence is counterposed to the larger textual body that contains it, the sentence will also be rendered meaningless because it is dependent on other sentences, just as a word in a sentence is dependent

---

23. Bhartṛhari attempts to return to the Grammarians' foundation, Pāṇini's sūtra P 2.1.1, *samarthaḥ padavidhiḥ*: An operation (*vidhi*) on *padas* [takes effect] only when they are semantically and syntactically connected (*samarthaḥ*). Katre [1989: 105]. The MBh on P 2.2.1 is known by the name *samarthāhnika*, a day session for *samartha* and the whole *āhnika* discusses *samartha/sāmarthya*. Consult Joshi [1968] for a translation and the full-fledged study.

24. VPwr 64, 67; VPII 31, 55, 220:
vākyānāṃ samudāyaś ca ya ekārthaprasiddhaye /
sākāṅkṣāvayavas tatra vākyārtho 'pi na vidyate // VP 2.76
yathā padasarūpāṇāṃ vākyānāṃ saṃbhavaḥ pṛthak /
tathā vākyāntarābhāve syād eṣāṃ pṛthagarthatā // VP 2.112

on other words. Thus, in Bhartṛhari's theory, a sentence would become meaningless.

Although Bhartṛhari is definitely replying to this objection in VP 2.112, it appears that he basically accepts the main point of the objection. As the opponents point out, Bhartṛhari also holds that as parts of a larger text, sentences do not have independent meanings. However, the abstraction of a sentence from the textual body is similar to the abstraction of a word. Therefore, just as a word is considered to have some meaning when abstracted, an abstracted sentence also can be, although temporarily, considered to have its own independent meaning.

Despite Bhartṛhari's repeated emphasis on the predominance of a sentence and its meaning over its constituent words and their meanings, the meaning of the sentence must be subordinate to the meaning of the whole passage.

Bhartṛhari expresses the same idea elsewhere as follows:

> The feature of the meaning of each word [that constitutes a sentence] has its basis in the meaning of the sentence. However, if the meanings of sentences are dependent on each other (*sāpekṣa*) [to appear], they are the same as meanings of words; [therefore, their basis lies in the larger textual body where these sentences exist]. (VP 2.325)[25]

As long as a sentence belongs to a larger textual body and is dependent on other sentences to express a meaning, just as a word in a sentence, it is not a determinate.[26] Therefore, just like a word in a sentence, even a single grammatically complete sentence would be regarded as incomplete to communicate the determinate meanings when it is counterposed to a larger textual body or context. Moreover, in this case, the sentence does not result

---

25. VPwr 88; VPII 133, 278:
rūpaṃ sarvapadārthānāṃ vākyārthopanibandhanam /
sāpekṣā ye tu vākyārthāḥ padārthair eva te samāḥ // VP 2.325

26. As Bhartṛhari repeatedly states in the verses quoted in this paper (VP 2.8, 9, 450, and 212), he regards the interdependence (*sāpekṣa, sākāṅkṣa*) of the parts as the proof of their incompleteness. On the other hand, from the Mīmāṃsākas' point of view, the interdependence is a condition for establishing a single sentence or the single-sentence-ness among many sentences, as explicitly stated in their definition of a sentence mentioned in fn.15. VP 2.76 and 447 are based on a view similar to that of the Mīmāṃsākas. Although this is the conflictive point between the two, the latter position is not exclusive, since the Grammarians themselves interpret *sāmarthya* as single-meaning-ness (*ekārthībhāva*) and interdependence (*vyapekṣā*), as Joshi [1968: iv–xviii] clarified.

in a "sentence meaning" (*vākyārtha*); rather, it denotes something similar to a "word meaning" (*padārtha*). Therefore, the larger textual body or context is considered to bring about the "sentence meaning" (*vākyārtha*), namely, the instantaneous understanding of "what should be done," *pratibhā*.

However, it appears that Bhartṛhari rather carefully avoids applying the term *vākya* for context that expands beyond the scope of a sentence. It is not explicitly mentioned that what is expressed by the context is *vākyārtha*. Even for him, *vākya* is, primarily, a stretch whose main element is a verb in a certain conjugation form, as described by Kātyāyana. As a grammarian, all through his *Vākyapadīya*, he uses the term according to the grammatical tradition. As I have already stated, his focus is on the relation of *vākya* and *pada*, and everything that is related as whole and part is used to explain the relation or is examined in accordance with the relation.

It is clear that Bhartṛhari admits that a single sentence is not sufficient to serve for the purpose of proper communication in some cases; therefore, in VP 2.450–451, he defines *vākya* based on what it signifies but not on what form it takes. To him, a grammatical or formal definition similar to that of Kātyāyana is insufficient. Whether it is only one word,[27] a single complete sentence, a paragraph consisting of many sentences, or a larger text, if it expresses "what should be done" (*itikartavyatā*), Bhartṛhari considers it the same meaningful unit to be examined in his treatise—the *Vākyapadīya*.

5. Conclusion

In this paper, I have examined Bhartṛhari's arguments related to the issue of context—in particular, context as the determinate factor of the meaning of a word and context considered as the larger textual body surrounding a single sentence. Despite the fact that a certain complicated technical problem underlies both these arguments, Bhartṛhari's view on them, in both cases, is finally related to *pratibhā* as a flash of understanding that informs people what to do. It is completely different from a mere accumulation of the literal, if any, meanings of words that constitute a sentence, although it is described as the understanding of the sentence.

The understanding of a text is neither the understanding of the linguistic elements that constitute it nor that of their total sum; rather,

27. In the section beginning with the VP 2.325 above, Bhartṛhari takes up the issue of one word sentence such as "*vṛkṣaḥ*" (There is a tree). The argument also has a dispute with the Mīmāṃsakas as its background. For an observation of the section as a whole, see Iyer's translation [1977: 140–143].

it is an instantaneous and intuitive cognition extended to the complete understanding of the context. The meanings of its constituent sentences and words are understood only when they are analytically observed in the light of the larger context. Bhartṛhari's view can be regarded as an ancient Indian antecedent of modern contextualism, although he focuses exclusively on *vākya* as a sentence.

Abbreviations

MBh *Mahābhāṣya* in Abhyankar [1962–72].
P *Aṣṭādhyāyī* in Katre [1987].
VP *Vākyapadīya*, see VPII, VPwr.
VPII *Vākyapadīya*, Kāṇḍa 2 in Iyer [1983].
VPwr *Vākyapadīya* in Rau [1977].

Bibliography

Aklujkar, Ashok
1990 "Bhartṛhari: *Trikāṇḍī* or *Vākyapadīya*, with *Vṛtti* on Books 1 and 2," in Coward and Raja [1990: 121–174].

Abhyankar, K.V.
1962–72 (ed.) *The Vyākaraṇa-mahābhāṣya of Patañjali*, vols. 1–3, Poona: Bhandarkar Oriental Research Institute, (First edition by F. Kielhorn, 1880–1885).

Akamatsu, Akihiko
1998 *The Philosophy of Language in Classical India* (Annotated translation of the first and second volumes of Bhartrhari's *Vākyapadīya* and his *Vṛtti*), vols. 1–2, Tokyo: Heibonsha. [in Japanese]

Cardona, George
1983 *Linguistic Analysis and Some Indian Tradition*, Pandit Shripad Shastri Deodhar Memorial Lectures No. 20 (first series), Poona: Bhandarkar Oriental Research Institute.

Coward, Harold G. and K. Kunjunni Raja
1990 (ed.) *The Philosophy of the Grammarians: Encyclopedia of Indian Philosophies*, vol. V, Delhi: Motilal Banarsidass.

Hirano, Katsunori
2007 "The Constitution and Signification Structure of the Text," in

Shoichi Sato et al. (eds.), *Horizon of Integrated Text Science*, Nagoya: Graduate Schools of Letters, Nagoya University, pp. 253–273. [in Japanese]

Iyer, K.A. Subramania

1977 *The Vākyapadīya of Bhartṛhari, Kāṇḍa II, English Translation with Exegetical Notes*, Delhi: Motilal Banarsidass.

1983 (ed.) *Vākyapadīya of Bhartṛhari, Containing the Ṭīkā of Puṇyarāja and the Ancient Vṛtti, Kāṇḍa II*, Delhi: Motilal Banarsidass.

Joshi, S.D.

1968 *Patañjali's Vyākaraṇa-Mahābhāṣya: Samarthāhnika (P. 2.1.1) edited with Translation and Explanatory Notes*, Publications of the Centre of Advanced Study in Sanskrit, Class C, no. 3. Poona: University of Poona.

1980 (ed.) *Proceedings of the Winter Institute on Ancient Indian Theories on Sentence-meaning, held in March 1979*, Publications of the Centre of Advanced Study in Sanskrit, Class E, no. 6, Poona: University of Poona.

Katre, Sumitra M.

1987 (ed. and tr.) *Aṣṭādhyāyī of Pāṇini*, Austin: University of Texas Press.

Laddu, S.D.

1980 "The Concept of *Vākya* according to Kātyāyana and Patañjali," in Joshi [1980: 223–228].

Palsule, G.B.

1980 "Bhartṛhari's Concept of *Vākya* and *Vākyārtha*," in Joshi [1980: 1–8].

Raja, K. Kunjunni

1969 *Indian Theories of Meaning*, Adyar Library Series 17, Madras: Adyar Library.

1976 "Pāṇini's Concept of a Sentence," *Adyar Library Bulletin* 40: 165–170.

1990 "Philosophical Elements in Pāṇini's *Aṣṭādhyāyī*," in Coward and Raja [1990: 111–113].

Rau, Wilhelm

1977 (ed.) *Bhartṛharis Vākyapadīya*, Abhandlungen für die Kunde des Morgenlandes Bd. XLII. 4, Wiesbaden: Komissionsverlag Franz Steiner GMBH.

Recanati, François
2004 *Literal Meaning*, Cambridge: Cambridge University Press.

IV
NYĀYA AND VAIŚEṢIKA

CHAPTER 7

NEW LIGHT ON THE COMMENTARY TEXTS OF ANCIENT INDIA

Katsunori HIRANO

1. Introduction

We have various implements for expressing and conveying our thoughts to others: words, music, painting, dancing, etc. Among them, we carefully select a particular implement in order to give others information about something effectively. This means that often one implement is more appropriate to convey thoughts to others than another. In other words, each implement has a particular system, which is more suitable to show what we want to express. In this paper I will use the term 'text' to refer to one of these implements of communication, and we can hold the commentaries in ancient India to be commentary texts.

The purpose in this paper is to explore the system through which the commentary texts convey information and to advance a new theory to explain the genesis of commentary texts in ancient India. Allow me to summarize the main points that will be made in this paper. We will conclude that the commentary texts are generated via combination with already-known information, and that the commentary texts have a character of the texture of quotation (or "a mosaic of citations").[1] Then, taking the quotation theory into consideration, we will focus attention on the way in which information is quoted or drawn from the precedent commentary texts in detail. Added to this, a social context, as the necessary conditions for the genesis of the commentary texts, will be offered in this paper.

---

* This paper is a revision and expansion of my earlier studies: Hirano [2004; 2006].

1. See Kristeva [1969: 85], "*tout texts se construit comme mosaïque de citations, tout texte est absorption et tranformation d'un autre texte*".

I am mainly utilizing the 'inherence' (*samavāya*) chapter in the *Padārthadharmasaṃgraha* (*PDhS*) by Praśastapāda (ca. 550–600),[2] the *Vyomavatī* (*Vy*) by Vyomaśiva (ca. 900–960), the *Nyāyakandalī* by Śrīdhara (ca. 950–1000), and the *Kiraṇāvalī* (*Kir*) by Udayana (ca. 1050–1100). These thinkers belonged to the Vaiśeṣika school, one of the six orthodox philosophical schools in ancient India.

2. 'Inherence' as a Category

The philosophy of the Vaiśeṣika school is marked by categorization. The Vaiśeṣika school divides the world into six categories (*padārtha*) and claims that all entities can be listed and classified under a certain category. The original six categories are substance (*dravya*), quality (*guṇa*), activity (*karman*), universal (*sāmānya*), particular (*viśeṣa*), and inherence (*samavāya*). These six categories are further subdivided into nine kinds of substances, twenty-four kinds of qualities, five kinds of activities, and two kinds of universals. The number of particulars is endless, while there is only one inherence—the focus of our present discussion. Table I summarizes the kinds of categories.

Table I: The Kinds of Categories in Vaiśeṣika Philosophy

Category	Kinds
Substance	earth, water, fire, air, ether, time, space, soul, mind
Quality	color, taste, smell, touch, number, magnitude, distinctness, conjunction, disjunction, nearness, remoteness, cognition, pleasure, pain, desire, hate, effort, weight, fluidity, viscidity, tendency, unseen merit, unseen demerit, sound
Activity	throwing upwards, throwing downwards, contraction, expansion, locomotion
Universal	being-ness (highest universal), cow-ness etc. (lower universal)
Particular	[endless]
Inherence	[one]

Inherence, which is a relation, subsists between two inseparable entities: between substance and quality, between substance and activity, between a type of universal and a thing (*artha*: substance, quality, and activity), between particular and the eternal substance, and between the whole

2. On the dates of authors, see Potter (ed.) [1995 (1977): 9–12].

(*avayavin*) and its parts (*avayavas*). Take a blue pot as an example. The pot is a substance and the color blue is a quality. The relation, between the pot and its, inseparably connected, blue color is inherence. We can illustrate the structure of the example of the blue pot in Figure 1.

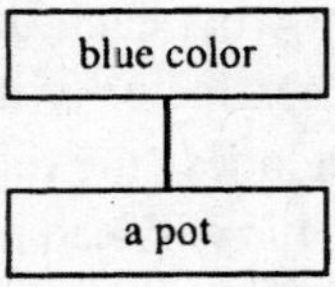

Figure 1

I will briefly explain how to read Figure 1. The rectangle labeled "blue color" represents property (*dharma*), and the rectangle labeled "a pot" represents its possessor (*dharmin*). The line between "blue color" and "a pot" represents a relation between the property and the possessor. In this case, the bold line between the rectangle labeled "a pot" and the rectangle labeled "blue color" represents inherence.[3]

The *PDhS* defines 'inherence' as follows:

> The relation, which subsists between entities that are incapable of existing separately [and] that stand as the contained and the container, is inherence, being a cause of the idea that '[this is] here (this is in that)' (*PDhS*, p. 2, no. 9: *ayuta-siddhānām ādhārya-ādhāra-bhūtānaṃ yaḥ sambandha iha-pratyaya-hetuḥ sa samavāyaḥ*.)

The preceding definition of inherence may be separated into four factors:

(I) entities that are incapable of existing separately (*ayuta-siddha*),
(II) entities that stand as the contained and the container (*ādhārya-ādhāra-bhūta*),
(III) the relation (*yaḥ sambandha*), and
(IV) a cause of the idea that '[this is] here' (*iha-pratyaya-hetu*).

The role of a definition may be defined as the decision of the meaning of a word, sign, or concept. A definition 'defines' the meaning of a particular word etc. However, a definition is not perfect when it is also applied to the meanings of other words etc. not explicitly defined. Accordingly, each factor of a definition has a function that prevents the definition from applying to

3. On this explanation of Figure, I have followed Tachikawa [1981: 18] and Wada [1990: 47–48].

other words that do not fit the particular meaning of the defined.[4] In other words, a definition defines the meaning of the defined object through the exclusion of other objects. Therefore, we will consider what each factor of the definition of inherence of the *PDhS* excludes in each commentary text.

Now, we will take a close look at what each of the three commentary texts on the *PDhS* excludes by a chosen factor of inherence's definition of the *PDhS*, as, for example, the *Vy* excludes "the relation between the bowl and the fruit of jujube" by factor (I). This will lead us to a discussion of how the commentary texts are generated, and exploring the understanding of the *PDhS*'s definition of inherence by the commentators might offer some insight into this particular implement of communication. I will outline based on the order from the *Vy*.

3. What is Excluded by Each Factor of the Definition of Inherence in the Commentary Texts

3.1. The *Vy*

The *Vy* first supposes that the definition of inherence is only composed of factor (IV)—inherence is a cause of the idea that '[this is] here' (*ihapratyayahetu*). However, this definition cannot exclude "the relation between the tree and the village," which is not inherence, since the relation causes the idea that "the trees are in the village" and technically fits factor (IV). Therefore, factor (III)—the relation (*yaḥ sambandha*)—is added to the definition that is composed of (IV) only in order to exclude this relation from the concept of inherence. When a man sees the trees and a village from a distance, he has the idea that there is a relation between the trees and the village. However, according to Vyomaśiva, there is in fact no relation between the trees and the village, since an intermediate space[5] is actually

4. On the consideration of the function of definitions in Indian philosophy, see Matilal [1990 (1985): 176–202] and Sato [1995].

5. The word of '*antarāla* (an intermediate space)' is found in the universal chapter of the *PDhS* (pp. 82–83, no. 368). The word is used in the discussion that universal, for instance, cowness (*gotva*), is not indicated in an intermediate space between individual entities, for instance, two cows, since the occurrence of conjunction and inherence is not there in an intermediate space between individual entities. Śrīdhara interprets '*antarāla*' as ether, space, motionless-air, or absence of material substance in the *NK*. (p. 317.16–17: *antarālam iti ākāśaṃ vā digdravyaṃ vā stimitavegamūrttadravyābhāvo vā ...*). Then, Vyomaśiva shows absence of material substance and ether as the examples of '*antarāla*' in the *Vy* (vol. II, p. 283.5–8:

between the trees and the village. Therefore, even if the delusive relation between the trees and the village does cause the idea that "the trees are in the village," it comes to be that the delusive relation is excluded from the concept of inherence by virtue of factor (III).[6]

Then, even if the definition is composed of (III) and (IV)—the relation, which is a cause of the idea that '[this is] here', is inherence—there is a deviation from the concept of inherence by virtue of "the relation between the ether and the flying bird," which is not inherence, since the relation causes the idea that "the bird is in the ether" and comes to fit the definition composed by (III) and (IV). In order to prevent the deviation, factor (II)—entities that stand as the contained and the container (*ādhāryādhārabhūta*)—must be added to the definition. According to the *Vy*, since "the relation between the ether and the flying bird" is regarded as that between the pervading (the ether) and the pervaded (the flying bird), the ether, which is a pervasive entity, cannot only be regarded as the container but also as the contained for the flying bird. Therefore, "the relation between the ether and the flying bird" is excluded from the concept of inherence by factor (II).[7]

The *Vy* criticizes "the idea that the bird is in the ether," which is caused by "the relation between the ether and the flying bird," from an epistemological viewpoint. Cognition of '[this is] here' for the ether is erroneous on the grounds that the ether is beyond the senses and the cognition of 'here' can only occur to an object that is grasped by a sense organ. Therefore, the erroneous cognition 'here' for the ether comes to be excluded by factors (II) or (III), since factors (II) and (III) fit in the perceivable entities. As a result, "the relation between the ether and the flying bird" cannot be regarded as the relation being "a cause of the idea that 'the bird is in the ether'" and subsequently as inherence by virtue of factors (II) or (III).[8]

---

tathā kim idam antarālaṃ nāma yatra sāmānyasyopalambhaprasaṅgaś codyate? yadi mūrttadravyābhāvaḥ? na tatra gotvādisāmānyam. abhāvatvād eva. atha śabdānumeyam atīndriyam ākāśam, antarālāvasthitaṃ vā ghaṭādidravyam, ...).

6. *Vy*, vol. I, p. 25,12–14: *ihapratyayahetutvaṁ antarālādarśanasyāpīti sambandhagrahaṇam. tathā hi, dūrād grāmārāmayor antarālam apaśyatām iha grāme vṛkṣā iti jñānaṃ dṛṣṭam, ...*

7. *Vy*, vol. I, p. 25,14–18: *tathāpy ākāśaśakunisambandhena vyabhicāraḥ. tad ihapratyayahetuḥ sambandhaś ceti. tathā hi, ihākāśe śakunir iti jñānaṃ dṛṣṭam, tadvyavacchedārtham ādhāryādhāragrahaṇam. na cākāśasyādhāratvam ādheyatvaṃ vā, adharottarabhāvasyābhāvāt. yatra hi saṃyogidravyeṣv adharottarabhāvas tatraivādhārādheyabhāvaḥ kuṇḍabadarādāv upalabdhas tadabhāvaś cākāśe, tasya vyāpakatvena śakuniṃ vyāpya sadbhāvāt.*

8. *Vy*, vol. I, p. 25,19–26: *athākāśasyātīndriyatvād iheti jñānaṃ na syāt, tasya hy aparokṣeṣv eva bhāvāt. tad asat. atīndriye 'py ākāśe iheti jñānaṃ kevalaṃ*

Moreover, to the definition, composed of (II), (III), and (IV)—the relation, which subsists between entities that stand as the contained and the container, is inherence, being a cause of the idea that '[this is] here'—factor (I)—entities that are incapable of existing separately (*ayutasiddha*)—had to be added for the purpose of excluding "the relation between the bowl and the fruit of jujube" from the concept of inherence. We can illustrate the structure of this relation in Figure 2.

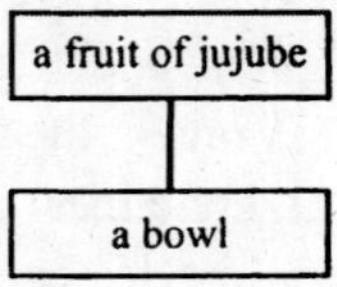

Figure 2

According to Vaiśeṣika philosophy, this relation is 'conjunction (*saṃyoga*)', subsisting between entities that are capable of existing separately (*yutasiddha*). However, the definition of inherence composed of (II), (III), and (IV) only, does not exclude "the relation between the bowl and the fruit of jujube." Because the bowl and the fruit of jujube are regarded as the container and the contained entities respectively (II), there is a relation between the bowl and the fruit of jujube (III), and this relation causes the idea that 'the fruit of jujube is in the bowl' (IV). Therefore, if the definition of 'inherence' was only composed of factor (II), (III), and (IV), "the relation between the bowl and the fruit of jujube" would come to be inherence. For the purpose of excluding this relation from the concept of inherence, the *Vy* interprets that factor (I)—entities that are incapable of existing separately (*ayutasiddha*)—must be added to the definition.[9]

Then, even if inherence was defined using (I) and (III) only—the relation, which subsists between entities that are incapable of existing separately, is

---

bhrāntam, tasya vyavacchedārtham upapannam ādhāryādhārapadam. iṣṭañ ca bhrāntehajñānasya vyavacchedārthaṃ sambandhapadam. anye tv asya codyasya parihārārtham ā samantāt kāśata ity ākāśam, varttata ity upacāreṇākāśaṃ raśmayo 'bhidhīyante. te ca pratyakṣam ity upapannam ihākāśe śakunir iti jñānam iti manyante. tac cāsat, mukhyasadbhāve 'py upacārakalpanāyām atiprasaṅgāt. uktañ cātīndriye 'py ākāśe 'parokṣajñānaṃ bhrāntaṃ tadvyavacchedārthaṃ viśeṣaṇam iti. mūrttadravyābhāvena cākāśena sambandhābhāva eveti.

9. *Vy*, vol. I, p. 26, 1–3: *tathā hy* ādhāryādhārabhūtānāṃ yaḥ sambandha ihapratyayahetuḥ sa samavāya ity ukte kuṇḍabadarasambandhena vyabhicāras tadartham ayutasiddhānām iti padam. yutasiddhir vakṣyamāṇā, sā vidyate yeṣāṃ te yutasiddhās tanniṣedhena cāyutasiddhās teṣām iti.* *According to the reading of *Vy* (K) (p. 108, 3), *tathā hy* is corrected by *tathā api*.

inherence—it would be applicable to the cases, "the relation of the denoted and the denoter (*vācyavācakabhāva*)" and "that of an object and the cognition of the object (*viṣayaviṣayibhāva*)."[10] The *Vy* provides specific relations under both of these cases: "the relation of largeness (*mahattva*) in the ether and the articulated word 'largeness' (*mahattvaśabda*) for largeness in the ether" under the former case, and "the relation of desire (*icchā*) in a soul and awareness of desire (*icchālambanavijñāna*) in the soul" under the latter case. We can illustrate the structure of both relations in Figure 3 and 4.

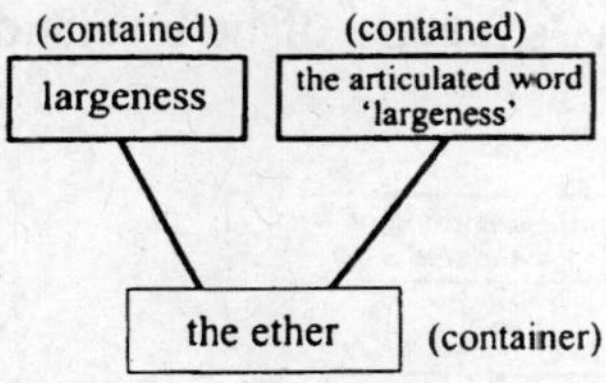

Figure 3

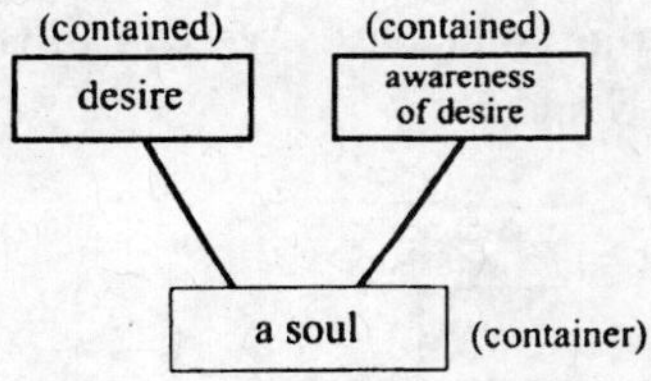

Figure 4

Now, the definition, composed of factor (I) and (III), would not be sufficient to exclude the case "the relation of largeness in the ether and the articulated word 'largeness' for largeness in the ether." The reason is that largeness and the articulated word 'largeness' are inseparably connected in the sense that they are inseparably connected to the same place (the ether) (I), and a relation subsists between them as one between the denoted and the denoter (III). Therefore, if the definition of inherence were only composed of factor (I) and (III), "the relation of largeness in the ether and the articulated word 'largeness' for largeness in the ether," which is not inherence, could not be excluded from the concept of inherence. Therefore, factor (II)—entities that stand as the contained and the container (*ādhāryādhārabhūta*)—needs to be added to the definition for the purpose of excluding the above relation from the concept of inherence. Since largeness and the articulated word 'largeness' are not related in the sense of the contained and the container, factor (II) can exclude the relation from the concept of inherence. With the same reasons mentioned above, "the relation of desire in a soul and awareness of desire in the soul," under the relation of an object and the

10. With regards to *viṣayaviṣayibhāva*, which is literally translated as the relation of object and object-possessor, it can be translated as the relation of an object and the cognition of the object, see Uno [1996: 96].

cognition of the object, is excluded from the concept of inherence by factor (II).[11]

Then, even though the definition composed of (I), (II), and (III)—the relation, which subsists between entities that are incapable of existing separately and that stand as the contained and the container, is inherence—it is still applicable to "the relation of the denoted and the denoter" and to "that of an object and the cognition of the object." The *Vy* again provides specific relations under both of these cases: the relation of the ether (*ākāśa*) and the articulated word 'ether' (*ākāśaśabda*) under the former case and the relation of a soul (*ātman*) and the cognition of the soul (*ātmālambanajñāna*) under the latter case. We can illustrate the structure of both relations in Figure 5 and 6.

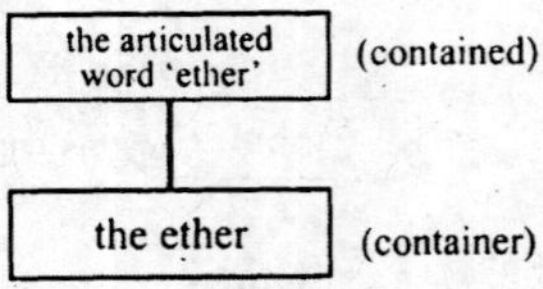

Figure 5

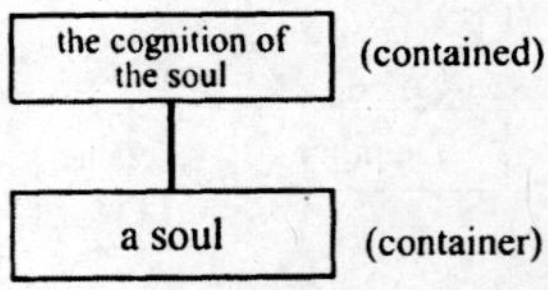

Figure 6

The relation of the ether and the articulated word 'ether' is inherence. However, not every relation of the denoted and the denoter, is inherence. As Figure 3 illustrates, "the relation of largeness in the ether and the articulated word 'largeness' for largeness in the ether," under the relation of the denoted and the denoter, is not inherence. The same is true of the relation of an object and the cognition of the object on the evidence of "the relation of desire in a soul and awareness of desire in the soul" in Figure 4. Therefore, the *Vy* insists that factor (II) must be interpreted as "*only* entities that stand as the contained and the container." The interpretation of factor

---

11. *Vy*, vol. I, p. 26,3–10: *tathāpy ayutasiddhānāṃ yaḥ sambandhaḥ saḥ samavāya ity ukte vyabhicārābhāvaḥ? tan na. vācyavācakabhāvena viṣayaviṣayibhāvena ca vyabhicārāt. tathā hy ākāśamahattvam ākāśe samavetaṃ mahattvaśabdavācyam ity ākāśamahattvatacchabdayor vācyavācakabhāvaḥ sambandho na ca yutasiddhir vibhinnāśrayasamavāyitvābhāvāt. tathā hy ākāśamahattvam ākāśe samavetaṃ tadvācakaś ca śabdas tatraivety ayutasiddhatvam. evam icchādyālambanaṃ vijñānam ātmani samavetam icchādayaś ca tatraivety ayutasiddhatve saty eṣāṃ viṣayaviṣayibhāva ity anayor vyavacchedārtham ādhāryādhārapadam. na cātrākāśamahattvaśabdas tanmahattvādhāraḥ. nāpīcchādyālambanavijñānaṃ tadādhāram iti.*

(II) with this restriction[12] serves to exclude both cases[13]—the relation of the denoted and the denoter and that of an object and the cognition of the object—since both may or may not subsist between entities that stand as the contained and the container.[14]

Moreover, the *Vy* interprets factor (I) as "*only* entities that are incapable of existing separately." By virtue of the interpretation of (I), with the restriction of the word 'only', the relation of the denoted and the denoter and that of an object and the cognition of the object come to be swept away from the concept of inherence, since both cases emphasize relations which do not always subsist between entities that are incapable of existing separately. Although the *Vy* does not provide specific relations for both cases, we can construct examples for both cases that do not subsist between entities that are incapable of existing separately. For example, the relation of taste and the articulated word 'taste', etc. under the relation of the denoted and the denoter, and the relation of a pot and the cognition of the pot, etc. under the relation of an object and the cognition of the object.[15] We can illustrate the structure of both relations in Figure 7 and Figure 8.

---

12. Regarding the function of 'only' (*eva*) in Indian philosophy, see Kajiyama [1966].
13. We can point out the narrow application (*avyāpti*) of the definition of inherence. That is to say, although the relation between the ether and the articulated word 'ether' and that between a soul and the cognition of the soul are inherence, both relations are excluded by factor (II) with a restriction in the *Vy*. However, even though the definition has the defect of narrow application, the definition is regarded as a correct definition in Indian philosophy. See Sato [1995: 25–27].
14. *Vy*, vol. I, p. 26, 11–17: *nanv evam apy ābhyām eva vyabhicāraḥ. tathā hy ayutasiddhānām ādhāryādhārabhūtānāṃ yaḥ sambandhaḥ saḥ samavāya ity ukte 'pi vācyavācakabhāvaviṣayaviṣayibhāvābhyām eva vyabhicāraḥ. tathā hy ākāśaśabdenākāśam abhidhīyata ity anayor ādhāryādhārabhāve sati vācyavācakabhāvaḥ, na cāsti yutasiddhiḥ. evam ātmālambanam aham iti jñānam ātmany evety ayutasiddhatve saty ādhāryādhārabhūtayor asti viṣayaviṣayibhāva iti tadvyavacchedārtham avadhāraṇam ādhāryādhārabhūtānām eva yaḥ sambandhaḥ sa samavāya iti. vācyavācakaviṣayaviṣayibhāvayoś cādhāryādhārabhūteṣu tadviparīteṣu ca sadbhāva iti vyavacchedaḥ.*
15. With regard to the relations for both cases that subsist between entities that are incapable of existing separately, see Figure 3 and Figure 4, and Figure 5 and Figure 6.

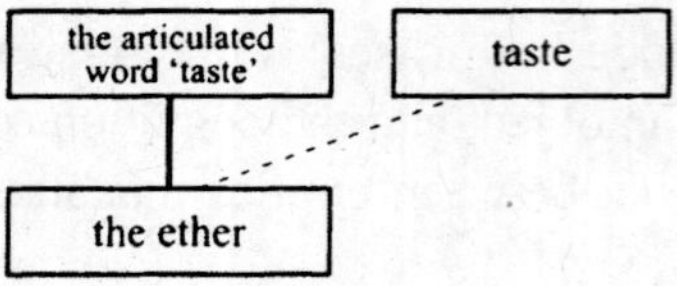

Figure 7

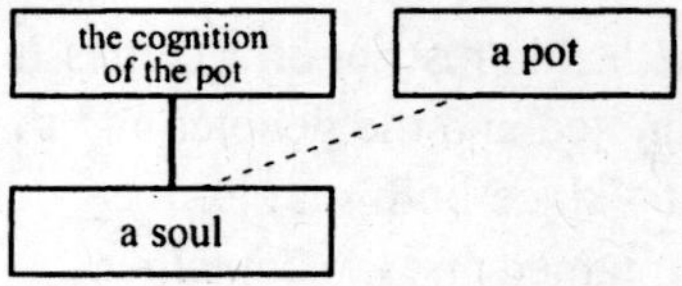

Figure 8

In Figure 7, the dotted line indicates a relation between taste and the ether, where taste does not exist in the ether. That is to say, the dotted line signifies that there is not any relation between taste and the ether. The same applies to the dotted line between 'a pot' and 'a soul' in Figure 8. The interpretation of factor (I), which explicitly says that inherence subsists between *only* entities that are incapable of existing separately, serves to exclude the relation of the denoted and the denoter and that of an object and its cognition, since both relations may or may not subsist between entities that are incapable of existing separately.[16]

3.2. The *NK*

Second we will consider the *NK*, focusing on what is excluded by the factors of the definition of inherence. The *NK* first supposes that the definition of inherence is composed of factor (I) only—inherence subsists between entities that are incapable of existing separately (*ayutasiddha*). In this case, "the relation of merit and pleasure" could reasonably be understood as inherence, since merit and pleasure, which are examples of Qualities (see Table I), are also entities that are incapable of existing separately in the sense that they are inseparably connected to the same place (a soul). That is to say, the residence of merit and pleasure is the same (*sāmānādhikaraṇya*). We can illustrate the structure of the aforementioned case in Figure 9.

16. *Vy*, vol. I, p. 26, 18–20: *nanu evam ayutasiddhānām iti vyartham eva, na. asyāpi sāvadhāraṇasya lakṣaṇāntaratvāt. tathā hy ayutasiddhānām eva yaḥ sambandhaḥ sa samavāya iti. vācyavācakaviṣayaviṣayibhāvau tu yutasiddhānām ayutasiddhānāñ ceti.*

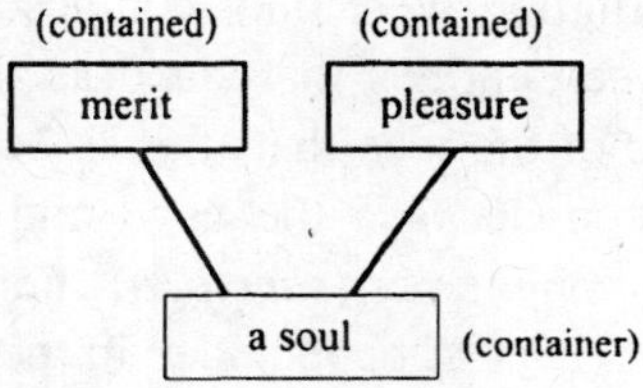

Figure 9

Although the relation between merit and a soul and that between pleasure and a soul is inherence in Vaiśeṣika philosophy, the relation of merit and pleasure is not inherence. Therefore, the *NK* insists that factor (II)—entities that stand as the contained and the container (*ādhāryādhārabhūta*)—must be included in the definition in order to exclude this relation from the concept of inherence. Since merit and pleasure are not related as the contained and the container, factor (II) can exclude "the relation of merit and pleasure" from the concept of inherence.[17]

Next the *NK* deals with "the relation between the ether and the flying bird" and insists that the relation is excluded by factor (I) without giving a detailed explanation, commenting that factor (II) does not have a role of excluding this relation.[18] It should be noted that the *Vy* and the *NK* disagree regarding this "relation between the ether and the flying bird," where the *Vy* interprets that the relation is explicitly excluded by factor (II) or (III).

Moreover, the *NK* deals with "the relation of the denoted and the denoter," for which the specific relation is the relation of the ether (the denoted) and the articulated word 'ether' (*ākāśaśabda*, the denoter). We can illustrate the structure of "the relation of the ether and the articulated word 'ether'" in Figure 5. The *NK* interprets that factor (IV)—a cause of the idea that '[this is]here' (*ihapratyayahetu*)—is included in the definition in order to exclude "the relation of the denoted and the denoter," which does not cause the idea that '[this is] here', from the concept of inherence.[19]

---

17. *NK*, p. 14,18–20: *ayutasiddhayoḥ sambandha ity ucyamāne dharmasya sukhasya ca yaḥ kāryakāraṇabhāvalakṣaṇaḥ sambandhaḥ so pi samavāyaḥ prāpnoti tayor ātmaikāśritayor yutasiddhyabhāvāt tadartham ādhāryādhārabhūtānām iti padam* ...

18. *NK*, p. 14,21: *na tv ākāśaśakunisambandhanivṛttyartham ayutasiddhipadenaiva tasya nivarttitatvāt.*

19. *NK*, p. 14,22–24: *evam apy ākāśasyākāśapadasya ca vācyavācakabhāvaḥ samavāyaḥ syāt tannivṛttyartham ihapratyayahetur iti vācyavācakabhāve hi tasmāc chabdāt tadartho jñāyate na tv ihedam iti.*

And, even if the definition were only composed of (II) and (IV)—inherence subsists between entities that stand as the contained and the container, being a cause of the idea that 'this is here'—it would still be applicable to "the relation between the bowl and the fruit of jujube." However, this relation is 'conjunction (*saṃyoga*)', not inherence. Therefore, the *NK* insists that factor (I) must be included in the definition in order to exclude the relation, which subsists between entities that are capable of existing separately, from the concept of inherence.[20]

3.3. The *Kir*

Finally, we will consider the *Kir*. The *Kir* interprets factor (I)—entities that are incapable of existing separately (*ayutasiddha*)—into "what are fused" (*prāpta*). Then, the relation between what are fused is understood as inherence, which has a distinction of fusion (*prāpti*). Factor (I), with such a meaning, excludes 'conjunction' from the concerned relation because 'conjunction' subsists between entities that are not fused.[21] Moreover, the *Kir* points out that the relation of the denoted and the denoter, etc., are not inherence because the relation of the denoted and the denoter, etc. does not have a distinction of fusion.[22]

4. Quotation Theory

The exclusions related to each factor of the definition of inherence in the three commentary texts are summarized in table II:

20. *NK*, p. 14,24–25: *ādhāryādhārabhūtānāṃ ihapratyayahetur iti kuṇḍabadarasambandho na vyavacchidyate tadartham ayutasiddhānām iti.*
21. *Kir*, p. 18,4–5: *ayutāḥ prāptāś ca te siddhāś cety ayutasiddhāḥ, prāptā eva santi na viyutkā iti yāvat. teṣāṃ sambandhaḥ prāptilakṣaṇaḥ samavāyaḥ. tena saṃyogo vyavacchinnaḥ, tasyāprāptipūrvakatvāt.*
22. *Kir*, p. 18,7: *prāptipadenaiva vācyavācakabhāvādilakṣaṇaḥ sambandho na prasajyate.*

Table II: What is excluded by the factors of the definition of inherence

	The *Vy*	The *NK*	The *Kir*
(I)	1. The relation between the bowl and the fruit of jujube (=Conjunction) 2. The relation of the denoted and the denoter * The relation of taste and the articulated word 'taste', etc. 3. The relation of an object and the cognition of the object * The relation of a pot and the cognition of the pot, etc.	1. The relation between the ether and the flying bird 2. The relation between the bowl and the fruit of jujube (=Conjunction)	1. Conjunction 2. The relation of the denoted and the denoter, etc.
(II)	1. The relation between the ether and the flying bird (=*vyāpakavyāpyabhāva*) 2. The relation of the denoted and the denoter <a> The relation of largeness (*mahattva*) in the ether and the articulated word 'largeness' (*mahattvaśabda*) for largeness in the ether <b> The relation of the ether (*ākāśa*) and the articulated word 'ether' (*ākāśaśabda*) 3. The relation of an object and the cognition of the object <a> The relation of desire (*icchā*) in a soul and awareness of desire (*icchālambanavijñāna*) in the soul <b> The relation of a soul (*ātman*) and the cognition of the soul (*ātmālambanajñāna*)	1. The relation of merit and pleasure (=*sāmānādhikaraṇya*)	
(III)	1. The relation between the trees and the village 2. The relation between the ether and the flying bird		
(IV)		1. The relation of the denoted and the denoter <a> The relation of the ether (*ākāśa*) and the articulated word 'ether' (*ākāśaśabda*)	

(I) entities that are incapable of existing separately (*ayuta-siddha*),
(II) entities that stand as the contained and the container (*ādhārya-ādhāra-bhūta*),
(III) the relation, (*yaḥ sambandha*).
(IV) a cause of the idea that '[this is] here (this is in that)' (*iha-pratyaya-hetu*).
The items with * in table II is not referred to in the text.

In the preceding chapter we observed the combination of the definition factors and what is excluded (the exclusion) between the three commentary texts. A quotation theory offers the key to relating the combination of both the definition factors and what is excluded with the genesis of commentary texts. That is to say, how the commentary texts are generated via combination with already-known information—both the factors of definition and what is excluded—which are quoted from the preceding texts.

This allows us to focus attention to the way in which information is quoted from the precedent texts and manipulated. The term 'quotation' can be defined as information in a precedent text moved to a subsequent text, implicitly or explicitly. Therefore, 'quotation' may then be further divided into two types: explicit quotation and implicit quotation.[23] Explicit quotation takes the form of the 'preservation', the 'substitution', and the 'permutation' of information between texts. In these cases we can perceive the movement of information from the precedent text to the following text. On the contrary, implicit quotation takes the form of the 'deletion' of information between the texts, where we cannot perceive the movement of information from the precedent text to the following text. The above can be schematized as follows:

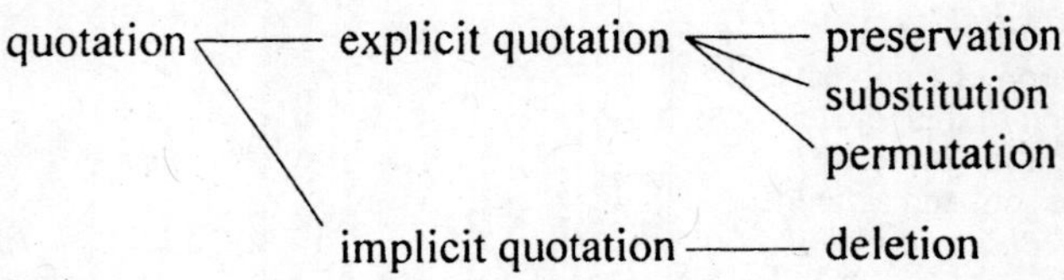

Having made this distinction, we shall explain each a kind of quotation with the combination of the definition factors (x and y) and what is excluded (a, b, and c) between the commentary texts (the precedent text α and the subsequent text β).

'Preservation' of a quotation, in view of the combination of the definition factor and what is excluded, refers to the unchanged combination of a specific factor and a specific exclusion in 2 or more different commentary texts. That is to say, a is excluded by the same factor x in α and β.

'Substitution' of a quotation refers to the changed combination of the definition factor and what is excluded between the commentary texts. The main character of substitution is that it paraphrases what is excluded.

23. With regard to the concept of quotation, see Sasaki [1990] and Matsuzawa [2003: 27–29], but the concept of quotation, which is offered in this paper, does not explain in their papers.

When the exclusion is paraphrased, it is denoted by a synonym. That is to say, where originally *a* or *b* are excluded by the factor *x* in α, *c* is excluded by *x* in β, where *c* covers the meaning of the original *a* or *b*. Therefore, substitution can be regarded as a variety of preservation.

'Permutation' of a quotation refers to the changed combination of the definition factor and what is excluded between the commentary texts. That is to say, while *a* is excluded by a factor *x* in α, *a* is excluded by a different factor *y* in β.

Implicit quotation takes the form of the 'deletion' of what is excluded in the subsequent text. That is to say, *a* is excluded by factor *x* in α, however, *a* is not mentioned in β.

Let me summarize the main points that have been made in the above.

Preservation—*a* is excluded by *x* in α,
a is also excluded by *x* in β.

Substitution—*a* or *b* are excluded by *x* in α,
but *c* is excluded by *x* in β.

Permutation—*a* is excluded by *x* in α,
but *a* is excluded by *y* in β.

Deletion——*a* is excluded by *x* in α,
but *a* is not mentioned in β.

Let us look closely at the 'preservation', 'substitution', 'permutation', and 'deletion' of quotations between the three commentary texts on the *PDhS*, using Table II.

With regard to 'preservation', we can point out one case in the commentary texts.[24]

(1) *Vy* (I) 1 → *NK* (I) 2

Let us look at case (1). "The relation between the bowl and the fruit of jujube" is excluded by factor (I) in the *Vy*. The relation is also excluded by (I) in the *NK*. Therefore 'preservation' of "the relation between the bowl and the fruit of jujube" can be pointed out between the *Vy* and the *NK*.

With regards to 'substitution', we can point out three cases in the three

24. On the reading of "*Vy* (I) 1" etc., in this paper, the name of the text is indicated at the beginning, next the number of the factors of the definition is indicated, and, last, the number or alphabet indicates what is excluded by each factor as indicated in table II.

commentaries.

(1) *Vy* (I) 1 → *Kir* (I) 1
(2) *Vy* (I) 2, (I) 3 → *Kir* (I) 2
(3) *Vy* (II) 2–a, (II) 3–a → *NK* (II) 1

Let us look at case (1) first. "The relation between the bowl and the fruit jujube" is excluded by factor (I) in the *Vy*. The relation is under the relation of conjunction. On the other hand, conjunction is excluded by factor (I) in the *Kir*. Therefore, substitution of "conjunction" for "the relation between the bowl and the fruit jujube" occurs between the *Vy* and the *Kir*.

Regarding case (2), "the relation of the denoted and the denoter" is excluded by factor (I) in the *Vy*. Although the *Vy* does not provide a specific relation for it, we constructed an example such as "the relation of taste and the articulated word 'taste' in Figure 7. The *Kir* excludes "the relation of denoted and the denoter, etc." by factor (I) without providing a specific relation for it. However, we can assume that the *Kir* implies the same specific relation for it as the *Vy*. The reason for this assumption is that other specific relations under the relation of the denoted and the denoter—the relation of largeness in the ether and the articulated word 'largeness' for largeness in the ether as Figure 3 indicates—are not excluded by factor (I). Moreover, when we consider that "the relation of an object and the cognition of the object" is paired up with "the relation of the denoted and the denoter" in the *Vy*, it may safely be assumed that the word 'etc.' (*ādi*) in "the relation of the denoted and the denoter, etc." excluded by factor (I) in the *Kir*, implies "the relation of an object and the cognition of the object." With regard to the specific relation under the relation of an object and the cognition of the object, we may say that the *Kir* implies "the relation of a pot and the cognition for the pot" in Figure 8 with the same reasoning that is mentioned for "the relation of the denoted and the denoter" above. It follows from what has been said that substitution of "the relation of the denoted and the denoter, etc." for "the relation of the denoted and the denoter" and "the relation of an object and the cognition of the object" occurs between the *Vy* and the *Kir*.

Let us look at case (3) last. Both "the relation of largeness in the ether and the articulated word 'largeness' for largeness in the ether," under the relation of the denoted and the denoter, and "the relation of desire in a soul and awareness of desire in the soul," under the relation of an object and the cognition of the object, are excluded by factor (II) in the *Vy*. Each relata in these relations exists in the same place as Figure 3 and Figure 4 indicate.

"The relation of merit and pleasure," whose relata also exist in the same place, as Figure 9 indicates, is excluded by factor (II) in the *NK*. Therefore, substitution of "the relation of merit and pleasure" for two relations in the *Vy* can be pointed out between the *Vy* and the *NK*.

Regarding 'permutation', we can point out three cases in the commentary texts.

(1) *Vy* (II) 1 → *NK* (I) 1
(2) *Vy* (III) 2 → *NK* (I) 1
(3) *Vy* (II) 2–b → *NK* (IV) 1

Let us look at case (1) and (2) first. "The relation between the ether and the flying bird" is excluded by factor (II) and (III) in the *Vy*. But the relation is excluded by (I) in the *NK*. Therefore 'permutation' can be pointed out between the *Vy* and the *NK* with reference to this relation.

Let us look at case (3) next. "The relation between the ether and the articulated word 'ether'" is excluded by factor (II) in the *Vy*. The same relation, however, is excluded by factor (IV) in the *NK*. Therefore, permutation can be pointed out between the *Vy* and the *NK* with reference to the relation.

With regards to 'deletion', we can point out nine cases in the three commentaries.

(1) *Vy* (I) 2 → *NK*
(2) *Vy* (I) 3 → *NK*
(3) *Vy* (II) 1 → *Kir*
(4) *Vy* (II) 2–a → *Kir*
(5) *Vy* (II) 2–b → *Kir*
(6) *Vy* (II) 3–a → *Kir*
(7) *Vy* (II) 3–b → *NK*, *Kir*
(8) *Vy* (III) 1 → *NK*, *Kir*
(9) *Vy* (III) 2 → *Kir*

For the moment let us look closely at (8). "The relation between the trees and the village" is excluded by factor (III) in the *Vy*. But the relation is not mentioned in the *NK* and the *Kir*. Therefore, with regard to this relation, 'deletion' can be pointed out between the *Vy* and the subsequent texts, the *NK* and the *Kir*. Regarding the other 8 cases too, what are excluded, which are mentioned in the *Vy*, are not mentioned later. That is to say, they are deleted in the subsequent texts, the *NK* or the *Kir*.

It follows from what has been said that, when we analyze the genesis of commentary texts from the viewpoint of quotation theory, the commentary texts themselves are generated by quotation. They are the result of preservation, substitution, permutation, and deletion of already-known information from preceding texts. However, we should not conclude that only the oldest text, in this case the *Vy*, has presented original thought. If it is emphasized that the commentary texts are generated by quotation of already-known information, the same is true of the original. That is to say, we can think that the *Vy*, although it does not have preceding commentary texts, is also composed of information drawn from different earlier texts.

The classification of quotation into four forms—preservation, substitution, permutation, and deletion—is based on the way in which information is conveyed. From this viewpoint, let us then consider the qualities of the information that is conveyed by each of these four forms of quotation. Preservation takes the form of the unchanged combination of old information. Therefore, information which preservation conveys can be regarded as that information which has been restricted from being re-interpreted, and is therefore non-violated. Substitution and permutation take the form of the changed combination of old information. Information, which substitution and permutation convey, can therefore be regarded as new information, produced via the new combination of old information. Deletion takes the form of old information not perceived in a new commentary text. Since brief and simple explanation was demanded in Indian philosophy, there was a tendency for the commentary texts to omit or delete common and already-known information. Taking this tendency into consideration, information conveyed via deletion can be regarded as common, already-known, and prevalent information, which probably is of no value for making specific reference to.

Furthermore, when comparing the three commentary texts on the *PDhS*, we notice that the amount of commentary on each category decreased over time.[25] If we combine and measure the amount of comments on the definition of inherence in the *PDhS* and compare it to the three commentary texts, the *Vy* is roughly 49 times longer, the *NK* is 31 times longer, and the *Kir* is 8.5 times longer than the *PDhS*. An increase of 'deletion' between the three commentary texts helps to account for the decrease in the amount of comments on inherence between the three commentary texts.[26] If we view it from a different perspective, we may see that it implies an expansion and communalization of knowledge about inherence in the Vaiśeṣika school between the period from the *Vy* to the *Kir*.

25. We can also point out the decrease in the amount of comments of the three commentary texts at the definition chapter of substance, quality, activity, and particular.
26. We should also consider that 'substitution' contributes to the decrease in the amount of comments on inherence between the three commentary texts as well.

5. Conclusion

(1) The commentary texts are generated by combining information quoted and drawn from precedent texts. When new commentary texts are generated, some preexisting information is preserved, substituted, permuted, and deleted, as we have observed using the definition of inherence in the three commentary texts on the *PDhS*. However, this does not mean that new generated commentary texts do not convey new and original information. Original information occurs from the combination of old information. That is to say, the combination of the definition factors and what is excluded is re-combined in a newer commentary text; showing a new interpretation of inherence.

(2) When comparing the three commentary texts on the *PDhS*, it is clear that the amount of commentary on the definition of inherence decreases over time. Deletion of information between the three commentary texts can be regarded as a main cause of this decrease in the amount of commentary between the three commentary texts. We can assume that the deleted information can be regarded as already-known, prevalent, and common information for the commentators. Therefore, it is often omitted or deleted in the commentary texts on the basis of demand for brief and simple explanations. In other words, it is likely that the deleted information is of no value for making reference to, but is instead conveyed orally.

On the other hand, we have to admit that there is information that must have been written in the commentary texts, even though it is already-known, prevalent, and common. Conjunction, a relation well known as the antithesis of inherence in the Vaiśeṣika school and others, is treated as such a kind of information in the three commentary texts. The fact that information regarding conjunction is quoted explicitly in the three commentary texts shows that information regarding conjunction must have been indispensable to understanding inherence. Therefore, it seems reasonable to say that conjunction is quoted in the form of preservation and substitution between the commentary texts. Preservation refers to the unchanged combination of information (the definition factors and what is excluded). And although substitution refers to the changed combination of information, it is a variety of preservation. In other words, this analysis may show that conjunction was not allowed to be re-interpreted, or at least much-re-interpreted, in the discussion of inherence by the commentators, and then we may regard preserved or substituted information as non-violated information. In addition, although the concept of 'tradition' is ambiguous, one may say that traditional views point to information that is conveyed through preservation and substitution.

(3) When we admit that already-known and common information, which is regarded as unworthy of quotation, is deleted in new commentary texts, a new commentary text loses its character as an autonomous text. The 'deleted' information, which the new commentary text does not quote, cannot be known by reading the new commentary text only. Hence, if a reader desires basic information regarding inherence, they must refer to not only the new text, but also to the old texts. On the other hand, if the reader refers to the old texts only, they would miss the latest information. Viewed in this light, commentary texts on the same original source material should be regarded as one whole, where complete information is conveyed by the commentary texts group.

(4) Moreover, if we look at deletion from a different perspective, not bound by the texts only, we see that a group and community, which memorizes and holds 'deleted' information in common, must have been formed. It is difficult to imagine that the commentary texts were made, not for the public, but for individuals only. In other words, the deleted information was well-known and common, not only for the commentator himself, but also for the group and community. Viewed in this light, although the concept of 'school' in Indian Philosophy is not clear, we can regard an aspect of 'school' as a group or community which memorizes deleted information in common.

Finally, I would like to offer one caveat. Since the characteristic of the commentary texts, mentioned in this paper, is derived from a consideration of the chapter regarding the definition of inherence in the *Vy*, the *NK*, and *Kir* only, it is obvious that there is not enough evidence to conclude whether or not the characteristic of the commentary text explored herein could be applied to the all commentary texts in ancient India. This question needs further consideration. However, it is certain that this exploration shows a way of reading the text and offers a compelling hypothesis for the characteristic of the commentary text in ancient India.

Bibliography

Primary Sources

Kiraṇāvalī (*Kir*) of Udayana, in *Praśastapādabhāṣyam with the Commentary Kiraṇāvalī of Udayanācārya*, edited by J.S. Jetly, Gaekwad's Oriental

Series 154, Vadodara: Oriental Institute, reprint, 1991.

Nyāyakandalī (*NK*) of Śrīdhara, in *the Praśastapāda Bhāshya with Commentary Nyāyakandali of Sridhara*, edited by Vindhyesvari Prasad Dvivedin, Sri Garib Dass Oriental Series 13, Delhi: Sri Satguru Publications, 1984.

Padārthadharmasaṃgraha (*PDhS*) of Praśastapāda, in Bronkhorst and Ramseier [1994].

Vyomavatī (*Vy*) of Vyomaśiva, in *Vyomavatī of Vyomaśivācārya*, edited with the *Praśastapādabhāṣya* by Gaurinath Sastri, 2 vols, M.M. Śivakumāraśāstri-Granthamālā 6, Varanasi: Sampurnanand Sanskrit University, 1983, 1984.

Vyomavatī (*Vy*\[K]) of Vyomaśiva, in *Praśastapādabhāṣyam*, edited with Commentaries (up to Dravya) *Sūktī* of Jagadiśa Tarkālaṃkara, *Setu* of Padmanābha Miśra and *Vyomavatī* of Vyomaśivāchārya (to the end) by M. M. Gopīnath Kavirāj and Panditraj Dhundhirāj Shāstri, Chaukhamba Sanskrit Series 61, Varanasi: Chaukhamba Amarabharati Prakashan, 1983.

Secondary Literature

Bronkhorst, Johannes and Yves Ramseier

1994 *Word Index to the Praśastapādabhāṣya: A Complete Word Index to the Printed Editions of the Praśastapādabhāṣya*, Delhi: Motilal Banarsidass.

Kajiyama, Yuichi

1966 "Bukkyotetugaku niokeru Meidaikaishaku—eva no Buniseigen-kinou—" (The Interpretation of the Proposition in Buddhist Philosophy), *Kanakurahakase Kokikinen Indogaku Bukkyogaku Ronsyu*, Kyoto: Heirakuji Shoten. (in Japanese)

Kristeva, J.

1969 *Σημειωτική: Recherches pour une Sémanalyse*, Paris: Éditions du Seuil.

Hirano, Katsunori

2004 "Originality and Quotation: A Study of a Commentary Text's Genesis in Vaiśeṣika Philosophy", *SITES: Journal of Studies for the Integrated Text Science*, 2 (1): 59–74.

2006 "The Genesis of Commentary Texts in Ancient India: From a Quotation Theory Viewpoint", *Conflict between Tradition and Creativity in Indian Philosophy: Text and Context*, 21st Century COE Program International Conference Series 7, pp. 37–46.

Matilal, B.K.

1990 (1985) *Logic, Language and Reality*, 2nd edn., Delhi: Motilal Banarsidass.

Matsuzawa, Kazuhiro

2003 *Seiseiron no Tankyu* (Inquiry into Genesis), Nagoya: Nagoya University Press. (in Japanese)

Potter, K.H.

1995 (1977) (ed.) *Indian Metaphysics and Epistemology: The Tradition of Nyāya-Vaiśeṣika up to Gaṅgeśa:* Encyclopedia of Indian Philosophies, vol. II, Delhi: Motilal Banarsidass.

Sasaki, Ken-ichi

1990 "Inyou wo Meguru Sansei no Porifoni" (Polyphony of Three Voices on Quotation), in H. Ichikawa et. al. (eds.), *Translation*, Adventure in Modern Philosophy 5, Tokyo: Iwanami Publisher. (in Japanese)

Sato, Hiroyuki

1995 "Teigi no Teigi" (On the Concept of the Definition in Indian Philosophy), *Bukkyo Bunka* 33: 3–29. (in Japanese)

Tachikawa, Musashi

1981 *The Structure of the World in Indian Realism*, Studies of Classical India 4, Dordrecht: D. Reidel Publishing Company.

Uno, Atsushi

1996 *Indo Ronrigaku* (Indian Logic), Kyoto: Hōzōkan. (in Japanese)

Wada, Toshihiro

1990 *Invariable Concomitance in Navya-Nyāya*, Sri Garib Dass Oriental Series 101, Delhi: Sri Satguru Publications.

* I would like to thank Mr. Matthew Pelowski for correcting my English.

CHAPTER 8

TEXT, CONTEXT AND AUTHOR'S INTENTION: TWO FRAMES OF REFERENCE IN THE VAIŚEṢIKA SCHOOL

Takanori SUZUKI

1. Introduction

One of the main features of Indian thought is its way of development, continued under the scheme of commentarial activities. The six orthodox philosophical schools, which typically followed this way of development, handed their original tenets, written in the shape of *sūtra*s, down to the next generations through commentarial activities. Indian philosophical schools are often considered to be conservative, because, in this system, the next generations had to hold their *sūtra*s as absolute fundamentals, and this consideration is somewhat true. However, this does not mean that each and every theory of the six schools, written in the *sūtra*s and handed down to the next generation was always the same. Keeping the system of commentarial activities as its framework, the contents of commentaries varied due to the social or periodical contexts in which commentators lived.

Among the six orthodox schools that developed their theories through commentaries and sub-commentaries etc. from their *sūtra*s, the Vaiśeṣika school, which is focused on in this paper, has some particular features in its way of development. The *Vaiśeṣikasūtra* (*VS*), the fundamental text of the Vaiśeṣika school, seems to be regarded as less authoritative than the *Padārthadharmasaṅgraha* (*PDhS*), which was written in the 6th century in order to summarize the Vaiśeṣika school's tenets. Three well-known Vaiśeṣika texts, Vyomaśiva's *Vyomavatī* (*Vy*, middle of the 10th century), Śrīdhara's *Nyāyakandalī* (*NK*, end of the 10th century), and Udayana's *Kiraṇāvalī* (*Kir*, second half of the 11th century), were written as commentaries on the *PDhS*. When we investigate the history of the Vaiśeṣika school, it is necessary to consider the fact that some commentaries were written on the *VS*, but regarded as less authoritative after the emergence of the *PDhS*.

Another point which characterizes the history of the Vaiśeṣika school is its fusion with the Nyāya school. The Nyāya school, which mainly investigated questions of logic and epistemology, had an intimate relationship with the Vaiśeṣika school, which categorically analyzed the structure of the world. From their early stage, both schools gradually deepened their sharing of theories to eventually reach the stage where some texts were made in common. It was necessary to have some consistency between each theory among the two schools in order to compose common texts, however, both schools had differing tenets and argued about some topics before they started to have common texts and to be practically considered as one school.

One of the biggest arguments between the two schools regards what is considered to be the means of valid cognition (*pramāṇa*). The Nyāya-Vaiśeṣika school, which was a practical union of the two schools, regarded perception (*pratyakṣa*), inference (*anumāna*), analogy (*upamāna*), and verbal cognition (*śabda*) as *pramāṇa*s in its texts, such as the *Tarkasaṅgraha* (*TS*, ca. A.D. 15c). This classification was adopted in the Nyāya school since the period of the *Nyāyasūtra* (*NS*, ca. A.D. 2–5c), while the Vaiśeṣika school grouped the latter two kinds of cognitions as inference, and held that they both cannot be established as independent *pramāṇa*s. Thus, it is reasonable to think that the Vaiśeṣika school approached the Nyāya school as far as regarding the topic of what is to be regarded as *pramāṇa*s, and that there should have been some argument done between these two schools to reconcile the differences between their theories so that they could eventually become *one* school.

Although there has not been much research focusing on theoretical consistency, for the sake of unification, of the Vaiśeṣika school and the Nyāya school, Dr. Anantalal Thakur has mentioned the existence of branches in the Vaiśeṣika school,[1] which seems to be relevant to this topic. Dr. Thakur has recently published *Origin and development of the Vaiśeṣika system*, in which he confirms details of the history of the Vaiśeṣika school. In this paper, I would like to suggest, mainly based on the above prior research, the possibility that there was an innovative movement that tried to modify the Vaiśeṣika school's tradition and another movement that differed from it in the process of inheritance of its tenets. This investigation is focused on the two schools' theories of verbal cognition, or the location

1. Thakur [1957] [1961].

of words as means of verbal cognition.

2. Verbal Cognition in the Vaiśeṣika School from the *VS* to the *PDhS*

Both the *VS*[2] and the *PDhS*[3] hold that words are to be included as means of inference (this opinion is called the 'theory of inclusion' from here onwards), and they find its ground in the sameness of the process in which verbal cognition and inference occur.

┌ *VS*: Both inference and verbal cognition require a cognition:
 "This is ... of that (*asyedam*)"[4]
└→ *PDhS*: Both inference and verbal cognition require cognitive process
 : perception of relationship (*sambandha*) + perception of a relatum
 → remembrance (*smṛti*) of relationship → cognition of the other relatum

Figure 1: The ground for the theory of inclusion in the *VS* and the *PDhS*: the sameness of cognitive process

While the description of both texts is simple, some other texts describe the ground of the theory of inclusion in detail. For example, the *NS*, which holds that verbal cognition is to be differentiated from inference (this opinion is called the 'theory of differentiation' from here onwards), introduces three grounds for the theory of inclusion enumerated by its

---

2. *VS* (C) 9.18–21: *asyedaṃ kāryaṃ kāraṇaṃ sambandhi ekārthasamavāyi virodhi ceti laiṅgikam//* 18 *etena śābdaṃ vyākhyātam//* 19 *hetur upadeśo liṅgaṃ nimittaṃ pramāṇaṃ kāraṇam ity anārthāntaram//* 20 *asyedam iti buddhyapekṣatvāt//* 21
3. *PDhS*, p. 206, 11–13: *śabdādīnāṃ apy anumāne 'ntarbhāvaḥ samānavidhitvāt/ yathā prasiddhasamayasya liṅgadarśanaprasiddhyanusmaraṇābhyām atīndriye 'rthe bhavaty anumānam; evaṃ śabdādibhyo 'pīti/*
   On the process of an inferential cognition, the *PDhS* describes it in the following way. Knowledge of the rule (*samaya*) that "wherever there is *x*, there is *y*. wherever there is no *y*, there is no *x*." (Knowledge of the relationship of *x* and *y*) → Firm cognition of *x* → Remembrance of the rule → (Reconsideration (*parāmarśa*) of *x*) → Cognition of *y*. In verbal cognition, when one who knows the relationship, for instance, between the word (*śabda*) "cow" and its meaning (*artha*), hearing the sequence of the sound "c-o-w", he cognizes its meaning after remembering the relationship. This sameness of process where both cognitions occur is the ground of the *VS* and the *PDhS*'s assertion. cf. *PDhS*, p. 197, 3–7; Appendix.
4. Cognition of '*asyedam*' is equal to that of relationships in general since the word '*asya*' which has a six case-ending, signifies *sambandhamātra*, relationships in general. cf. *Pāṇinisūtra* 2.3.50: *ṣaṣṭhī śeṣe/*

opponents,[5] while the *Nyāyavārttika* adds three more.[6] From the fact that the Candrānanda's *Vaiśeṣikasūtravṛtti* (*CV*) shares four among these six grounds,[7] we can probably trace the discussion made by the two schools from the time of the *NS* to the sixth century, the period that the *NV* and the *CV* were written. Relevant arguments can be found also in some texts of other schools, especially Kumārila's *Ślokavārttika* (*ŚV*) deals with this topic at some length. Kumārila, a proponent the theory of differentiation, mentions the Buddhist school and the Vaiśeṣika school as his opponents,[8] and in the Śabdapariccheda 35–37 he summarizes the opponents' opinion.[9]

The grounds of the theory of inclusion shown in the above texts are quite similar and have more elaboration than what is written in the *VS*. This fact allows us to conclude that the discussion on this topic had become bigger after the time of the *VS*, and taking this development of the discussion, the *PDhS* gave a more systematized explanation under the reflection of the epistemological theory of inference, especially the relationship between a mark and what is to be inferred.

3. Location of Means of Verbal Cognition in the *Vy* and the *NK*

3.1. Difference of Opinions in the Vaiśeṣika School

Before its description of the ground for the theory of inclusion, the *PDhS* briefly shows its basic standpoint which does not allow words to be a

---

5. *NS* 2.1.49–51: *śabdo 'numānam arthasyānupalabdher anumeyatvāt//* 49 *upalabdher advipravṛttitvāt//* 50 *sambandhāc ca //* 51
6. *NV*, p. 246,16–20.
7. *CV*, p. 69,19–70,9: ***etena śābdaṃ vyākhyātam****/ yathā kāryādismṛtisavyapekṣam anumānaṃ trikālaviṣayam atīndriyārthaṃ ca tathaiva śābdaṃ saṅketasmṛtyapekṣaṃ trikālaviṣayam atīndriyārthaṃ ca/ ... evaṃ śabdaḥ kāraṇaṃ sadarthasya pratipattau kuta iti cet/* ***asyedam iti buddhyapekṣatvāt****/ ... evam upamā[nā]dīnām antarbhāvaḥ/ evaṃ dve eva pramāṇe/ pramāṇatvaṃ ca pramīyate 'neneti pramāṇaṃ pramā pramāṇam iti vā/*
8. *ŚV*, p. 290,20: *tatrānumānam evedaṃ bauddhavaiśeṣikaiḥ śritam/*
9. *ŚV* śabdapariccheda 35cd–37, p. 194: *śabdānumānayor aikyaṃ dhūmād agnyanumānavat//* 35cd *anvayavyatirekābhyām ekapratyakṣadarśanāt/ sambandhapūrvakatvāc ca pratipattir ito yataḥ//* 36 *pratyakṣānyapramāṇatvāt tadadṛṣṭārthabodhanāt/ sāmānyaviṣayatvāc ca traikālyaviṣayāśrayāt//* 37
The interpretation that the seven phrases which end in ablative case-ending should all be regarded as referring to 'aikyam' is based on Pārthsārathi's comment. cf. *NRA* ad *ŚV* śabdapariccheda 110: *anvayavyatirekajatvaṃ sambandhapūrvakatvaṃ sāmānyaviṣayatvaṃ cāsiddham, anyaś ca hetucatuṣṭayam upamānādibhir anaikāntikam iti/*

pramāṇa.[10] The *Vy*, which is the first main commentary of the *PDhS* that we have been able to obtain so far, gives interesting comments on the passage of the *PDhS* as follows:

- Now, to describe the nature of knowledge (*vidyā*), there is a section which starts with [the words] "Knowledge is also of four kinds ..." in addition to un-knowledge (*avidyā*).
  <objection> verbal cognition (*śābdajñāna*) also has the shape of knowledge. Why, then, is it not examined here [in the *vidyā* section]?
  <answer> To let the difference of opinions be known. Precisely, the difference of opinions that some (*kecit*) include verbal cognition as inference whereas the others (*anye*) consider it as an individual *pramāṇa* exists among Vaiśeṣikas, and because of this fact, verbal cognition is not mentioned here [in the *vidyā* section].[11]

As is shown in the above passage, Vyomaśiva clearly says that there were different opinions with reference to the eligibility of words as a *pramāṇa*. This is confirmed also in the section of *parīkṣā* in which he gives comments so as to show that the *PDhS*'s description can be taken in both meanings, that is, as a meaning which stands for the theory of inclusion and as one which stands for the theory of differentiation. The *PDhS*'s description and the comments of the *Vy* are as follows.

(*PḌhS*, p. 203, 11)
śabdādīnām apy anumāne 'ntarbhāvaḥ samānavidhitvāt/ yathā prasiddhasmayasya liṅgadarśanaprasiddhyanusmaraṇābhyām atīndriye 'rthe bhavaty anumānam; evaṃ śabdādibhyo 'pīti/

1) *Vy*'s comment on '*api*'

The word '*api*' in the sentence "*śabdādīnām apy anumāne 'ntarbhāvaḥ*" is to be connected with the word '*anumane*'. Thus the sentence should be interpreted to mean that verbal cognition is included *also* with inference.[12]

---

10. *PDhS*, p. 183,6: *vidyāpi catruvidhā pratyakṣalaiṅgikasmṛtyārṣalakṣaṇā/*
11. *Vy*, p. 137,6: *athedānīṃ vidyāsvarūpanirūpaṇārthaṃ na kevalam avidyā* ***vidyāpi caturvidhā*** *ityādi prakaraṇam/ ... nanu śābdajñānasyāpi vidyārūpatvād ihānupanyāse kiṃ prayojanam? vipratipattijñāpanam iti/ tathā hi, śābdam anumāne 'ntarbhavatīti kecit, anye tu pramāṇāntaram iti vaiśeṣikāṇāṃ vipratipattis tenehānabhidhānam/*
12. This interpretation can be seen also in the *Kir* but not in the *NK*. The latter, which holds the theory of inclusion, does not seem to even allow that there is a possibility for it to be interpreted another way in contrast to the *Vy*.

2) *Vy*'s comment on '*śabdādi*'

The word '*śabdādi*' in the sentence is analyzed as "*śabda ādau yeṣāṃ tāni tathoktāni*", a *bahuvrīhi* compound, which can be interpreted both as *tadguṇasaṃvijñāna* and as *atadguṇasaṃvijñāna*.[13] In the former interpretation, verbal cognition is considered to be included with inference. while in the latter, verbal cognition is considered as an independent *pramāṇa*.

3.2. Arguments between the Two Theories Seen in the *Vy* and the *NK*

The *Vy* first introduces the theory of inclusion, as a case where compound '*śabdādi*', appearing in the above *PDhS*'s passage, is interpreted as *tadguṇasamvijñāna*. It also presents the ground for inclusion, which is based on the sameness of the cognitive process with that of inference,[14] after which discussion between the theory of inclusion and that of differentiation follows (Table 1). Vyomaśiva next discusses the validity of Veda as a *pramāṇa*, and eventually declares that words are to be established as a *pramāṇa* and to be differentiated from inference.[15]

---

13. *Vy*, p. 163,16–18: *tatra śabda ādau yeṣāṃ tāni tathoktāni. atas teṣām anumāne 'ntarbhāvo lakṣaṇaikyam iti tadguṇasaṃvijñānabahuvrīhyabhyupagame śabdasyāpy anumāne 'ntarbhāvaḥ/ atadguṇasaṃvijñāne śabdaṃ vinā apareṣām iti/*
14. *Vy*, p. 164,6–7: *ayam gośabdaḥ kakudādimadarthavān gośabdatvāt pūrvolabdhaivaṃvidhagośabdavad iti sambandhāvagamenārthapratipādakatvāc ca dhūmavat/*
15. *Vy*, p. 170,12–13: *śeṣañ cātra dūṣaṇapratisamādhānam* ***asmadgurubhir*** *vistareṇābhihitam iti nehoktam/ ataḥ śabdasyāptoktatvena prāmāṇyān nānumāne 'ntarbhāvaḥ/*
    Although Vyomaśiva uses the expression, "it is not to be stated here because our teacher already explained in detail" in several places (p. 140,25; 149,17; 173,18–19), it is not clear whom the word '*asmadguru*' refers to. However, the fact that he uses this expression after his criticism against *trairūpya* theory that is closely similar to that of the *NV* (*Vy*, p. 149,17) implies something related to the connection between Vyomośiva and Nyāya school.

Table 1: Summary of the argument between the theory of differentiation and the theory of inclusion in the *Vy*

	Theory of differentiation	Theory of inclusion
A	• An inferential mark like smoke conveys a cognition of fire through an essential relationship (*svābhāvikasambandha*), whereas a word conveys its meaning through a denotator-denoted relationship (*vācyavācakabhāva*) for those whom knows the conventional rule (*saṅketa*). • When sounds or words have specific order (*viśiṣṭānupūrvī*), they become *vācaka* and the others become *vācya*. • Words which have the shape of a sentence do not require even a conventional relationship (*samaya*).	• A conventional rule can be regarded as a constant one like an essential relationship. • '*śabda*' is a means of inference for the space.[16] • A word as a result of speaker's intention (*vivakṣā*) is regarded as a means of inference for the speaker's intention.
B	• An inferential mark requires three characters (*trairūpya*) to become valid, whereas a means of verbal cognition requires a character that is uttered by a trustworthy person (*āptoktatva*).	

In contrast to the *Vy*, the *NK* holds the theory of inclusion and refutes some opponent (*kaścit*) whose opinion is introduced in *pūrvapakṣa*. According to the *NKT* and the *NKP*, the commentaries of the *NK*, this '*kaścit*' is to be identified with Vyomaśiva (Table 2).

16. According to the Vaiśeṣika tenets, '*śabda*' is considered to be an inferential mark of space because it is what inheres into the space (*ākāśasamaveta*). This statement seems to be a sophistry to this argument.

Table 2: *Pūrvapakṣa* by 'somebody (*kaścit*)' in the *NK*

pūrvapakṣa A	(1) In inference, a *dharmin* (subject of cognitive event) which is qualified by its *sādhyadharma* is cognized through its *liṅga*, whereas in verbal cognition, this cognitive structure is not the case since both a word and its meaning can not be a *dharmin*. (2) There is no invariable relationship (*avinābhāva*) or inevitable rule (*niyama*) between a word and its meaning. Ground 1: Some words are used with deviation of place or time. Ex.) the word 'Yudhiṣṭhira' in the period that Yudhiṣṭhira does not exist; the word 'Laṅkā' in India. Ground 2: Some words are used in a deviated sense in other places. Ex.) The word '*caura*' means 'rice' in the south area, whereas it means 'thief' in the sacred area. * (2) is similar to the theory of inclusion A in the above *Vy*'s argument.
pūrvapakṣa B	If a means of verbal cognition were an inferential mark, it would become a *pramāṇa* by satisfying *trairūpya*. However, in reality, the validity of verbal cognition is established by satisfying not *trairūpya* but by the character to be uttered by a trustworthy person (*āptoktatva*). * This is equal to *Vy*'s theory of differentiation B.

There is no corresponding description with the *pūrvapakṣa* A (1) found in the *Vy*, but A (2), which pays attention to the difference between the relationship required in inference and the one in verbal cognition, and B, which points out the difference between main conditions for each cognition—one is *trairūpya* and the other is *āptoktatva*—can be traced to some statements in the *Vy*.[17] After this *pūrvapakṣa* shown in Table 2, the *NK* presents a discussion between one who holds the theory of differentiation and one who holds the theory of inclusion. The following Table 3 summarizes Śrīdhara's opinion against the *pūrvapakṣa*.

17. However, *pūrvapakṣa* A is more similar to the grounds for the theory of differentiation that Kumārila gives in his *ŚV* and that Jayanta Bhaṭṭa gives in his *NM*. It is to be noted that there is no determinate evidence that Śrīdhara intended Vyomaśiva with the word '*kaścit*', despite the description of the *NKT* and the *NKP*.

Table 3: The answer of Śrīdhara: theory of inclusion

Answer to *pūrvapakṣa* A	(1) Meaning of a word is understood under the cognitive structure of inference, where a speaker is considered to be a *pakṣa*, the uttered word a *liṅga*, the speaker's intention (*vivakṣā*) a *sādhya*. Ex.) (*pratijñā*) The person who is being cognized as *dharmin* has a intention to convey the meaning of what has a hump on its back. (*hetu*) Because he is uttering the word 'cow.' (*dṛṣṭānta*) Like me [when I utter 'cow']. (2) There is no essential relationship between a word and its meaning. (This idea shares its content with *pūrvapakṣa* A) It is no use making distinction that the word '*caura*' directly conveys the meaning of thief to *āryans*, whereas it becomes a *liṅga* for the southern inhabitants to let them infer the meaning of rice.[18] * Both (1) and (2) are similar to Table1's theory of inclusion.[19]
Answer to *pūrvapakṣa* B	Like smoke, which works as a *liṅga* of fire only when it is qualified by some specific natures such as 'going upwards with continuation', the word 'cow' conveys its meaning only when it is qualified by 'being uttered by a trustworthy person.' Under this fact, an undesirable situation, like the meaning of a word not conveyed by insanity or fraud, can be avoided.

4. Relevant Discussion in Other Texts

4.1. Description in the *NV* and the *CV*

The theory of differentiation itself had been already presented before the *Vy* and the *NK* as an answer to the opponents introduced in the *NS* 2.1.49–51. Its assertion can be summarized into two points: (1) relationships required in each cognitive process are different, and (2) the validity of verbal cognition depends on the condition that the word is used by a trustworthy person (*āptoktatva*), not on three conditions for a valid inferential mark (*trairūpya*). Uddyotakara discusses especially the first point at some length, in which he denies a permanent relationship, such as a natural relationship and inherence, between a word and its object. Then he attributes the reason that each word conveys its meaning into the existence

18. Śrīdhara presents the following syllogism: *āryāṇāṃ api cauraśabdād arthapratītiḥ liṅgapūrvikā, cauraśabdajanitapratipattitvāt, ubhayābhimatadākṣiṇātyaprayujyamānacauraśabdajanitapratipattivat/* (*NK*, p. 504, 1–2).
19. However, as far as answer (1) is concerned, it seems to have similarity with the theory of inclusion presented by Buddhists, especially that of Dharmakīrti. cf. *PV*, I, k. 213 and *PVSV*, p. 107,20–25.

of a 'conventional relationship (*samaya*)' between them. He eventually asserts that this conventional relationship is different from the one that is the ground for inference because it is variously established according to places or people.[20]

On the other hand, Candrānanda, who attributes the reason for the validity of verbal cognition to a 'conventional rule (*saṅketa*)', holds that words are to be included in inference because the process of occurrence of both cognitions is the same anyway, whether the relationship between two things is conventional or essential.[21] The Vaiśeṣika school already argued conventionality of relationship between a word and its meaning in the *VS* 7.2.19–24.[22]

As is shown above, the points of argument between the theory of inclusion and that of differentiation, which can be summarized into two points—relationships required in each cognitive process are different, and the main condition(s) of validity for each cognition are different—had been discussed before the period of the *Vy* and the *NK*, since the time of the *NS*. Although the two advocates faced against each other for a long time, their opinions are, in practice, almost the same at the point where they both regard a relationship between a word and its meaning as a conventional one (*samaya*, *saṅketa*) and admit that '*āptoktatva*' is a factor for both cognitions. Their differences regard whether *samaya* or *saṅketa* can be identified with the ground of inference or not, and whether '*āptoktatva*' should be regarded as a qualifying factor of a logical mark or as a main condition that directly conveys a word's meaning to a listener. Besides, it is to be noted here that the *NV* and the *CV* deal with this topic focusing on the cognition of a word and there seems to be no discussion in the *Vy* and the *NK* that *support*s the theory of inclusion in terms of a verbal cognition being considered as a

---

20. *NV* ad *NS* 2.1.55. There is a similar discussion found also in the *NM* (*NM*, p. 591, 22–p. 592, 3).

21. *CV*, p. 70, 1–8: *evaṃ śabdaḥ kāraṇaṃ sadarthasya pratipattau kuta iti cet/ asyedam iti buddhyapekṣatvāt/ yathā 'arthasya' pratipattāv iyaṃ hastaceṣṭā kāraṇaṃ pratipattavyā iti vṛttasaṅketaḥ tāṃ hastaceṣṭāṃ dṛṣṭvā tataḥ śabdāt kāraṇād arthaṃ pratipadyate evam 'asyārthasya pratipattāv ayaṃ śabdaḥ kāraṇam' iti prasiddhasaṅketas tataḥ śabdāt kāraṇād arthaṃ pratipadyate, yathā abhinayāder api arthaṃ pratipadyante laukikā evaṃ śabdo 'rthasya saṅketavaśena vyañjakatvāt kāraṇam iti vṛttikāraḥ/*

22. *VS* 7.2.19–24: *śabdārthāv asambaddhau//* 19 ... *sāmayikaḥ śabdād arthapratyayaḥ//* 24. It is to be noted here that the *Upaskāra* lacks three *sūtra*s of *VS* 7.2.21–23 preserved in the *CV* and that this is one of the parts that has a significant difference in the *sūtra*'s preservation in each commentary.

cognition of a sentence, not a word.

4.2. Description in the *ŚV* and the *Kir*

Kumārila, who asserts the differentiation of verbal cognition from inference, refutes the theory of inclusion in his *ŚV*. The following Table 4 is a summary of the argument.

Table 4: Location of verbal cognition in the *ŚV*: theory of differentiation and respect for sentence-cognition

A	Verbal cognition cannot have the same cognitive structure as inference. Ground: (1) A word cannot work as a *pakṣa* (*ŚV* 59–68ab) (2) A word cannot work as a *liṅga* (*ŚV* 68cd–96) • A word does not have the first character of *trairūpya*. • A word does not have the second character of *trairūpya*.
B	Understanding of the meaning of a word (*pada*) can not be regarded as a *pramāṇa* because it is nothing but remembrance.

Kumārila begins the discussion on the relationship between verbal cognition[23] and inference, under the level of consideration that verbal cognition is equal to cognition of a word. He then proves that means of verbal cognition cannot be either *pakṣa* or *liṅga* through argument A. He concludes with argument B that understanding of the meaning of a word is nothing but a remembrance (*smṛti*) and cannot be a *pramāṇa*. After further discussion, he comes to say that when *śabda* is talked about, what is to be discussed is not cognition of a word, but that of a sentence and eventually affirms that all the discussions in the argument A and B are not essential for what is relevant to the differentiation or inclusion of verbal cognition.[24] As he says:

> Whether cognition from a word (*pada*) is a *pramāṇa* or not, there's no defect for those who hold that *āgama* is a *pramāṇa* (*āgamavādin*) because the meaning of *āgama* is the meaning of a sentence (108).
> In fact, knowledge with reference to the meaning of a sentence occurs

---

23. *ŚV*, śabdapariccheda 54cd: *pade tāvat kṛto yatnaḥ parair ity atra varṇyate|*
24. However, it is to be noted here that the Nyāya and the Vaiśeṣika referred to the word in general including daily language by their use of the word '*śabda*', whereas the Mīmāṃsā referred to the Veda by the same word. The former attributed the ground for validity of *śabda* to *āptoktatva* (in case of Vaiśeṣika, validity of *śabda* as inference), whereas the latter attributed it to *apauruṣeyatva*.

> through words [which constitute a sentence] without experience of any relationship. Therefore, this [verbal cognition] is different from [inference] (109).
> The ground of the above will be established in the *vākyādhikaraṇa* section. Besides, all that others have pointed out [as the ground of the theory of inclusion] cannot be established with reference to cognition of a sentence (110).
> Those who were afraid of differentiating [verbal cognition] from inference in considering that a sentence can be understood only from the knowledge of words [in the sentence], even though it is not seen before, suffered in vain when they tried to prove the sameness of cognition of a word [with inference].[25]

The above description in the *ŚV* signifies the denial of a discussion made in the *NV* and the *CV* that tried to prove the theory of inclusion under the grounds that the relationship required in both cognitions would be the same.[26]

Taking into account the *ŚV*'s description, it appears to be futile to argue the difference or the sameness between verbal cognition and inference focusing on cognition of a word. Therefore, it is to be noted here that the *NK* still adopted the theory of inclusion in terms of cognition of a word. Although some descriptions about cognition of a sentence appear in the *NK* after Table 3–(2) in the form of denial of theory that a word and its meaning have an essential relationship, it has, strangely enough, the same content with Vyomaśiva's statement which asserts that meaning of a sentence is conveyed by the denotative function of words which have specific word order (*viśiṣṭānupūrvī*).[27] Besides, more strangely, there are

---

25. *ŚV*, śabdapariccheda, 108–111: *pramāṇam anumānam vā yady api syāt padān mitiḥ/ vākyārthasyāgamārthatvād doṣo nāgamavādinām//* 108 *vākyārthe tu padārthebhyaḥ sambandhānubhavād ṛte/ buddhir utpadyate tena bhinnāsāv akṣabuddhivat//* 109 *vākyādhikaraṇe cāsya hetoḥ siddhir bhaviṣyati/ sarveṣāṃ ca paroktānāṃ vākyābuddhāv asiddhatā//* 110 *vākyeṣv adṛṣṭeṣv api sārthakeṣu padārthavinmātratayā pratītim/ dṛṣṭvānumānavyatirekabhītāḥ kliṣṭāḥ padābhedavicārāṇāyām//* 111
26. *NM*, pp. 403–409. Argument on the relationship between *śabda* and *anumāna* is already made in the Dignāga's *Pramāṇasamuccaya*. Dignāga, who denies *śabda* as an independent *pramāṇa*, discusses this issue in the auto-commentary on the verse 4, the first chapter of this text which held the theory of differentiation. However, in this argument he seems to be avoiding answering clearly the question on the differentiation of sentence-cognition from inference. See Kitagawa [1965: 90].
27. *NK*, p. 505, 7: *śabdasya hi nijaṃ sāmarthyaṃ śabdatvam, āgantukaṃ tu*

other passages in the *NK* which refers to mutual-dependence (*ākaṅkṣā*), proximity (*sannidhi*), and consistency (*yogyatā*), three necessary factors for verbal cognition in regarding it as the cognition of a sentence but without considering its relevance with inference.[28]

Unlike the *Vy* and the *NK*, where some similarity can be found between the discussion presented, in spite of their opposite standpoints, the description of the *Kir* is unique. It deals with this issue regarding verbal cognition as cognition of a sentence by quoting many passages from Udayana's own *Nyāyakusumāñjali*[29] and by referring to a theory of sentences, which seems similar to that of the Mīmāṃsā school and Vācaspati. Udayana's standpoint is handed down to the later Nyāya-Vaiśeṣika school, such as in the *TS*, which declares verbal cognition to be nothing but cognition of a sentence.[30]

5. Context of the *PDhS*'s Commentarial Texts

5.1. Vyomaśiva, Śrīdhara, Udayana

After Udayana's period, in which the Vaiśeṣika school and the Nyāya school practically merged into one school, Mithilā, where Udayana flourished, became a center of the Nyāya-Vaiśeṣika school. Whereas Bengal, where Śrīdhara is said to have had as his academic base, lost its fame and gave its academic position to Mithilā.[31] As has been seen above, the *Vy* takes the same route as the later Nyāya-Vaiśeṣika school in terms of its regarding means of verbal cognition as a *pramāna*, and the *Kir*, which takes verbal cognition as cognition of a sentence, also has similarity with the later Nyāya-Vaiśeṣika school texts. In contrast, the *NK* observes the *VS* and the *PDhS*, which advocate the inclusion of words into inference, in

---

sāmarthyaṃ saṅketo viśiṣṭā cānupūrvī/ tasmād eva ca sāmarthyadvitayāt tadarthapratyayopapateh, sambandhāntarakalpanāvaiyarthyam, dṛṣṭāt kāryopapatāv adṛṣṭakalpanānavakāśāt/

28. *NK*, p. 22, 6–8: ... *padārthānām eva yogyatāsannidhimatām anyonyākāṇ-kṣānibandhanaḥ sambandhaḥ/ tathā ca ... vākyārtho gamyata eva/ NK*, p. 18, 4 also is the statement of same type.

29. In the *Kir*, which might be considered as a compilation of Udayana's own texts, there are vast quotations from the *Nyāyavārttikatātaryapariśuddhi* and the *Nyāyakusumāñjali*.

30. *TS*, p. 54, 17: *vākyārthajñānaṃ śābdajñānam/ tatkaraṇaṃ śabdaḥ/*

31. At least Thakur [1957] [2003] advocates so. It is to be noted here that some *Navya-nyāya* scholars, such as *Jayadeva* and *Raghunātha Śiromaṇi*, flourished in Bengal.

taking verbal cognition as cognition of a word. The fact that the *NK* tries to protect the sameness between verbal cognition and inference through "a word-level" discussion, in spite of Kumārila's criticism, lets us suppose that Śrīdhara had some "intention" behind this commentarial activity.

As has been presented by Hirano [2003] and Wada & Hirano [2007], commentarial activities can be regarded as a kind of communication in which a receiver of messages in original texts sends his interpretation of them to another receiver. Whenever messages are interpreted, they are biased by social context, no matter what the messages may be. Although social context is something vast and ambiguous, at least as far as systematic messages passed down among limited communities, such as philosophical theory etc. are concerned, they are to be interpreted under the strong influence of individual and concrete contexts in which the theory was handed down. In other words, although each commentarial activity is no doubt an individual intentional act, it is not completely independent from the commentator's surroundings and done with reference to interpretations of his surroundings that are *psychologically* near him.[32]

With reference to the relationship between Vyomaśiva, Śrīdhara, and Udayana, that of the latter two has been well considered and it is commonly accepted that Udayana criticizes Śrīdhara. However, as for the relationship between Vyomaśiva and the latter two, it does not seem to have been investigated enough at least in western and Japanese research. Although Dr. Matilal says "Vyomaśiva is mentioned with respect by Śrīdhara and Udayana",[33] and this opinion seems to be tacitly accepted, the evidence for it does not seem to have been investigated since even Dr. Matilal himself does not refer to it.

In contrast, among Indian researchers, Dr. D.C. Bhattacharya already in 1958 pointed out some phrases of the *NK* in which Śrīdhara refers to Vyomaśiva by the word 'eke' etc. and declared "the scathing criticism

32. As is well known, R. K. Merton developed the theory of reference groups: the one to which an individual refers as a basis for conformity and comparison in terms of his judgment or a behavior pattern. According to his achievement, one's reference group is not always the same with his membership group: the one to which he practically belongs (Merton [1961]). In addition, it is obscure how much the notion of 'school'—a kind of indicator that is now used to discuss Indian thought—made scholars of that period have a sense of belonging. It should be remembered here that there are quite a few scholars who composed commentaries on several schools' fundamental texts such as Vācaspati. Thus their frame of reference should be investigated without limiting it to the notion of 'school' in common usage.

33. Matilal [1977: 68–69].

of the solution of an 'un-schooled' intellectual is also directed against Vyomaśiva".[34] Dr. Parikh, in the *NK*'s introduction, also asserts "Śrīdhara preferred to differ from Vyomaśiva" on the ground that the *NKP*, a commentary of the *NK*, identifies the opinion of 'somebody' critically quoted by Śrīdhara with Vyomaśiva.[35] In recent research, Dr. A. Thakur enumerates eighteen criticisms toward Vyomaśiva from the *NK*.[36]

The main points that have been pointed out about the three commentators of the *PDhS* in preceding research can be summarized as follows:[37]

(Vyomaśiva)[38]

- He is considered to be a Śaiva scholar who flourished in south India. His active period is thought to be the latter half of the10th century from the fact that his patron seems to be Śrīharṣa of Malava dynasty, who was a grandson of King Bhoja (K. Potter points out the possibility that he may be from Kashmir).
- Vyomaśiva's teacher seems to be a great scholar whose texts mentioned Buddhist opinions.[39]
- Udayana refers to him by the word '*ācārya*'.[40]

(Śrīdhara)

- He was from Bhurisrshti village, West Bengal, and had Pandudasa as his patron, who was his student also.

---

34. "The scathing criticism of the solution of an 'un-schooled' intellectual is also directed against Vyomaśiva" (D.C. Bhattacharya [1958: 12]). Since the original word is '*aśrutavyākhyātṛ*' (*NK*, p. 361, 11), 'untaught commentator(s)' would be a more literal translation. The *NKP* puts comment on this word as "*aśrutavyākhyātṛṇāṃ iti aśrutam eva gurubhyaḥ svamanīṣikayā ye vyācaṣṭe teṣāṃ vyomaśivādīṇāṃ*" to identify it with a group represented by Vyomaśiva that explains its tenets 'in being indifferent to a teacher's word.' Thakur [2003: 268] also points out the same *NK*'s comment so as to prove that Śrīdhara took critical position against Vyomaśiva.
35. Parikh [1991: intro. iii].
36. It is to be noted here that Vyomaśiva is referred to by name in the *NK*. Dr. Thakur's assertion is based on the fact that there are many passages which refer to the theory of the 'other[s]' by the word *eke*, *anye*, *kecit*, and the *NKP* identifies some of them with Vyomaśiva. He says the way of identification in the *NKP* is 'faithful' (Thakur [2003: 268]).
37. This summary is mainly based on D.N. Bhattacharya [1958], Potter [1977] and Thakur [2003].
38. Dating of the life-spans of the three scholars is based on Potter [1977].
39. Vyomaśiva refers to '*asmadguru*' in *Vy*, p. 130, 140, 149, 171, 173 etc.
40. Udayana also does not refer to Vyomaśiva by name. Vardhamāna, who is a commentator of the *Kir* identifies '*ācārya*' in the phrase "*viśeṣaguṇavattvāt pṛthivyādivad ity ācāryāḥ*" in the *Kir* with Vyomaśiva (*Kiraṇāvalīprakāśa* p. 350, 10).

- He composed the *NK* in A.D. 991, as its colophon says.
- Although his name was well-known by later scholars, the *NK* could not establish one stream. Padmanabha's *Nyāyakandalīsāra* is the only text known by us.[41]
- There are many expressions that signify 'other' such as *eke*, *anye*, *apare*, and *kecit*. They are almost all able to be identified by the *NKP* and most of them seem to be a refutation of Vyomaśiva. Some ironical expressions like 'uneducated commentator' and 'logician' are applied to Vyomaśiva.[42]
- According to Dr. Thakur, Śrīdhara thinks that Vyomaśiva does not understand Praśastapāda's intention.[43]

(Udayana)

- He was a well-known Mithila scholar from Kariyona, Bihar.

5.2. Groups in V-school, with N-school and Mīmāṃsā School

With reference to the social context in which the three commentators lived, Dr. Thakur introduced a noteworthy report. First, he presented the fact that the *Yaśastilakacampū* (*YTC*), of a Jaina scholar Somadeva Sūri, mentions two Vaiśeṣika schools, that is Saiddhāntika on one hand and Tārkika on the other.[44] In addition, in his assertion that the Vaiśeṣika school accepted

---

41. The *NKT*, the *NKP* and the *Nyāyakusumodgama* are known as three commentaries of the *NK*, two of which—the *NKT* and the *NKP*—are works of Jainas.
42. Śrīdhara uses this expression at least twice in his *NK* (*NK*, p. 17,3; p. 639,9). The word Tārkika may possibly signify one branch group in the Vaiśeṣika school. Refer to 5.2 of this paper.
43. Dr. Thakur seems to consider the following passage as its ground. *NK*, p. 359, 12: *durakṣaradurvidagdhānāṃ yukutim ācāryavacanaṃ cotsṛjatām andhānām iva pade pade kiyat skhalitaṃ upadarśayiṣyāmaḥ*/ Before this description, the opposition made by '*kecit*' is presented (*NK*, p. 359,7), which the *NKP* identifies with the opinion of Vyomaśiva (*NKP*, p. 357,18).
44. Thakur [1957: intro. 16] says that these two branches differed in their interpretations with reference to a cause of liberation. Although Dr. Thakur himself does not pick up the relevant passages, he seems to find the following passage of the *YTC* as evidence. *YTC*, p. 2: *sakalaniṣkalāptaprāptamantratantrāp ekṣadīkṣālakṣaṇāc chraddhāmātrānusaraṇān mokṣaḥ iti saiddhāntikavaiśeṣikāḥ, dravyaguṇakarmasāmānyasamavāyāntyaviśeṣābhāvābhidhānānāṃ padārthānāṃ sādharmyavaidharmyāvabodhatantrāj jñānamātrāt iti tārkikavaiśeṣikāḥ* ...*/* According to its Hindi commentary and introduction, pp. 16–17 (prastāvanā), Saiddhāntika, who was a Śaiva, emphasized *śraddhā* as the direct cause of liberation, whereas Tārkika regarded disappearance of suffering brought by knowledge of six categories as the cause.

theism under the influence of the Pāśupata school,[45] he points out that the Kauṇḍinya's *Pañcārthabhāṣya* classifies *pramāṇa* into perception, inference, verbal cognition, and that this classification has similarity with that of Vyomaśiva.

Dr. Thakur asserts also that Nyāya scholars who flourished in Kashmir did not have a favorable attitude toward the Vaiśeṣika school. Specifically he emphasizes that Jayanta tried to regard it as a follower of the Nyāya school.[46] In fact, when Jayanta mentions the difference of classification of *pramāṇa*s between some schools, he does not refer to the Vaiśeṣika school in spite of his referring to Buddhists as advocates of the theory of inclusion. This fact would support Dr. Thakur's opinion.[47]

Furthermore, Dr. Thakur gives a noteworthy indication about the relationship between the Vaiśeṣika school and Śālikanatha, a Prābhākara scholar. He implies that Śālikanātha, who flourished in Bengal, had an intimate relationship with the Vaiśeṣika school and that an anonymous author of the *Praśastapādabhāṣyavyākhyāna*, who is mentioned by Cinnambhaṭṭa in his commentary on the *Tarkabhāṣā*, can be identified with Śālikanātha.[48] He even presents fifteen fragments of the *VS* quoted in Śālianātha's *Ṛjuvimālā* and *Prakaraṇapañcikā* (*PrP*).[49] Although this is not pointed out by Dr. Thakur himself, the fact that Śālikanātha considers cognition based on the 'secular word (*laukikaśabda*)' as inference in his *PrP* seems to be noted. Śālikanātha declares that *laukikaśabda* is nothing

---

45. Bronkhorst [1996] also deals with the acceptance of theism in the Vaiśeṣika school.
46. Thakur [2003: 381]. Dr. Thakur presents the following passage as its ground. "*vaiśeṣikāh punar asmadanuyāyinaḥ eva* ...// *NM* (I), p. 9, 5".
47. *NM* (I), p. 75, 7–11: *pratyakṣam evaikaṃ pramāṇam iti cārvākāḥ/ pratyakṣānumāne dve eveti bauddhāḥ/ pratyakṣam anumānam āptavacanaṃ ceti trīṇi pramāṇānīti sākhyāḥ/ ādhikyam api pramāṇāṃ mīmāṃsakarabhṛtayaḥ pratipannavantaḥ/*
Jayanta ironically says in another place that, 'The wise (*vipaścitaḥ*) include words with inference." According to the *Tippaṇi*, the editor's own commentary, this '*vipaścitaḥ*' refers to the authors of the *VS*, the *PDhS*, and the *NK*. "*ata eva hi manyante śabdasyāpi vipaścitaḥ/ āptavādāvisaṃvādasāmānyād anumānatām//* *NM* (I), p. 403", "*vipaścitaḥ kaṇādapraśastpādayaḥ/ 'etena śabdaṃ vyākhyātam' ityādisūtrabhāṣyakandalādiṣu asya vistaro draṣṭavyaḥ/ Tippaṇi* (I), p. 403, p. 23."
However, the phrase '*āptavādāvisaṃvādasāmānyād*' lets us suppose, with the higher possibility, that this passage is a summarized opinion of Dignāga and Dharmakīrti. cf. *Pramāṇasamuccaya*, II, k. 5ab, *PVSV*, p. 108, 1–6.
48. Thakur [1957] [2003: 251].
49. Thakur [2003: 251–256]. Interestingly enough, some of them are accompanied by the phrase '*bhagavān kāśyapo*'.

but inference, using the descriptions of the *VS* as a proof.[50]

6. Investigation: Two Hypotheses

From the fact that the Vyomaśiva and the Śrīdhara took opposite standpoints, in spite of their knowing about the difference of views in the Vaiśeṣika school, we must interpret the authors' intentions for doing so.[51] In this section, what these *PDhS*'s commentators intended is suppositionally examined through the above philological work, with the help of the prior research.

Hypothesis 1: Innovation and Conservatism

First, the difference in their standpoints can be attributed to their degree of commitment to the Nyāya school and loyalty towards the Vaiśeṣika tenet. In this hypothesis, the innovative movement, in which orientation to a fusion of Vaiśeṣika with Nyāya, occurred practically existed at the period of Vyomaśiva, and Vyomaśiva himself followed the movement, or strategically showed his commitment to the Nyāya school, by taking the viewpoint of the theory of differentiantion.[52]

On the other hand, Śrīdhara, who advocated the theory of inclusion, is interpreted to have followed an orientation of loyalty towards traditional

50. *PrP*, p. 244,20–p. 245,9. The *MMU*, a later manual-book of the Bhāṭṭa Mīmāṃsā school criticizes the theory of Prābhākara Mīmāṃsā school and the Vaiśeṣika that regards a secure word as inference.
51. As for Śrīdhara, we cannot be convinced that he knew a difference of opinion existed in his period, for, as has been seen in section 4 of this paper, his criticism against the theory of inclusion cannot be determined to be directed to Vyomaśiva.
52. Here I am using the word 'strategically' and 'orientation' in while taking Habermas' theory of action into account. As is well known, Habermas divided action into two categories: one oriented toward reaching understanding (Verständigung) and one oriented toward success (Erfolg) and positioned the latter to be a strategic action in which the agent aims to achieve some aim through his statement itself. Among Indian commentarial texts, we often come across statements that seem to be made not because commentators oriented towards reaching an understanding with opponents but because they oriented to protect an original text's legitimacy. Especially distorted interpretations in which a commentator tries to connect fundamental texts' descriptions with the philosophical context of his period can be often found. This is a typical pattern of action oriented toward success in which a commentator tries to establish a universal validity of the fundamental text, where commentarial activity itself has more significant meaning than the contents of the commentary.

Vaiśeṣika theory or strategically showed his orientation.[53]

As we have seen in section 5.2, there is a statement in which Jayanta tries, according to Dr. Thakur, to put the Vaiśeṣika school under a subordinate position to that of the Nyāya school, and it is known from the *YTC* that there were two groups—Saiddhāntika and Tārkika—in the Vaiśeṣika school.[54] This distinction is made according to the difference of opinion about liberation, which, needless to say, should not be interpreted as parallel to differences of opinion about the location of verbal cognition in the *Vy* and the *NK*. However, the fact that these two texts have different opinions also on the topic of liberation,[55] could be taken into account as strengthening the possibility of this hypothesis.

Scholars are obliged to refrain from judging the period when an approach to the Nyāya school took place, for it is difficult to guess the situation inside the school at the period that the *VS* and the *PDhS* were written. This is due to their simple description, even though both texts present the theory of inclusion as their own.

However, given that the *PDhS* had a role as a manual and that there must have been some branches in the Vaiśeṣika school before the text, the possibility is undeniable that there had been a theory of inclusion before the *PDhS* drew *Vaiśeṣika theories* together and, as it were, gave *the Vaiśeṣika theory* a new point of departure.[56]

---

53. In reality, as we have seen in section 3.2, Śrīdhara himself does not refer to Vyomaśiva by name and the intimacy of the *NK*'s criticism to the *Vy*'s assertion is not very high. Thus, it is not clear whether the former took the latter as its target of criticism or not. Their comments may possibly be an interpretation that the commentators made up in order to explain the situation of the Vaiśeṣika school at their period.
54. *YTC*, p. 2, 5–7 and *YTC*, introduction, p. 26. According to *YTC*'s introdution, Jaina scholar Haribhadra Suri in his *Saddarśanasamuccaya* says that both the Nyāya school and the Vaiśeṣika school are Śaiva, Guṇaratna, who is a commentator of the text, identifies the Nyāya school with the Śaiva (*sadāśivabhakta*) and Vaiśeṣika with the Pāśupata.
55. There is also a significant difference between the *Vy* and the *NK* regarding the theory of liberation. The former uses an intellectualistic point of view in terms of the means of liberation, whereas the latter emphasizes the necessity of *śravaṇa*, *manana*, and *nidhidhyāsana* and regards both knowledge and religious acts as essential for liberation. The *SDS* introduces the theory of liberation, which is near Śrīdhara's, as the Vaiśeṣika theory (*SDS*, p. 210, 2–p. 211, 8).
56. W. Ruben [1928: 4, note 23] points out the possibility that the Vaiśeṣika school considered verbal cognition as another independent *pramāṇa*.

Hypothesis 2: Distance to Prābhākara Mīmāṃsā School

Secondly, the fact that Śrīdhara adopted the theory of inclusion can be regarded not as a sign of observing Vaiśeṣika theory, but as his preference for Prābhākara Mīmāṃsā theory. As has been pointed out by Dr. Thakur, Śālikanātha, who was from Bengal, shows his commitment toward the Vaiśeṣika theory. In addition, Śālikanātha, who belonged to the Prābhākara Mīmāṃsā school that regarded secure words as inference, quotes the *VS* passages in order to support Prābhākara theory in the *PrP*. These facts let us imagine an intimate relationship between Śrīdhara and Śālikanātha, both of whom adopted the theory of inclusion, not to mention the relationship between the Vaiśeṣika school and the Prābhākara Mīmāṃsā in Bengal.[57] In this case, the reason why Śrīdhara adopted the theory of inclusion is attributed to a reference to a group, formed on the basis of region beyond the difference of schools rather than a reference to a group formed on the basis of the scholarly notion of 'schools'.

Of course the above two ideas are still in the hypothetical stage, and further investigation remains necessary. The following Figure 2 is an illustration of the above two hypotheses.

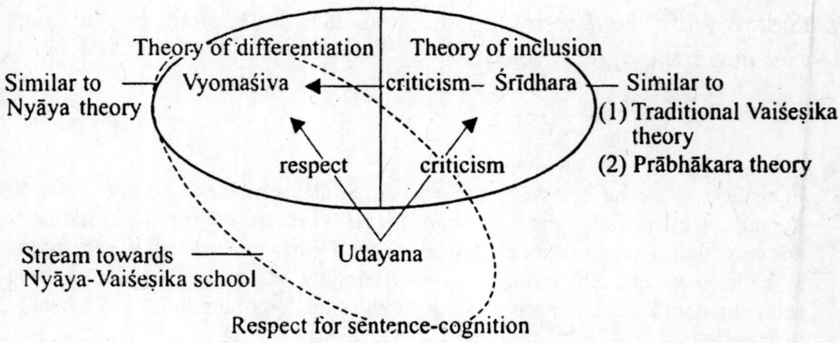

Figure 2: Relationships between the *PDhS* commentaries: groups in the Vaiśeṣika school

57. The *NK*'s similarity with the Prābhākara school can be found also in argument about the necessity of *liṅgaparāmarśa*. Refer to Appendix.

7. Appendix: Difference of Opinion with Reference to the Theory of *Liṅgaparāmarśa*

In the *anumāna* section of the *PDhS*, there are some traces that the *Vy* and the *Kir* imported the theory of reconsideration of inferential marks (*liṅgaparāmarśa*) from the Nyāya school to incorporate it into the Vaiśeṣika system,[58] whereas the *NK* denied the necessity of this cognition.[59] In brief, the former two texts asserted cognitive process:

vyāptismaraṇa → *liṅgaparāmarśa* → *anumiti*

whereas the *NK* asserted one:

vyāptismaraṇa → *anumiti*

Another description of the same content can be found also in the *smṛti* section of the *PDhS*. It appears as follows:

> *liṅgadarśanecchānusmaraṇādyapekṣād ātmamanasosaṃyogaviśeṣāt paṭvābhyāsādarapratyayajanitāc ca saṃskārāt dṛṣṭaśrutānubhūteṣv artheṣu śeṣāvyavasāyecchānusmaraṇadveṣahetur atītaviṣayā smṛtir iti/.*[60]

From the above passage, the following inferential cognitive process can be reconstructed.

liṅgadarśana → *smṛti* → *śeṣānuvyavasāya*

The set of the *Vy* and the *Kir*, and the *NK* give different comments on the above *PDhS*'s passage, that is to say, the *Vy* and the *Kir* interpret the word '*śeṣa*' to mean '*anumeya*', the word '*śeṣa-anuvyavasāya*' to mean '*liṅgaparāmarśa*' or '*vyāptipakṣadharmatopapannaliṅgavijñānam*',[61]

---

58. *PDhS*, p. 197,3–6: *vidhis tu yatra yatra dhūmas tatra tatrāgnir agnyabhāve ca dhūmo 'pi na bhavatīti/ evaṃ prasiddhasamayasyāsandigdhadhūmadarśanāt sāhacaryānusmaraṇāt tadanantaram agnyadhyavasāyo bhavati. evaṃ sarvatra deśakālāvinābhūtam itarasya liṅgam//*
   Both the *Vy* and the *Kir* interpret '*agnyadhyavasāya*' in the above passage of the *PDhS* as Bahuvrīhi and paraphrase it as *liṅgaparāmarśa*. (*Vy*, p. 156,3: *agnir adhyavasīyate aneneti agnyadhyavasāyaḥ parāmarśajñānam/ Kir*, p. 198,7: *agnir adhyavasīyate 'neneti adhyavasāyaḥ parāmarśaḥ/*).
59. This passage in which the *NK* denies necessity of *parāmarśa* has been pointed out by Marui [2005: 88–89]. However, my opinion differs in terms of his having an idea that the whole Vaiśeṣika school rejected *parāmarśa* theory.
60. *PDhS*, p. 243, 8–11.
61. *Vy*, p. 212, 15: *upayuktāl liṅgād anumeyaḥ śeṣaḥ, so 'nuvyavasīyate aneneti*

whereas the *NK* interprets the same word '*śeṣa-anuvyavasāya*' to mean that '*anumeyajñānam*'.[62]

We are here able to confirm the fact that the *Vy* and the *Kir* put the theory of *liṅgaparāmarśa* into the Vaiśeṣika system, whereas the *NK* rejected it probably due to Śrīdhara's reference to Vaiśeṣika traditional theory or due to his commitment to Prābhākara's theory,[63] with which the above two hypotheses can be strengthened.[64]

References

Primary Sources

Kiraṇāvalī (*Kir*) of Udayana, edited with *Padārthadharmasaṅgraha* (*PDhS*) by Jitendra S. Jetly, Vadodara: Oriental Institute, 1971 (rpt. 1991).

Kiraṇāvalī of Udayana, edited with *Kiraṇāvalīprakāśa* of Vardhamāna by Narendra Chandra Vedantatirtha, Fasc. 2, Calcutta: Bibliotheca Indica, 1956.

Mānameyodaya (*MMU*) of Nārāyaṇa, edited by Kunhan Raja and Suranarayan Ṣastri, Madras: Adyar Library and Research Centre, 1975.

Nyāyamañjalī (*NM*) of Jayanta Bhaṭṭa, edited with *Tippaṇī* by K.S. Varadacharya, Vol. I, Madras: Oriental Researh Institute, 1969.

Nyāyakandalī (*NK*) of Śrīdhara, edited with *Tippaṇa* (*NKT*), *Pañjikā* (*NKP*), *Nyāyakusumodgama* by R. T. Vyas, Vadodara: Oriental Institute, 1991.

Nyāyasūtra (*NS*) of Gautama, edited with *Bhāṣya* of Vātsyāyana by Anantalal Thakur, Delhi: Indian Counsil of Philosophical Research, 1996.

Nyāyabhāṣyavārttika (*NV*), Uddyotakara, edited by Anantalal Thakur, Delhi: Indian Counsil of Philosophical Research, 1997.

Prakaraṇapañcikā (*PrP*) of Śālikanāthamiśra, edited by Mukunda Shastri,

---

śeṣānuvyavasāyaḥ parāmarśajñānam, tasya hetur avinābhāvasambandhasmaraṇam .../, *Kir*, p. 243, 21: '*śeṣaḥ*'—*pariśeṣaḥ*, '*anuvyavasitaḥ* (*anuvyavasāya?*)'—*vyāptipakṣadharmatopapannaliṅgavijñānam; tasya vyāptismṛtiḥ hetuḥ/*

62. *NK*, p. 600, 9–10: ... *anuvyavasāyaḥ, prathamopajātaliṅgajñānāpekṣayā tadanantarbhāvyanumeyajñānam, tasya hetuvyāptismaraṇam/*

63. The Prābhākara denies the necessity of *liṅgaparāmarśa* and asserts that cognition of *pakṣadharmatā* after invariable relationship's being grasped is the direct factor of inference. Śrīdhara's view is similar to this.

64. The *Vy* criticizes at least twice those who deny the necessity of *liṅgaparāmarśa* (*Vy*, p. 156, 7–8; *Vy*, p. 164, 1–3).

Chaukhamba Sanskrit Series 61, Varanasi: Chaukhamba Sanskrit Book Office, 1903.

Pramāṇavārttika (*PV*) of Dharmakīrti, the First Chapter with the Auto commentary (*PVSV*), edited by Raniero Gnoli, Roma: ISMEO, 1960.

Sarvadarśanasaṅgraha (*SDS*) of Mādhava, edited by V.S. Abhyaṅkar, Poona: Bhandarkar Oriental Research Institute, 1978.

Ślokavārttika (*ŚV*) of Kumārila, edited with *Nyāyaratnākara* (*NRA*) by Ganga Sagar Rai, Varanasi: Ratna Publications, 1993.

Tarkasaṅgraha (*TS*) of Annambhaṭṭa, edited with *Dīpikā* and *Nyāyabodhinī* by Y.V. Athalye, Poona: BORI, 1974.

Upāsakādhyayana of Somadevasūri, a part of *Yaśastilakacampū* (*YTC*), edited by Kailāśacandra Śāstrī, Varanasi: Bhāratīya Jñānapītha Prakāśana, 1964.

Vyomavatī (*Vy*) of Vyomaśiva, edited by Gaurinath Śastri, Varanasi: Sampurnand Sanskrit University, 1963.

Vaiśeṣikasūtra (*VS*) of Kaṇāda, edited with *the Commentary of Candrānanda* (*CV*) by Muni Jambuvijaya, Vadodara: Oriental Institute, 1982.

Secondary Sources

Bhattacharya, Dineshchandra

1958 *History of Navya-Nyāya in Mithilā*, Darbhanga: Mithila Institute of Post-Graduate Studies and Research in Sanskrit Learning.

Bronkhorst, Johanness

1996 "God's arrival in the Vaiśeṣika System", *Journal of Indian Philosophy* 24 (3): 281–294.

Chemparathy, Geroge (Trans. into Japanese by Yuusho Wakahara)

1986 *L'autorite du Veda selon les Nyāya-Vaiśeṣikas*, *Bukkyogaku Kenkyuu* 42: 43–70.

Habermas, Jurgen (Trans. into Japanese by Rinitsu Kawakami, M. Hubrichit and Toshihiko Hirai)

1985 *Theorie des kommunikativen Handelns*, Miraisha.

Hirano, Katsunori

2003 "On the System of the Commentary *Text* in Indian Philosophy", *SITES: Journal of Studies for the Integrated Text Science* 1 (1): 81–92.

Kataoka, Kei

2003 "Budda no Jihi to Ken'i wo meguru Seitenkaishakugaku to

Bukkyouronrigaku no Tairitsu" (Dialogue of Mīmāṃsā and Buddhism on the Buddha's compassion and authority), *The Memoirs of the Institute of Oriental Culture* 142: 198–158.

Kitagawa, Hidenori
1965 *Indo koten ronrigaku no kenkyu—Jinna no taikei (A Study of Indian Classical Logic-Dignaga's System)*, Suzuki Gakujutsu Zaidan.

Matilal, Bimal K.
1977 "Nyāya-Vaiśeṣika", *A History of Indian Literature, vol. VI: fasc. 2*, ed by J. Gonda, Wiesbaden: Otto Harrassowitz.

Marui, Hiroshi
2005 "Ronshoushiki ni okeru Upanaya no Imi ni tsuite—Shoki Niyaaya Gakuhashi Saikousei ni mukete no Shiryou" (A study of the function of the fourth member upanaya of the Nyaya's five-membered syllogism: Toward reconstruction of the early stage of Nyaya system of logic), *Journal of Indian and Buddhist Studies* 53 (2): 82–90 (L).

Merton, Robert K. (Trans. into Japanese by Tougo Mori)
1961 *Social Theory and Social Structure: Toward the Codification of Theory and Research*, Misuzushobou.

Nozawa, Masanobu
2007 "On the Vaiśeṣika Definition of Mokṣa", *Expanding and Merging Horizons: Contributions to South Asian and Cross-Cultural Studies in Commemoration of Wilhelm Halbfass*, Wien: Verlag der Osterreichischen Akademie der Wissenschaften, pp. 385–399.

Parikha, V.
1991 Introduction to *Nyāyakandalī* edited by R.T. Vyas, Vadodara: Oriental Institute.

Potter, Karl H.
1977 *Nyāya-Vaiśeṣika:* The Encyclopedia of Indian Philosophies, vol. II, Delhi: Motilal Banarsidass.

Ruben, Walter
1928 *Die Nyaya-Sutras: Text, Übersetzung, Erläuterung und Glossar*. Leipzig: Deutsche Morgenländische Gesellschaft, 18 (2).

Sjödin, Anna-Pya
2006 *The Happening of Tradition: Vallabha on Anumāna in Nyāyalīlāvatī (South Asian Studies 1)*, Uppsala: Uppsala University Library.

Thakur, Anantalal

1957 (ed.) *Vaiśeṣikadarśana of Kaṇāda with an anonymous commentary*, Darbhanga: Mithila Institute.

1982 Introduction, to *Vaiśeśikasūtra of Kaṇāda with the Commentary of Candrānanda*, edited by Muni Jambuvija,'a, Baroda: Oriental Institute.

2003 *Origin and Development of the Vaisesika System* (*History of Science, Philosophy and Culture in Indian Civilization, vol. II. Life, thought and culture in India, part 4–a*), New Delhi: Project of History of Indian Science, Philosophy, and Culture: Centre for Studies in Civilizations.

Wada, Toshihiro and Katsunori Hirano

2007 "Indotetsugaku ni okeru Tyuushakutekusuto no Seisei—In'youriron no Tekiyoukanousei" (The Genesis of Commentary Texts in Indian Philosophy: A New Light Based on Quotation Theory), *Horizon of Integrated Text Science* (*21st Century COE Program, Studies for the Integrated Text Science*), pp. 73–115.

* I express my gratitude to Mr. M. Pelowski for correcting my English.

CHAPTER 9

THE GENESIS OF SANSKRIT TEXTS AND THEIR CONTEXT IN NAVYA-NYĀYA: FROM GAṄGEŚA'S *TATTVACINTĀMAṆI* TO ITS COMMENTARIES

Toshihiro WADA

1. Introduction

In discussing the genesis of a Text in general and a commentary Text in particular we cannot help but think about quotation. Among those working in the field of semiology it is generally accepted that a Text is a 'texture' of quotations. Here the concept of quotation is taken in the broadest sense to include the adoption of ideas from other sources. From this viewpoint even an innovative Text would not be truly original. I do not intend to discuss here the issue of originality, which is problematic and beyond the scope of this paper. Instead, I will focus on the concept of quotation and examine the relationship between two commentary Texts. To put it another way, I will clarify how the latter commentary Text emerges as a 'texture' of the former one by means of quotation in a particular linguistic context. I also aim at discussing the relationship between those Texts and their 'context'.

I have used 'quotation' and 'context' both in a technical sense. Quotation generally means a complete or incomplete repetition of some other Text with or without quotation marks. Here I have taken it in the broader sense to include the adoption of ideas from others. This idea may be presented in a different wording so that it is difficult to establish from which author it was adopted. Moreover, if a particular portion of one Text (A) appears in another Text (B) and this portion in Text (B) includes new information, we regard this new information also as a quotation. This is because the whole of that portion including this information is regarded as a quotation from Text (A) in Text (B).[1]

1. More precisely, this new information appears to be new, but it may be a quotation from other Text(s).

The other concept 'context' is concerned not only with the linguistic structure surrounding a particular expression, but also with the non-linguistic structure surrounding it, such as the speaker, the hearer, the social or cultural circumstances, etc., of that expression. It is in the latter sense that I have used the term 'context' in the following discussion.

When thinking about different types of 'quotation', Hirano's paper [2004] is helpful to a large degree. He first divides it into two types: explicit and implicit. Explicit quotation is further divided into preservation, permutation, and substitution, while implicit quotation has no sub-division and is nothing more than deletion. In the discussion below I have not needed to make use of permutation and substitution but have required a new type of quotation: exemplification. Thus I will employ preservation, exemplification, and deletion in examining the relationship between the commentary Texts and will formulate the definition of these terms at the end of this section. In the following sub-section we discuss the Texts to be used in this study.

1.1. Sanskrit Texts

I will deal with three Sanskrit texts of the New School of Indian Logic, which is called "Navya-nyāya" and which influenced all philosophical traditions from a methodological point of view from the 14th century onwards. The main text of my analysis is the *Tattva-cintāmaṇi* (*TC*) of Gaṅgeśa Upādhyāya, who lived in the 14th century and consolidated the system of Navya-nyāya. Two commentaries thereon are; (1) the *Tattva-cintāmaṇi-sārāvalī* (*TCS*) of Vāsudeva Sārvabhauma (latter half of the 15th century), which is commonly called the *Sārāvalī*, and (2) the *Tattva-cintāmaṇi-prakāśa* (*TCPK*) of Rucidatta Miśra (first half of the 16th century)[2]. Rucidatta does not mention Vāsudeva or his commentary the *TCS* in his own commentary, but a general comparison of the two commentaries shows conclusively that Rucidatta was using Vasudeva as his main source.

The *TC* is comprised of four books entitled "Perception" (Pratyakṣa-khaṇḍa), "Inference" (Anumāna-khaṇḍa), "Analogy" (Upamāna-khaṇḍa), and "Language" (Śabda-khaṇḍa) respectively. This is a voluminous text, and we do not have a translation of the whole text in a modern language. The above-mentioned commentaries are also vast in size, and there is no

---

2. For an edition and translation of the Vyāptipañcaka of the *TCS*, see Wada [2003] [2005] [2006]. For an edition and translation of that of the *TCPK*, see Wada [forthcoming b]. See also notes 10 and 11.

comprehensive existing research on them. It is difficult to even draw a rough sketch of their content. We do not even know whether these two commentaries are complete or not; many commentaries of the *TC* have been published but in incomplete form. As a result, we cannot carry out our research on the whole *TC* and its commentaries and will have to focus instead on a particular section dealing with a particular concept.

Focusing on the section dealing with the definition of invariable concomitance, or pervasion (*vyāpti*: logical subsumption), which plays an important role in inference theory in Indian logic, I will attempt to clarify the relation between the two commentaries. For this task I have taken up the "Five Definitions of Invariable Concomitance Section" (Vyāpti-pañcaka) of the three texts. This section is placed in the beginning of the "Invariable Concomitance Chapter" (Vyāpti-vāda), which in turn forms the second chapter of the "Inference Book" (Anumāna-khaṇḍa), the second book of Gaṅgeśa's *TC* and the two commentaries. The "Five Definitions of Invariable Concomitance Section" of the *TC* is a small text; this section consists only of five provisional definitions of invariable concomitance and concludes that none of them is satisfactory for one reason only. The simple structure and small size of this section make it particularly suitable for our purposes here.

1.2. Invariable Concomitance (*vyāpti*)

To understand the content of the "Five Definitions of Invariable Concomitance Section" of the *TC* and the two commentaries, it is necessary to clarify the concept of invariable concomitance. In Indian logic inference is fundamentally given in the following form: "*A* possesses *B*, because *A* possesses *C*".[3] Here *A* is called the "subject" (*pakṣa*), *B* the "object whose existence is to be proved" or "probandum" (*liṅgin*, *sādhya*, *sādhya-dharma*), and *C* the "logical reason" or "probans" (*liṅga*, *sādhana*, *sādhana-*

3. Let us call this type (1). The other fundamental type of inference is as follows: "*B* exists in *A*, because *C* exists in *A*". Let us call this type (2). We may encounter an inference of the following form: "*D* is *E*, because *D* is *F*". A well-known example of this form is "This is a tree, because it is a Śiṃśapā tree". In the case of this form Navya-nyāya considers that the probans is the state of being *F*, or *F*-ness, and that the probandum is the state of being *E*, or *E*-ness. Accordingly, the inference of the above form is written as "*A* possesses *E*-ness, because *A* possesses *F*-ness" or as "*E*-ness exists in *A*, because *F*-ness exists in *A*". On the form of inference, see Ingalls [1951: 36]; A. Uno [1978: 436], which is reproduced in A. Uno [1996: 255]. On the relationship between the form of syllogisms (or inference) and inferential conginition (*anumiti*), see K. Bhattacharya [2001: 22–23].

dharma, hetu). When a relation of invariable concomitance between *B* and *C* is established, one can infer the existence of *B* on the basis of *C* in *A*. The following is the standard example of invariable concomitance: Smoke and fire exists in this relation; because of this relation, it is possible to infer the existence of fire from smoke somewhere, e.g., on a mountain. Thus, the relation of invariable concomitance is regarded as one of the most important grounds for the validity of inference. By using the terms "probans" and "probandum", this relation is usually expressed as follows: Wherever a probans exists, its probandum also exists.

Invariable concomitance is the relation of a probans to its probandum, and not the relation of the latter to the former. A valid probans necessarily exists in the locus of its probandum, but the reverse is not true. For instance, let us suppose that one infers fire from smoke on the mountain. The probans is smoke, which is a valid probans because the above inference is valid. The probandum is fire. It is true that wherever smoke exists fire also exists, but it is not true that wherever fire exists smoke also exists. We know an example which possesses fire but not smoke, namely a red-hot iron ball. Thus, smoke can prove the existence of fire, but fire cannot prove the existence of smoke. From this case we understand that the property of proving the existence of the other resides in smoke and not in fire. In other words, invariable concomitance is regarded as a property possessed by a probans, e.g., smoke, and not by the probandum. In Indian philosophy it is common to consider relation as a property residing in one of its relata.

Navya-nyāya attempted to define the relation of invariable concomitance as a property residing in a valid probans. The first definition, which Gaṅgeśa provides in his "Five Definitions of Invariable Concomitance Section", is the "state of not existing in the possessor of the absence of a probandum" (*sādhyābhāvavadavṛttitvam*).[4]

1.3. Preservation, Exemplification and Deletion

Preservation is defined as employing a particular expression or idea of Text *A* in Text *B*. If Vāsudeva's reason why Gaṅgeśa provides the third definition is stated by Rucidatta also, this is a case of preservation between Vāsudeva's *TCS* and Rucidatta's *TCPK*. Exemplification is defined as giving an example. If Vāsudeva employs a general term such as "incomplete occurrent" in explaining the defect of the fourth definition and Rucidatta provides as an example of an incomplete occurrent contact, this is a case of

4. For all the five definitions, see section 3.

exemplification. Deletion is simply what it means and needs no example.

We will take up the reasons assumed in Vāsudeva's *TCS* and Rucidatta's *TCPK* for why Gaṅgeśa provides the five definitions in a particular order. We will apply the concepts of preservation and deletion to the analysis of these reasons.

2. The Definition of Invariable Concomitance and Its Logical Form

2.1. The Definition of Invariable Concomitance

When Gaṅgeśa seeks the definition of invariable concomitance ('definition' being here a rendering of *lakṣaṇa*), he examines whether it applies to a valid probans (*sad-dhetu*) or not. This fact implies that he regards the valid probans as the definiendum (*lakṣya*). Since invariable concomitance can be considered as the coexistence of a valid probans with its probandum (*sādhya*), such coexistence is a property residing in the valid probans. That the *lakṣaṇa* applies to a valid probans (definiendum) means that the *lakṣaṇa* exists in or on a valid probans. A valid probans is the probans of a valid inference. Since invariable concomitance is a property residing in a valid probans, invariable concomitance and its *lakṣaṇa* exist in one and the same locus, the valid probans.

If the property regarded as the definition exists in a valid probans, the definition is proved correct. However, Gaṅgeśa and Vāsudeva in fact test whether the 'definition' exists in a valid probans or in an invalid probans. If it does not exist in a valid probans, it suffers from the defect of narrow-application (*avyāpti*). If it exists in an invalid probans, it suffers from the defect of over-application (*ativyāpti*). If it does not exist in any probans, it suffers from the defect of non-application (*asaṃbhava*). By overcoming these defects one by one, the given definition is improved upon.

2.2. Logical Form of the Definitions

It is important to show the formal structures of the definitions of invariable concomitance. These formal structures have in the past been expressed mostly in terms of symbolic logic. This method is, of course, valuable, but in the present paper I would like to demonstrate another method of illustrating the formal structure of the definitions. This method is to use diagrams such as Figure 1 below.[5]

---

5. On the system of the diagrams, see Wada [1990] [1995a] [2001] [2004] [2007: 38–42]. On the history of the diagrams, see Wada [1995a] [2007: 42–46].

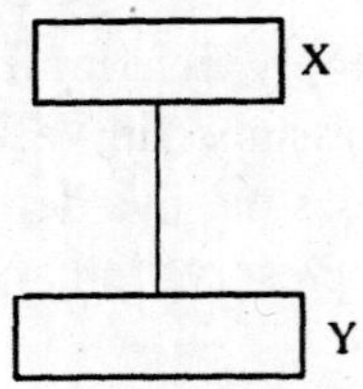

Figure 1

In Figure 1 rectangle X represents a property (*dharma*), and rectangle Y represents its possessor (*dharmin*). The line between X and Y indicates the relation between the entity (*x*) denoted by X and the entity (*y*) denoted by Y. A property is that which exists in something, and its possessor is that in which the property exists, or it is the locus of the property. For example, we look at a blue pot. The blue color of the pot is a property of the pot, and the pot is the property-possessor of this color. This is an example in which a property is abstract. To give an example in which a property is concrete, suppose we look at a book on a table. The book is the property of the table, and the table is the property-possessor of the book.

Since I regard the property and property-possessor relation as the most basic in Navya-nyāya analysis, I have drawn the diagram representing this relation first.

In Figure 2, the dotted line indicates the relation through which the entity denoted by X does not exist in or on the entity denoted by Y. In other words, the dotted line implies the relation whose existence is negated between these two entities.

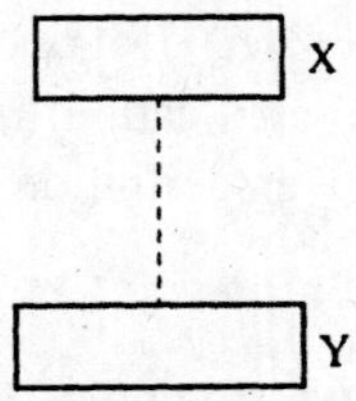

Figure 2

In order to demonstrate a diagram applied to an example of this, let us take the above-mentioned inference: the mountain possesses fire, because it possesses smoke. The probans is smoke, and the probandum is fire. To deal with a case in which something is absent somewhere, suppose that there is no tree on the mountain. We can illustrate the connection among the mountain, smoke, fire, and the absence of a tree in Figure 3.

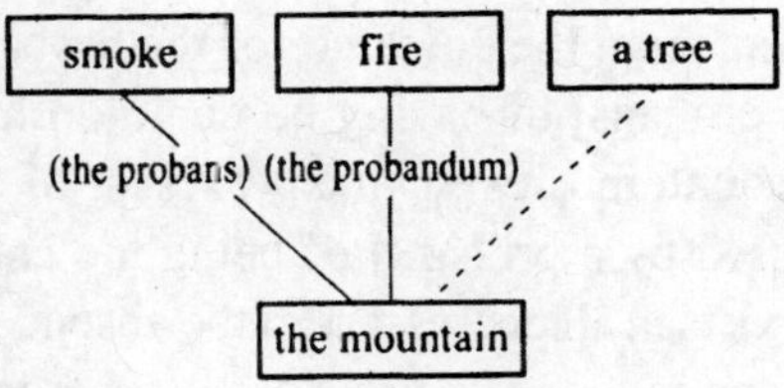

Figure 3

Navya-nyāya employs several basic concepts concerning relation, and we require more diagrams to illustrate those concepts. However, it is not necessary to demonstrate those diagrams here, and they will be shown later when needed.

The two advantages of using symbols stated by Goekoop also apply to my use of diagrams: "(1) It enables us to prove the logical equivalence or divergence of the definition of pervasion," and (2) "We can easily distinguish, among the definitions of pervasion, the logical variants from the verbal variants".[6] I would like to add a third advantage, which is that the diagrams enable us to easily confirm whether the definitions to be tested are properly applied to valid or invalid probantia. Moreover, the diagrams serve as a visual aid and help readers to more easily understand the complicated structure compressed in the definitions.

3. The "Five Definitions of Invariable Concomitance Chapter" of Gaṅgeśa

TEXT: *nanu anumitihetuvyāptijñāne kā vyāptiḥ na tāvad avyabhicaritatvaṃ, tad dhi na sādhyābhāvavadavṛttitvaṃ sādhyavadbhinnasādhyābhāvavadavṛttitvaṃ sādhyavatpratiyogikānyonyābhāvāsāmānādhikaraṇyaṃ sakalasādhyābhāvavanniṣṭhābhāvapratiyogitvaṃ sādhyavadanyāvṛttitvaṃ vā kevalānvayiny abhāvāt.* (*TC*, Vol. 2, Pt. 1, pp. 27,1 – 31,2.)

TRANSLATION: What is invariable concomitance in [that] cognition of invariable concomitance which is the cause of an inferential cognition? Indeed, [it is] not non-deviation [of a probans from the probandum]. The reason for this is that it is not [non-deviation defined as] (1) the non-occurrence [of a probans] in the possessor of the absence of the probandum, (2) the non-occurrence of [a probans] in

6. Goekoop [1967: 30].

the possessor of the absence of the probandum [which absence occurs] in what is different from the possessor of the probandum, (3) the state [possessed by a probans] of having no common locus with a mutual absence whose counterpositive is the possessor of the probandum, (4) the state [possessed by a probans] of being the counterpositive of an absence which exists in all possessors of the absence of the probandum, or (5) the non-occurrence [of a probans] in what is different from the possessor of the probandum, since [any of these five states] does not exist in an unnegatable [probans].

The definitions of invariable concomitance provided by Gaṅgeśa here are the first five among the twenty-one provisional definitions (*pūrvapakṣa-lakṣaṇa*) in his *TC*. Of these five, we can illustrate the structure of the first one in Figure 4. The arrow of the double line indicates that the absence[7] denoted by the rectangle where the arrow is rooted is the describer (*nirūpaka*) of the probandum denoted by the rectangle to which the arrow points. Here it is sufficient to understand that this arrow is used to indicate the relation between absence and its absentee, i.e., the entity whose existence is negated.

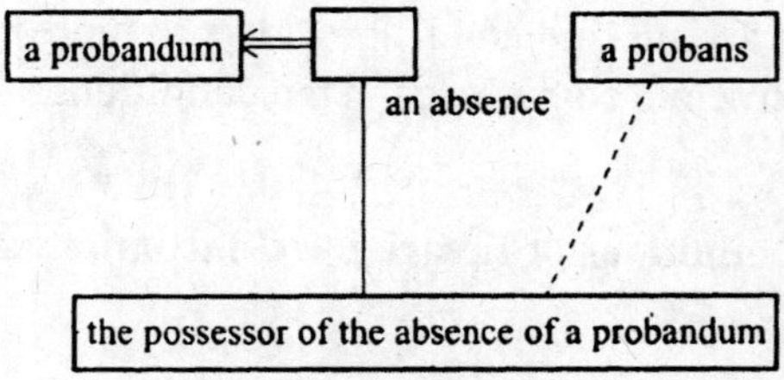

Figure 4 (The first definition)

Let us test the first definition first. We will apply this definition to the well-known valid inference in Indian logic "the mountain possesses fire, because it possesses smoke" (*parvato vahnimān dhūmāt*). (1) The

7. According to Matilal [1968: 101], Śrīdhara in the 10th century and Udayana in the 11th century approved the reality of absence. But it is Udayana who introduced the category of absence (*abhāva*) to the ontological list of the Vaiśeṣika School, which list was accepted by the Nyāya School also. These two schools were gradually synthesized into the Navya-nyāya School, and hence Navya-nyāya also accepts the category of absence. Absence occurs somewhere and it is necessarily the absence of something. The place in which absence occurs is called the locus of absence (*anuyogin*); that whose existence is negated is called the counterpositive (*pratiyogin*).

probandum of this inference is fire. (2) The probans is smoke. (3) The absence of the probandum is the absence of fire, and it exists, for example, in a lake. (4) In a lake smoke does not exist. (5) Smoke is the probans of the inference, so we can say that the probans does not exist in a lake, i.e., the possessor of the absence of the probandum. All the conditions stated in the definition have been met, and thus the definition applies to the present valid probans. We can illustrate the connection among the entities referred to in the above process in Figure 5.

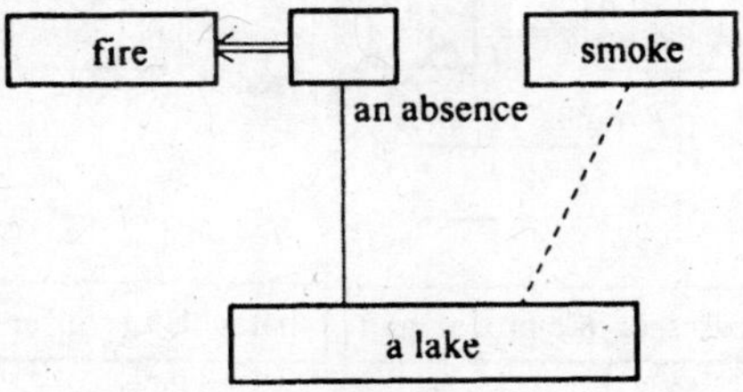

Figure 5

We will then examine whether the first definition applies to the invalid probans of the inference "the mountain possesses smoke, because it possesses fire" (*parvato dhūmavān vahneḥ*), which is naturally invalid. (1) The probandum is smoke. (2) The probans is fire. (3) The absence of the probandum is the absence of smoke, and it exists, for example, in a red-hot iron ball (*taptāyogolaka*), for this ball produces flames but not smoke. (4) A red-hot iron ball possesses fire, which is the probans. Hence, the probans does not fulfill the condition stated in the definition that it should not occur in the possessor of the absence of the probandum, and thus the definition does not apply to the invalid probans. It has been proved that the first definition does not suffer from the defect of over-application (*ativyāpti*) at least in the present case. We can illustrate the connection of the entities referred to in the above application in Figure 6.

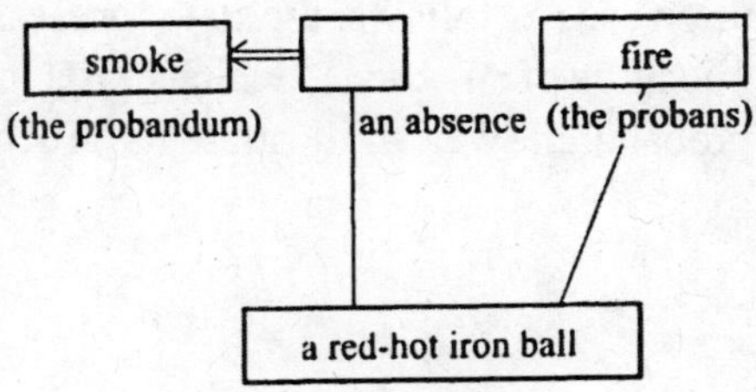

Figure 6

We will illustrate the structure of the remaining four definitions one by one. The second definition runs as follows: the non-occurrence of [a probans] in the possessor of the absence of the probandum [which absence occurs] in what is different from the possessor of the probandum. Figure 7 represents the structure of this definition. The mutual absence referred to in the figure is obtained from an analysis of "different" (*bhinna*) in the definition. That which is different is the possessor of difference (*bhedavat*), and difference is a mutual absence (*anyonyābhāva*).

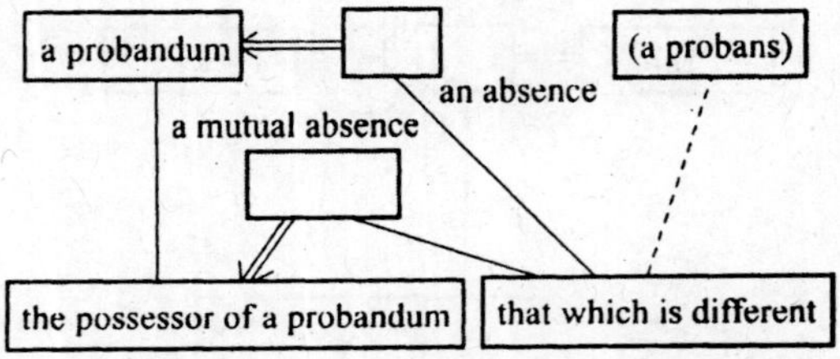

Figure 7 (The second definition)

The third definition runs as follows: the state [possessed by a probans] of having no common locus with a mutual absence whose counterpositive is the possessor of the probandum. We can illustrate the structure of this definition in Figure 8.

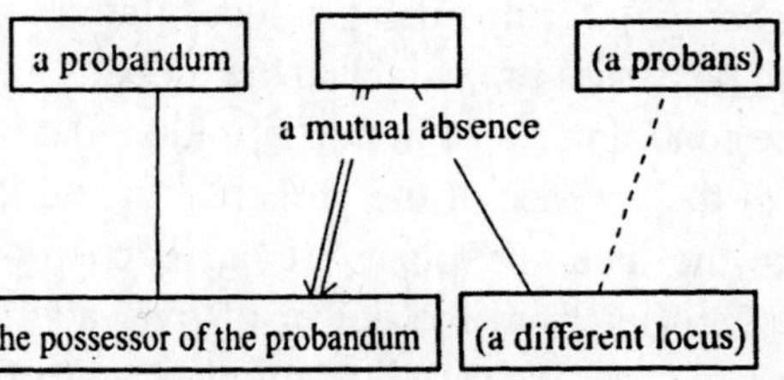

Figure 8 (The third definition)

The fourth definition runs as follows: the state [possessed by a probans] of being the counterpositive of an absence which exists in all possessors of the absence of the probandum. We can illustrate its structure in Figure 9.

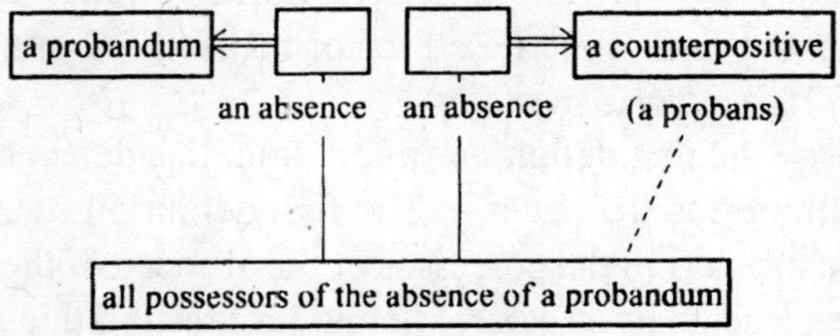

Figure 9 (The fourth definition)

The fifth definition runs as follows: the non-occurrence [of a probans] in what is different from the possessor of the probandum. We can illustrate its structure in Figure 10.[8]

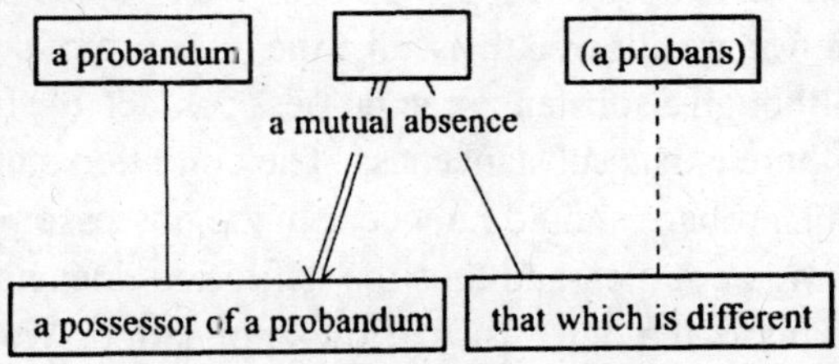

Figure 10 (The fifth definition)

4. The Reason for Presenting the Second Dedinition after the First Definition: Vāsudeva's Case

Gaṅgeśa does not say why a latter definition is more satisfactory than the former definition among the five. Commenting on these five definitions, Vāsudeva and Rucidatta explain why the latter definitions are superior to the former. We do not have enough space to examine all their reasons here, so we will look at only one case, that in which Vāsudeva points out the defect of the first definition. According to Vāsudeva, the first definition suffers from the defect of narrow-application to the valid probans whose probandum is an incomplete occurrent (*avyāpyavṛttin*). An incomplete occurrent is that which occurs in part of its locus. For example, contact between two substances is an incomplete occurrent, because it exists only in the physically connected parts of these two substances, and not in

8. Figures 8 and 10 appear to show that both the third and fifth definitions have the same logical structure. Wada [forthcoming a] has discussed the structure of both definitions.

the whole of the two. The valid inference which includes contact as the probandum is that "This is the possessor of contact, because it possesses substance-ness" (*saṃyogī dravyatvāt*).[9]

Let us see why the first definition suffers from this defect and then how the second definition is free from it. The first definition runs as the non-occurrence of a probans in the possessor of the absence of the probandum, and Figure 4 represents its structure. Let us start testing this definition by using the above inference. (1) The probandum is contact. (2) The absence of the probandum is the absence of contact. (3) The possessor of this absence is, for example, a substance. Contact is an incomplete occurrent, so it can share a locus with its absence. To give an example, when we touch a pot with the hand, the pot possesses contact with the hand. But the parts of the pot which the hand does not touch possess the absence of contact with the hand. Hence, we are allowed to assume the 'absence of contact' to exist in a substance although a substance can possess contact. (4) In such a locus of this absence there exists substanceness. The condition stated in the first definition that the probans should not occur in the possessor of the absence of the probandum is not met, and thus the definition does not apply to the valid probans. This is the defect of narrow-application. We can illustrate the connection among the entities referred to above in Figure 11.

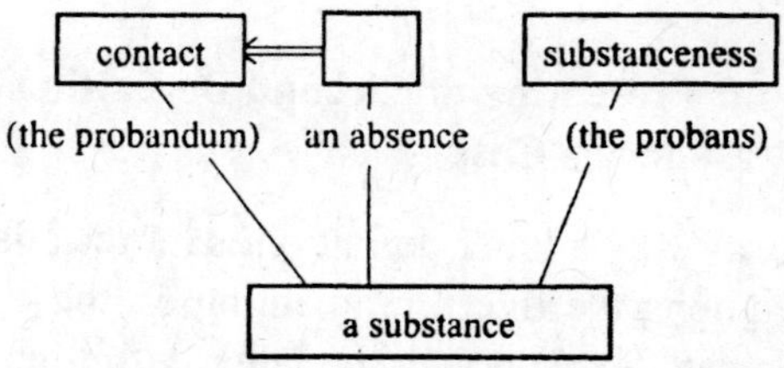

Figure 11

We will next see how the second definition removes the above defect. It runs as follows: the non-occurrence of [a probans] in the possessor of the absence of the probandum which absence occurs in what is different from

9. This inference is reconstructed from *Nyāyasiddhāntadīpa* (*NSD*, p. 66,1–3) of Śaśadhara, who flourished in the 13th century just prior to Gaṅgeśa's time: *saṃyogādyavyāpyavṛttau ca sādhye sādhyātyantābhāvasāmānādhikaraṇye 'pi dravyatvasya vyāpter iṣyamānatvāt* (When contact etc., which are incomplete occurrents, are the probanda, substanceness [the probans] possesses invariable concomitance [with the contact] in spite of [substanceness] sharing a locus with the constant absence of the probandum).

the possessor of the probandum. For the structure of this definition, see Figure 7.

The application of this definition will start as follows. (1) The probandum is contact. (2) The possessor of the probandum is, for example, a substance such as a pot. (3) What is different from a substance is, for example, a quality (*guṇa*). Here we have to determine why we cannot take another substance, like cloth, as what is different from the possessor of the probandum (a substance). Vāsudeva seems to consider that the expression 'what is different from the possessor of the probandum' implies that the probandum occurs in its possessor but not in what is different from its possessor. Hence, "the possessor of the probandum" includes all substances, and they all are ruled out from "what is different from the possessor of the probandum". As a result, we cannot take cloth as "what is different from the possessor of the probandum". (4) Since contact does not exist in a quality, the absence of contact exists in a quality. (5) In a quality there is no substanceness, and substanceness is the probandum. All the conditions stated in the second definition are met, and thus it applies to the present valid probans. We can illustrate the connection among the entities referred to in the above application in Figure 12.

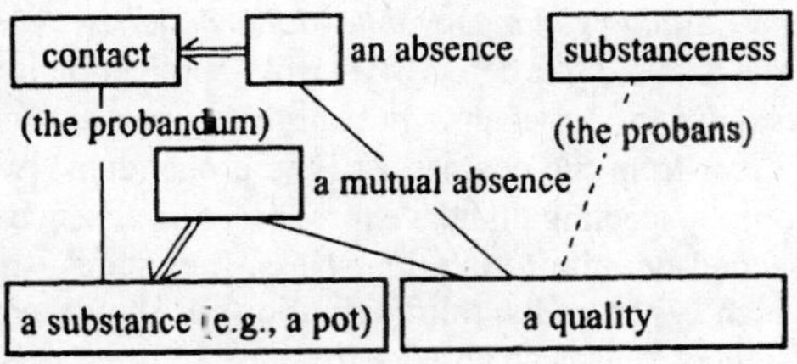

Figure 12

5. The Reason for Presenting the Latter Definitions: Vāsudeva and Rucidatta

Vāsudeva states that the first definition suffers from the defect of narrow-application to a valid probans whose probandum is an incomplete occurrent, and that the second one avoids this defect. He continues to say that the second definition contains the purposeless expression "the possessor of the absence of the probandum". The third definition does not have such an expression, but, according to him, if the absence used in the definition is mutual absence, this definition suffers from the defect of narrow-application to the probans of the valid inference "the mountain possesses fire, because it possesses smoke". The fourth definition suffers from the defect of narrow-application to a valid probans, such as substanceness, whose probandum is an incomplete occurrent; furthermore, the same definition suffers from the defect of over-application to the probans of the invalid inference "this possesses cognition, because it possesses contact".[10]

---

10. Vāsudeva's *TCS* on Gaṅgeśa's "Five Definitions of Invariable Concomitance Section" reads: ... *avyāpyavṛttisādhyake saddhetāv avyāptivāraṇāyāha sādhyavadbhinneti. sādhyābhāvapadasya vaiyyarthyam āśaṃkyāha sādhyavad iti. na cāyam abhāva etattvād ity atrāvyāptiḥ, abhāvatvāśrayapratiyogikānyonyābhāvānab hyupagamād iti vācyam, anyonyābhāvavyavahāraniyāmakaṃ svarūpabhedam ādāyaiva tatra lakṣaṇāgateḥ. tathāpi yatkiñcitsādhyavatpratiyogikānyonyābh āvasamānādhikaraṇe dhūme 'vyāptiḥ syād ity ata āha sakaleti. sākalyam iha sādhyābhāve tadvati vā vivakṣitaṃ, tena na dhūme 'vyāptir na vā dhūmābhāvav ajjalahradaniṣṭhābhāvapratiyogitayā vahnāv ativyāptiḥ. ihāpy ayaṃ samavāyabhinno ghaṭatvād ity atrāvyāptiḥ syāt. sādhyābhāvatvāvacchedena vartate yo 'tyantābhāvas tatpratiyogitvam iti vivakṣaṇe guṇo 'dravyaṃ saṃyogavadbhinnatvād ity atrāvyāptiḥ, dravyatvābhāvābhāvatvāvacchedena saṃyogavadanyonyābhāvātyantābhāvasya saṃyogasyāvṛtteḥ. sakalapadasyāśeṣānekavācino 'śeṣamātraparatve 'vyāpyavṛttisādhyake dravyatvādāv avyāptiḥ, ayaṃ jñānavān saṃyogād ity atrātivyāptiś cety ata āha sādhyavadanyeti. sādhyavattvāvacchedakāvacchinnapratiyogikabheda iha vivakṣitaḥ. ato dhūme nāsiddham sādhyavadanyāvṛttitvaṃ sādhyavadanyonyābhāvādhārānādheyatvād iti bhāvaḥ....* (Trans.: ... In order to avoid [the defect of] narrow-application [of the first definition given by Gaṅgeśa] to a valid probans whose probandum is an incomplete occurrent, [he states] 'different from the possessor of the probandum' [which is part of the second definition]. Suspecting that the expression 'the absence of the probandum' [stated in the second definition] is purposeless, [he] states 'the possessor of the probandum' [which is part of the third definition]. It should not be argued: in the case of [the inference] "this is an absence, because [it possesses] the state of being [called] 'this'", [the third definition suffers from the defect of] narrow-application; the reason [for this defect] is that mutual absence whose counterpositive is the locus of absenceness is not admitted. The reason [for our rejection of the above argument] is: based only on the determining factor of the use of the expression 'mutual absence', [which determining factor is] the particular nature [of mutual absence], the [third] definition [should] be applied in that [case]. Despite [the above discussion, the third definition] would [still suffer from the defect of] narrow-application to smoke, which has a common locus with a mutual absence whose counterpositive is a particular possessor of the probandum. Therefore [Gaṅgeśa states] 'all possessors' [which is part of the fourth definition]. 'Being all' here [in the fourth definition] is meant [to exist] in 'the absence of the probandum' or 'the possessor of the absence of a probandum'. Therefore, [this definition does] not [suffer from the defect of] narrow-application to smoke, nor [does it suffer from the defect of] over-application to fire, which is the counterpositive of an absence which exists in a lake possessing an absence of smoke. This [definition] will also [suffer from the defect of] narrow-application in the case of the inference "this is

Rucidatta, on the other hand, mentions that the first definition suffers from the defect of narrow-application to a valid probans whose probandum is contact, which is an incomplete occurrent. He keeps silent about the defect of the second definition. The third definition suffers from the defect of narrow-application to the probans of the valid inference "the mountain possesses fire, because it possesses smoke" if the absence used in the definition is mutual absence. The fourth definition is free from this defect, but suffers from the defect of narrow-application to the probans of the valid inference whose probandum is contact, i.e., an incomplete occurrent.[11]

---

different from inherence, because [it possesses] potness". If [to remove the defect mentioned above, the fourth definition] means 'the state [possessed by a probans] of being the counterpositive of a constant absence which exists with that which is qualified by the state of being an absence of the probandum [i.e., with an absence of the probandum, the definition suffers from the defect of] narrow-application in the case of the inference "a quality is not a substance, because [it possesses] the state of being different from the possessor of contact". This is because with that which is qualified by the state of an absence of an absence of substanceness [i.e., with the absence of an absence of substanceness] contact, which is a constant absence of a mutual absence of the possessor of contact, does not exist. If the word 'all', which means 'without exception' or 'plural', means only 'without exception' [in the fourth definition], [the definition will suffer from the defect of] narrow-application to substanceness and so forth in the case of [the inference whose] probandum is an incomplete occurrent. In addition [the fourth definition will suffer from the defect of] over-application in the case of [the inference] "this possesses cognition, because [it possesses] contact". Therefore, [Gaṅgeśa states] 'what is different from the possessor of a probandum' [which is part of the fifth definition]. Here [in the fifth definition 'the state of being what is different from the possessor of the probandum' is] intended to mean 'a difference whose counterpositive is qualified by the delimitor of the state of being the possessor of the probandum'. [This clarification] means that accordingly 'the non-occurrence [of the probans] in what is different from the possessor of the probandum' is not unobtained in smoke [which is the valid probans of the inference "the mountain possesses fire, because it possesses smoke"], because [smoke possesses] the state of not being an entity contained by the container of a mutual absence of the possessor of the probandum....

11. Rucitadda's *TCPK* on Gaṅgeśa's "Five Definitions of Invariable Concomitance Section" reads: *nirūpaṇaprayojakatvenāha anumitihetv iti. saṃyogasādhyakasaddhetāv avyāpter lakṣaṇāntaram āha sādhyavad iti. nanu yatkiṃcitsādhyavatpratiyogikāṇyoṇyābhāvasāmānādhikaraṇyaṃ dhūmādav apy astīty arucer āha sakaleti. sakalapadam aśeṣaparam, na tv anekāśeṣaparam. ato yatraikam eva sādhyaṃ tatra na sākalyāprasiddhir iti dhyeyam. nanu saṃyogādisādhyakasaddhetāv avyāptir ity anuśayenāha sādhyavad iti. sādhyavattvāvacchinnapratiyogitākānyonyābhāvavadavṛttitvam ity arthaḥ. anyonyābhāvaś ca vyāpyavṛttir iti noktadoṣaḥ. atra vṛttimattve satīti viśeṣaṇam. ato nākāśādāv ativyāptiḥ. kevalānvayinīti. kevalānvayidharmasādhyaka ity arthaḥ.* (Trans.: [Gaṅgeśa,] who explains [the cause of an inferential cognition], says, "[What is invariable

We can show the above reasons given by Vāsudeva and Rucidatta for presenting the later definitions, which are also the defects of the former definitions, in the following table:

Def.	Vāsudeva's reason	Rucidatta's reason
1	narrow-application to a valid probans whose probandum is an incomplete occurrent	narrow-application to a valid probans whose probandum is an incomplete occurrent such as contact
2	the purposeless expression "the possessor of the absence of the probandum"	none
3	narrow-application to the probans of the valid inference "the mountain possesses fire, because it possesses smoke"	narrow-application to the probans of the valid inference "the mountain possesses fire, because it possesses smoke"
4	(1) narrow-application to the probans, such as substanceness, whose probandum is an incomplete occurrent; (2) over-application to the probans of the invalid inference "this possesses cognition, because it possesses contact"	(1) narrow-application to the probans of the valid inference whose probandum is contact; (2) none

concomitance in that cognition of invariable concomitance which is] the cause of an inferential cognition?" Since [the first definition of invariable concomitance suffers from the defect of] narrow-application to a valid probans whose probandum is contact, [he] states another definition, [which includes the expression] "the possessor of the probandum". An undesirable consequence [will arise which is that someone may object that] even in smoke there exists the state of having a common locus with that of a mutual absence whose counterpositive is the possessor of some probandum. Therefore [he states] 'all possessors' [which is part of the fourth definition]. The word 'all' [employed in the fourth definition] means 'without exception', and not 'either plural or without exception'. That is why [we] should consider that the state of being all is not unobtained when only one probandum is [available]. Since [someone objects that the fourth definition suffers from the defect of] narrow-application to valid probantia whose probanda are contact etc., [Gaṅgeśa] states with regret 'the possessor of the probandum' [which is part of the fifth definition]. [The fifth definition] means 'the non-occurrence [of a probans] in the possessor of a mutual absence whose counterpositiveness is delimited by the state of being the possessor of the probandum'. A mutual absence is a complete occurrent, so [the fifth definition does] not [suffer from] the above-mentioned defect. Here [in all the five definitions presented by Gaṅgeśa] 'when [the probans] is an occurrent' is the qualifier [of each definition]. That is why [the revised fifth definition containing constant absence does] not [suffer from the defect of] over-application to space and so forth. The expression 'in an unnegetable' [in the *TC*] means 'in [the probans] whose probandum is an unnegatable property'.)

Vāsudeva's reason why the first definition is not satisfactory is also used by Rucidatta with his clarification of Vāsudeva's word "incomplete occurrent" as "contact". This is a case of exemplification. Vāsudeva's reason why the second definition is not satisfactory is not mentioned by Rucidatta. This is a case of deletion. Vāsudeva's reason why the third definition is not satisfactory is repeated; this is a case of preservation. One of Vāsudeva's two reasons why the fourth definition is not satisfactory is almost same as Rucidatta's; while Vāsudeva provides an example of a probans to which the definition should apply, Rucidatta provides an example of the probandum of such a probans. This is a case of exemplification. Vāsudeva's other reason for the other defect of the fourth definition is not referred to by Rucidatta. The reason for this is probably that since Vāsudeva presents a complete form of the inference which includes the invalid probans, Rucidatta does not need to do this in order to point out the second defect. This is a case of deletion.

6. Concluding Remarks

Preservation between the two commentary Texts indicates that the information deserves to be transmitted however simple it may look. Exemplification shows that even if the added information is not new, it looks fresh in its textual new context. When exemplification occurs, some information which they bear upon is not mentioned in the latter commentary Text and in this regard it resembles deletion. Deletion occurs when the information does not deserve to be transmitted. This does not always mean that the deleted information has become useless or unnecessary. Deletion often occurs when the information has become common knowledge to the readers of the later commentary Texts. This is the 'context' of commentary Texts.

As deleted information increases in successive commentary Texts, the size of the Texts decreases. Accordingly, when we read a commentary Text, we should infer that there is deleted information in the Text with reference to the former commentary Texts, and we can supply the information from them. When thinking about cases of exemplification, we have to consider with reference to what these cases occur. This leads one to the conclusion that to understand one of the commentary Texts on a main Text deeply, we have to read the other commentary Texts also. If follows that to recognize cases of preservation, exemplification, and deletion in the commentary Texts, we may have to regard them as one whole, as Hirano [2004: 73] states.

References

Primary Sources

Nyāyasiddhāntadīpa (*NSD*) of Śaśadhara, in *Śaśadhara's Nyāyasiddhāntadīpa with Ṭippana by Guṇaratnasūri*, edited by B.K. Matilal, L.D. Series 56, Ahmedabad: L. D. Institute of Indology, 1976.

Tattvacintāmaṇi (*TC*) of Gaṅgeśa Upādhyāya, in *Tattvacintāmaṇi of Gaṅgeśa Upādhyāya*, 4 volumes, edited with extracts from the Commentaries of Mathurānātha Tarkavāgīśa and Jayadeva Miśra by Kāmākhyānātha Tarkavāgīśa, Vrajajivan Prachyabharati Granthamala 47, Delhi: Chaukhamba Sanskrit Pratishthan, 1990.

Tattvacintāmaṇiprakāśa (*TCPK*) of Rucidatta Miśra, in *Tattvacintāmaṇi of Gaṅgeśopādhyāya with Prakāśa of Rucidattamiśra and Tarkacūdāmaṇi on Prakāṣā of Dharmarājādhvarin*, edited by N.S. Ramanuja Tatacharya, vol. 2, Pt. 1, Kendriya Sanskrit Vidyapeetha Tirupati Series 33, Tirupati: Kendriya Sanskrit Vidyapeetha, 1982.

Tattvacintāmaṇisārāvalī (*TCS*) of Vāsudeva Sārvabhauma, in G. Bhattacharya [1967].

Secondary Sources

Bhattacharya, Gopikamohan

1967 "Tattvacintāmaṇiṭīkā", *Anvīkṣā: Research Journal of the Department of Sanskrit* 3(2)/4(1): 171–205.

Bhattacharya, Kamaleswar

2001 "A Note on Formalism in Indian Logic", *Journal of Indian Philosophy* 29: 17–23.

Goekoop, C.

1967 *The Logic of Invariable Concomitance in the Tattvacintāmaṇi*, Dordrecht: D. Reidel Publishing Company.

Hirano, Katsunori

2004 "Originality and Quotation: A Study of a Commentary Text's Genesis in Vaiśeṣika Philosophy", *Journal of Studies for the Integrated Text Science* 2(1): 59–74.

Matilal, Bimal K.

1968 *The Navya-nyāya Doctrine of Negation*, Harvard Oriental Series 46, Cambridge, Mass.: Harvard University Press.

Uno, Atsushi

1978 "Indo no Suiron Shiki" (A Study of Indian Syllogism), in *Orientogaku Indogaku Ronshū* (Studies Dedicated to Professor Atuuji Ashikaga on the Occasion of His Seventy-seventh Birthday), Tokyo: Kokusho Kankokai, pp. 433–446. (in Japanese)

1996 *Indo Ronrigaku* (Indian Logic), Kyoto: Hozokan. (in Japanese)

Wada, Toshihiro

1990 *Invariable Concomitance in Navya-Nyāya*, Sri Garib Dass Oriental Series 101, Delhi: Sri Satguru Publications.

1995a "The Structure of the World in Indian Realism and Its Schematization", in M. Deshpande and S. Bhate (eds.), *Vācaspatyam: Pt. Vamanshastri Bhagavat Felicitation Volume*, Pune: Vaidika Samshodhana Mandala, pp. 150–158.

1995b "Gaṅgeśa and Mathurānātha on Siṃhavyāghralakṣaṇa of *vyāpti* (1)", *Journal of Indian Philosophy* 23: 274–279.

2001 "The Analytical Method of Navya-nyāya", *Journal of Indian Philosophy* 29: 519–530.

2003 "The Generation of Sanskrit Texts in the New School of Indian Logic (1): From Gaṅgeśa's Tattvacintāmaṇi to Its Commentaries", *Journal of Studies for the Integrated Text Science* 1(1): 63–80.

2004 "The Origin of Navya-nyāya and Its Place within the History of Indian Logic", in S. Hino and T. Wada (eds.), *Three Mountains and Seven Rivers: Prof. Musashi Tachikawa's Felicitation Volume*, Delhi: Motilal Banarsidass, pp. 439–462.

2005 "The Generation of Sanskrit Texts in the New School of Indian Logic (2): From Gaṅgeśa's *Tattvacintāmaṇi* to Its Commentaries", *Journal of Studies for the Integrated Text Science* 2(1): 43–58.

2006 "Vāsudeva on the Vyāptipañcaka Section of Gaṅgeśa's *Tattvacintāmaṇi* (1)", *Indologica Taurinensia* 31: 277–300.

2007 *The Analytical Method of Navya-Nyāya*, Gonda Indological Series 14, Groningen: Egbert Forsten Publishing.

forthcoming a "The Logical Structure of the Third and Fifth Definitions in the Vyāptipañcaka Section of Gaṅgeśa's *Tattvacintāmaṇi*", *J.L. Shaw Festschrift*.

forthcoming b "Rucidatta Miśra on the Vyāptipañcaka Section of Gaṅgeśa's *Tattvacintāmaṇi*", *Prof. John Vattanky Festschrift*.

* I wish to thank Dr. Charles Pain for correcting my English.

INDEX